For Conspicuous Gallantry

The Register of the Conspicuous Gallantry Medal 1855 - 1992

Compiled by
Phil McDermott

To Karen, Katharyn and Kerry

Foreword

It is a privilege to introduce this volume knowing how many hours of diligent research and hard work it has taken to compile. The persuasion of Government departments and other semi-official organisations is an art in itself, but the contribution of numerous individuals must also have been of great value.

It is a story of the old and the new, or nearly new. Two medals in one, two colours under the same name. No wonder there is an air of confusion surrounding these awards. Even some of the recipients, at the time, had little idea of the significance of the medal, at least as far as the Royal Navy was concerned.

On behalf of all C.G.M. holders I should like to thank those involved for producing this Register. A record such as this can never be 'finished' but the coverage is amazing bringing alive the courage, devotion and comradeship shown by so many.

Finally a thought for all those acts of Gallantry which went unrecorded, I salute them and all the other C.G.M. holders mentioned in this book.

Don Bunce C.G.M.

Acknowledgements

Many people have helped me and contributed to this work. Thanks are due to The Rt. Hon John Major M.P.; Major J.C. Cowley O.B.E., D.C.M.; Mr Don Bunce C.G.M.; Mr J.D. Coughlan C.G.M.; Mr C.C. Corder C.G.M.; Mr M.J. Dyas, Ian Bolton and his staff at Birmingham Central Library; Naval Secretary's Department, Second Sea Lord & Commander-in-Chief Naval Home Command; Headquarters Personnel and Training Command, Royal Air Force; Commander Tall of the Royal Navy Submarine Museum; Christine Gregory of The Royal Air Force Museum; The Royal Marines Museum; The Royal Naval Museum; Imperial War Museum; National Maritime Museum; The Public Records Office.

Special thanks are due to Karen for her help and understanding during many hours researching the various publications and countless hours spent walking around the various Museums and to my daughters Kerry and Katharyn who often thought there were better things to do!

It was important that this work covered all of the C.G.M.'s and I am deeply indebted to Mrs Douglas-Morris for being allowed to extract the citations from her husband Captain Douglas-Morris' excellent work 'Naval Medals 1857-1880'. This work contains a wealth of information about the campaigns for which the early C.G.M.'s were awarded.

Bibliography

Abbott, P.E. (1975) *Recipients of the Distinguished Conduct Medal 1855-1909*. London: J.B.Hayward & Son.

Abbott, P.E. and Tamplin, J.M.A. (1981) *British Gallantry Awards*. London: Nimrod Dix & Co.

Cooper Alan W (1986) *In action with the Enemy*. London: William Kimber & Co. Ltd.

Douglas-Morris, K.J. *Naval Medals 1857 -1880*. London: Private printed

Douglas-Morris, K.J. *Naval Medals 1793 -1856*. London: Private printed

Fevyer, W.H. (1982) *The Distinguished Service Medal 1914-1920*. London: J.B.Hayward & Son

Fevyer, W.H. (1981) *The Distinguished Service Medal 1939-1946*. London: J.B.Hayward & Son

HMSO (1855-1992) *The London Gazette*. London HMSO.

HMSO (1855-1992) *The Navy List*. London HMSO.

McDermott, P *For Distinguished Conduct in the Field*. London: J.B.Hayward & Son.

Royal United Services Institution, Journal of the - TheConspicuous Gallantry Medal by Commander W.B.Rowbotham August 1954.

Simenstad, A. (1990) *Norwegian War Decorations*. London: The London Stamp Exchange

Waldron, T. & Gleeson J. *The Frogmen*

Warren, C.E.T. and Benson, J. *Above us the Waves*

Introduction

This work is not intended to be about statistics, it has a primary function of being a catalogue of the eyewitness accounts, recording outstanding acts of courage performed by members of Naval and Air Forces during times of war, which have led to the men identified in these pages being awarded the Conspicuous Gallantry Medal.

As the recipients of these and other gallantry awards will be quick to point out, a large number of gallant acts take place during the major and minor conflicts which afflict our world from time to time, a great deal of these pass unnoticed. These pages pay tribute to those who *were* noticed and were awarded what is for N.C.O.'s and other ranks a *'near miss'* for the Victoria Cross.

The information in these pages has been compiled from primarily the London Gazette and the official recommendations/citations that were passed through for approval of the award and in some instances by extracting information from the various despatches published in the London Gazette, an example is shown in the appendices. Further research involved scouring the National and local newspapers of the time of the awards and subsequently for information on the individuals, this information has then been cross-referenced to a number of publications both official and private including the catalogues of the major auction houses for the past twenty years. Along with this has been information from some of the recipients themselves.

Some editorial standardisation has taken place and obvious errors in the original text have been corrected, however there may still be errors which I have carried forward to this work and for which I apologise in advance. A number of the original award recommendations no longer survive and in some cases were destroyed after approval.

Where the London Gazette preamble provided extra information as to theatre of war etc. this information has been included in *italics* before the citation.

I have identified where possible all other awards received and these are detailed in the notes section along with other relevant information on the man and his medals, I cannot however guarantee that this is complete.

Research is a never ending task and I would be grateful for any further information readers may have on any of the individuals included in this work.

Phil McDermott
Honorary Archivist
Gallantry Medallists' League

The
Conspicuous Gallantry
Medal

The C.G.M. was first introduced in 1855 as a reward for members of H.M. Naval forces who had distinguished themselves during the Crimean War. The Naval forces were lacking in any means of recognition for gallant and distinguished service in the Crimea, the Army had the Distinguished Conduct Medal (D.C.M.) at their disposal which had been instituted in 1854 and the V.C. did not come into being until 1856.

The initial medal utilised the existing Navy Meritorious Service Medal which bore on the reverse, in raised lettering, the wording "For Meritorious Service" the words "Meritorious Service" were erased and the wording "Conspicuous Gallantry" was engraved in their place. Following the initial awards for the Crimea, twelve medals to eleven recipients, the medal fell into disuse.

The medal was revived for the Ashantee wars of 1873-1874 this medal was suspended by initially a straight suspender, later Victorian issues had an ornate scroll suspender as featured on the medal of 1855. The suspension was changed back to be straight from the Edward VII issues until the last issue in 1991.

The next major change to the medal occurred in 1921 when the ribbon was changed form being three equal stripes blue, white, blue to the white ribbon with dark blue edges. This change had been made to distinguish it more clearly from the D.S.C. which also had a ribbon of three equal stripes blue, white, blue.

The final change in the medals history which is required to be mentioned in this work, was the introduction of the Conspicuous Gallantry Medal (Flying) by Royal Warrant in November 1942. The medal itself remained the same in design as that of the C.G.M., the difference being in the ribbon which was light blue with dark blue edges. The award is an extension to the medal of 1874 to cover members of the Military and Air Forces for acts of conspicuous gallantry while flying. The holders of this branch of the award are shown in section two.

During its history, the medal has been awarded very scarcely, in fact there are nearly four times as many Victoria Crosses!

For those readers wishing to study the history of the medal in more detail I would advise reading the publication 'British Gallantry Awards' by P.E.Abbott and J.M.A.Tamplin.

Numbers Awarded

The following tables brings shows the numbers of CGM's Awarded by Period.

Naval Awards

	Royal Navy	Royal Marines	Army	R.N.A.S. F.A.A.	R.N.R. R.F.R.	R.N.V.R.	Dominion Navies	Foreign Navies	Totals
1854-55 Crimea	11	1							12
1874-75 Ashantee	12	11							23
1876 Perak	3								3
1881 S.Africa	1								1
1883-85 Egypt	3	9							12
1889 Indoni	1								1
1894 Benin	2								2
1901 S.Africa & China	9	1							10
1904 Somaliland	1	1							2
1914-19	50	21		3	17	18			109
1927 Shangai	2								2
1940-46	56	7		2	3		4	8	80
1982 S.Atlantic			1						1
1991 Gulf	1								1
	152	51	1	5	20	18	4	8	259

Flying Awards

All awards, except one, of the C.G.M. (Flying) were made for service during World War Two and break down as follows

R.A.F., R.A.F.V.R. and R.Auxiliary Air Force.	82
R.A.A.F.	10
R.C.A.F.	12
R.N.Z.A.F.	4
Glider Pilot regiment	1
Foreign Nationals	2

This gives a total number of awards for the medal of 111.

Soldiers Died in the Great War
1914-1919

NOW AVAILABLE ON CD-ROM

There can hardly have been a family in Britain which was not touched in some way by the tragedy of the First World War, the "Great War for Civilisation". Great Britain, alone among the major European nations, went to war in 1914 with an army based on voluntary enlistment, numbering just over 247,000 at the outset with 486,000 Reserves and Territorials. By November 1918 almost a further 5,000,000 had enlisted, over half of them volunteers. For the first time since Napoleon, Britain had become a nation in arms and, in January 1916, for the first time in the country's history, conscription was introduced. The war developed into one of attrition as the allies strove to break through the formidable enemy defences, and by the end casualties on both sides were on a scale hitherto unparalleled.

In 1921 81 volumes embracing every regiment and corps of the British Army were published listing approximately 635,000 Soldiers and 37,000 Officers who died in the war, and it is this immense undertaking which is now published by The Naval & Military Press on one fully-relational database **CD-ROM**.

Soldiers Died on CD-ROM contains the complete set of all 81 volumes with software that allows searching of every element in each record. Searches can be executed for Regiments, Battalions, surnames, christian name(s), initial(s), born (town), born (county), enlisted (town), enlisted (county), regimental number, rank, killed in action, died of wounds, died, theatre of war of death, date(s), supplementary notes.

"Complete relational database of all 665,000 soldiers and 37,000 officers who died in the great war. Originally published in eighty volumes in 1921"

Searches of elements can be made by one or as many elements as you wish. For example, you could search for every soldier who died of wounds on the second day of the Battle of the Somme, every soldier killed at the Battle of Neuve Chappelle, 10th - 13th March 1915, all the soldiers born in Belfast, all the men killed in actions in France and Flanders, all the men 'died' in India, all the men with the surname Buckland. As you will see, you will have at your fingertips what would have been months of toil and a very hefty card index system on the screen in a matter of seconds.

The software package has been designed with scroll down menu bars for Regiments and Battalions and on screen buttons for you to click on with your mouse for other elements within the search field to keep typing to a minimum. In fact, if you can read and type with one finger, however slowly, you will be able to use this database to its full potential.

After completing your search you can view and sort the data on screen and print out your results.

We cannot emphasise too greatly that this essential reference work has now been transformed into a fully searchable cross reference relational database.

The price of £220 represents a saving of over £1000 on the traditional published work in book form. (Price plus VAT where applicable.)

Orders to: **The Naval & Military Press, PO Box 61, Dallington, Heathfield, East Sussex, TN21 9ZS, England**
Telephone: 01435 830111 Fax: 01435 830623
Email: order.dept@naval-military-press.co.uk Website: http://www.great-war-casualties.com

By using digital technology *The Naval & Military Press* have created a permanent and substantial record of those who fell during the years 1914 - 1919, when the Great War was taking its heavy toll on the British Army, and this will now be available to future generations in an easily accessible format. *"Lest we forget"*

A

ACKERMAN O.N. 301992 Stoker Petty Officer William
H.M.S. Vivid, Royal Navy

"For services rendered by Petty Officers and men of the Grand Fleet in the action in the North Sea on the 31ˢᵗ May - 1ˢᵗ June, 1916."

Stoker Petty Officer William Ackerman evidenced considerable aptitude and bravery in clearing a suction box in a damaged compartment and freeing the rods in use to keep it clear. It was necessary at one time for him to descend in a diving suit for the purpose.

LONDON GAZETTE 15.9.1916

NOTES: With an annuity of £10.

Awarded French Medaille Militaire 17.3.1919.

Entitled to 1914-15 Star, British War Medal and Victory Medal.

ADAMS C/MX.68801 Acting Chief Motor Mechanic Leslie Charles Thomas
ML139, Royal Navy

"For Gallantry, resolution and seamanship when H.M. Air/Sea Rescue Craft were heavily attacked by enemy aircraft in the straits of Dover."

For great bravery when a fire broke out in one of H.M. Motor Launches. These two ratings, in the face of the greatest danger, entered a compartment and put out a fire. This action saved the ship.

LONDON GAZETTE 29.9.1942

NOTES: Able Seaman Guy Aundrie Sandford was also awarded the CGM for this action.

Published in the Gazette as Royal Naval Reserve it has been confirmed by the Naval Secretary that Adams was in fact Royal Navy. His award was presented on 24.11.1942.

FOR CONSPICUOUS GALLANTRY

ADE O.N. K.14283 Stoker, 1ˢᵗ Class, Arthur James
Royal Navy

"For services rendered by Petty Officers and men of the Eastern Mediterranean Squadron between the time of landing in the Gallipoli Peninsula in April, 1915, and the evacuation in December, 1915 - January 1916."

His picket boat was struck by a shrapnel shell on 9ᵗʰ August, 1915, and the steam pipe perforated. Stoker Ade - though the engine-room was full of steam - went down, shut off steam and brought up the Leading Stoker, who was severely wounded and scalded.

LONDON GAZETTE 15.5.1916

NOTES: Awarded French Medaille Militaire 17.3.1919.

Entitled to 1914-15 Star, British War Medal and Victory Medal.

ANDERSON O.N. F.12676 Leading Mechanic (E) Sydney Francis, D.S.M.

Royal Naval Air Service

For conspicuous gallantry, initiative and courage displayed by him on the 19ᵗʰ March, 1918, when the petrol system of his machine sustained extensive damage in action with enemy aircraft. After repairing the damage to the petrol system he noticed that the starboard engine was boiling violently. After reporting to the officer in charge and requesting that the engine be throttled down as far as possible, he climbed out on the lower plane, and effected extensive repairs to the water circulation system, and thus enable the engine to be opened out to the desired number of revolutions. Leading Mechanic Anderson's work, which was carried out entirely in the open in a wind force of ninety miles per hour, and occupied 1¾ hours undoubtedly saved the machine.

LONDON GAZETTE 26.4.1918

NOTES: Awarded D.S.M. 11.8.1917.

Entitled to British War Medal and Victory Medal, medals issued to him in Australia.

FOR CONSPICUOUS GALLANTRY

ATTWOOD O.N. M.B.1915 Chief Motor Mechanic James
Royal Naval Volunteer Reserve

"In recognition of distinguished services during the operations against Zeebrugge and Ostend on the night of the 22nd-23rd April 1918."

Leading Deckhand Weeks with Chief Motor Mech. Attwood and Chief Motor Mech. Fox. These three ratings were amongst those who volunteered to man the motor launches detailed to rescue the crews of the blockships, and it was largely due to the coolness and courage with which the crews of these motor launches carried out their duties that so many officers and men were rescued. These three men displayed most conspicuous gallantry in the face of intense gun and machine-gun fire at short range.

LONDON GAZETTE 23.7.1918

NOTES: With an annuity of £10.

Leading Deckhand Weeks and Chief Motor Mechanic Fox were also awarded the C.G.M for this action.

Awarded Croix de Guerre (France) 28.8.1918. Also entitled to British War and Victory Medals.

B

BACHE C/SR.8070 Ordnance Artificer Fourth Class John
H.M.S. Naiad, Royal Navy

"For outstanding gallantry , fortitude and resolution during the battle of Crete."

The ship in which Ordnance Artificer Bache was serving was attacked by aircraft and damaged. A messdeck was flooded and water began to enter the magazine beneath it, so the magazine crew were ordered to leave. As he could not reach the magazine access hatch, because of the flooding messdeck, Ordnance Artificer Bache climbed down into the magazine through the ammunition supply trunk, and managed to shut the hatch. Then the lights went out. Ordnance Artificer Bache climbed up the ammunition trunk, found a torch, and again went down to the flooding magazine. Though he knew he was shut in, with a flooded messdeck above him, he began to send ammunition to the guns, enabling them to remain in action, and at length to drive off the enemy, up the ammunition trunk, found a torch, and again went down to the flooding magazine.

LONDON GAZETTE 8.1.1942

NOTES: Award presented 13.4.1943.

BARNES P/JX.186520 Able Seaman John Richard
M.G.B. 77, Royal Navy

"For bravery and skill when H.M. Motor Gun Boats attacked and sank a laden enemy tanker, and severely damaged two escorting trawlers off the French Coast."

For coolness and bravery as Gunner in one of H.M. Motor Gun Boats. When his loader was wounded, he, though himself wounded in the leg, re-loaded his gun, and then, seeing the magazine ablaze and the flames spreading to the ammunition, he helped his Commanding Officer to put out the fire, and thus saved the ship.

LONDON GAZETTE 8.9.1942

NOTES: Awarded M.I.D. for service in M.G.B. 64 on 19th November 1941, published in the London Gazette 10.2.1942.

Medal presented on 13.4.1943.

BARRICK FAA/FX.76495 Petty Officer Airman Leonard Francis
884 Squadron, H.M.S. Victorious, Fleet Air Arm

"For bravery and dauntless resolution while serving in H.M. Ships Ashanti, Bramham, Cairo, Charybdis, Fury, Icarus, Intrepid, Ithuriel, Kenya, Laforey, Ledbury, Nelson, Nigeria, Pathfinder, Penn, Rodney, Rye, Somali, Speedy, Tartar, and Wolverine and in H.M. Aircraft-Carriers, Merchantmen and Oilers when an important Convoy was fought through to Malta in the face of relentless attacks by day and night from enemy submarines, aircraft and surface forces."

Who, though gravely wounded, fought his gun, and gave warning to his pilot of the approach of enemy fighters, until he fainted.

LONDON GAZETTE 10.11.1942

NOTES: Awarded D.S.M. 31.7.1945 for service on board H.M.S. Indefatigable in Operation Iceberg in the Pacific.

The C.G.M. was awarded for action in Operation Pedestal which was the convoy sent to supply Malta. He was presented with the medal on 18.5.1943.

BARRY Able Seaman David
H.M.S. Cracker, Royal Navy

"14th October 1855, Kinburn, Black Sea."

Recommended by Rear Admiral Stewart. The original recommendation no longer survives but the Digest Book states ' Stewart reports excellent conduct of crews of Cracker, Diamond & Leander and submits certain names for reward'. The Admiralty minute reads 'David Barry, A.B., Spitfire to be granted medal and gratuity.', dated 25th January 1856. No further details surrounding this award have yet been found.

LONDON GAZETTE Not published in the gazette.

NOTES: Awarded second medal, see below.

BARRY Able Seaman David
H.M.S. Cracker, Royal Navy

"4th-6th November 1855, Glofira & Gheisk, Sea of Azoff."

No precise details exist surrounding the act or act of bravery which resulted in this award of this medal which appeared in a list at the end of Captain Sherard Osborn's dispatch dated 7 November 1855, from H.M.S. Vesuvius off Gheisk when acting as Senior Officer in the Sea of Azoff. This list includes Thomas Kerr and Peter Hanlan who also received the C.G.M.

LONDON GAZETTE 8.12.1855

NOTES: Mentioned in Despatches, 8.12.1855.

BARTLETT Po. 15558 Private Henry George
Royal Marine Light Infantry

For conspicuous gallantry at the capture of Salif on the 12th June, 1917. Single-handed he entered a hut occupied by two unwounded and one wounded Turks and three Arabs and took them prisoner.

LONDON GAZETTE 11.8.1917

NOTES: Awarded French Medaille Militaire 28.8.1918.

BEELEY O.N. M.B.2108 Chief Motor Mechanic, Hugh
Royal Naval Volunteer Reserve

In recognition of his conspicuous gallantry, coolness and skill under extremely difficult conditions in action.

LONDON GAZETTE 22.8.1919

NOTES: Entitled to British War Medal and Victory Medal.

FOR CONSPICUOUS GALLANTRY

BEESE O.N. J.103009 (Dev.) Able Seaman Clifford
H.M.S. Kiawo, Royal Navy

"In recognition of their services at Wanhsien, Yangtse River, China, on the 5th September, 1926 , and connected events."

For conspicuous courage amongst the survivors of the boarding party.

LONDON GAZETTE 6.5.1927

BELDING Leading Seaman George
H.M.S. Firefly, Royal Navy

"8th August 1855, Gulf of Bothnia."

No further information is available concerning this award.

LONDON GAZETTE Not published in the gazette.

BENDALL O.N. Po./K5343 Stoker 1st Class, Henry Cullis
H.M. Submarine C3, Royal Navy

"In recognition of distinguished services during the operations against Zeebrugge and Ostend on the night of the 22nd-23rd April 1918."

Sto.1st Class Bendall, P.O. W.Harner, Ldg.Smn W.G.Cleaver and E.R.A. 3rd Cl. A.G. Roxburgh.

The ratings above mentioned were members of the crew of Submarine C.3, which was skillfully placed between the piles of the Zeebrugge mole viaduct and there blown up, the fuse being lighted before the submarine was abandoned. They volunteered for and, under the command of an officer, eagerly undertook this hazardous enterprise, although they were well aware that if the means of rescue failed, and that if any of them were in the water at the time of the explosion, they would be killed outright.

LONDON GAZETTE 23.7.1918

NOTES: P.O Harner, Ldg Seaman Cleaver and E.R.A Roxburgh were also awarded the C.G.M. for this action. Lt Howell-Price received the D.S.O. and Lt. Sandford the V.C.

Awarded Croix de Guerre (France) 28.8.1918.

Stoker Bendalls medals comprising C.G.M., 1914-15 Star, British War Medal, Victory Medal, Navy L.S.G.C. and Croix de Guerre are now on display in the Submarine Museum at Gosport.

BENNETT C.S. 71853 Able Seaman Harry
H.M.S. Philomel, Naval Brigade

"For services rendered during recent operations against Malays in the Straits of Malacca."

On 4th January 1876 during the attack made by the Malays at Kotalama on Brigadier General J. Ross Indian General Service. Perak 1875-1876 Henry Thompson and Harry Bennett saved the life of Doctor Townsend attached to the Buffs, by cutting down the Malays who were about to spear him when he was on the ground in a helpless condition, these seaman at the time being separated from the main body, caused through the thickness of the bush.

The despatch published on February 18th 1876 expands the action as follows;

I have the honour to report that yesterday morning the forces as per margin was taken by me, for the purpose of disarming the village of Kota Lama, $1\frac{1}{2}$ miles distant, on the opposite side of the Perak River.

This village, in July last, was visited by Mr. Birch, when the inhabitants came down in considerable numbers, loading their arms, and warning him not to come near. Having no force with him, he was obliged to withdraw.

For long this village has been the haunt of all the worst disposed and turbulent Malays. The Queens Commissioner, deeming it necessary to disarm the inhabitants and destroy the houses or certain known leaders, I made the following arrangements.

The village of Kota Lama is on the left bank of the river. Lieutenant-Colonel Cox crossed with his party in boats, and moved up the bank a little more than a mile, when he extended the men, the left of the line keeping close to the river, and skirmished through the village.

Mr. Maxwell, Deputy-Commissioner, accompanied Lieutenant-Colonel Cox.

Captain Young moved his party in a similar manner up the right bank, to a village of the same name; his orders were to collect any arms, but not to destroy or injure houses or property, as the inhabitants have been well disposed.

Captain Speedy, Assistant-Commissioner, accompanied Captain Young.

Major McNair, I, and my staff went with Captain Garforth's party of the Naval Brigade.

We landed on the left bank just above the village, and, leaving a few blue jackets in charge of the boats, we moved in the direction of the village, expecting there to find Lieutenant-Colonel Cox's party.

Twenty blue jackets landed with us, and we were joined by Lieutenant Hare, R.E., with 4 Goorkhas, who had been assisting him to measure the distance along the bank.

We proceeded some distance before we came to some houses which I desired should be searched for arms they were, with few exceptions, deserted; after about an hour and a half we came upon several houses close to each other, the largest being occupied by women and children.

It being necessary to ascertain whether any men also were in it, Major McNair sent in two of his Malay followers, and himself looked in.

After satisfying himself that there were only women and children, he had just got down from the steps telling those inside not to be alarmed as they would not be harmed, when he heard several shots, and from the jungle close by some 50 Malays rushed out upon us, a few with fire-arms and the rest with spears.

The attack was so sudden that we were almost surrounded and had to retire.

The conduct of the marines and sailors was deserving of all praise. If it had not been for their steadiness few if any of us would have escaped.

As it was I regret to say that our loss was heavy in proportion to the numbers engaged. A report with return of casualties is attached.

Just before this attack was made several officers moved away in the direction of the river, two hundred yards distant. Major Hawkins was, it is supposed, following them when he was fatally wounded with a spear. No one seems to have seen him fall, but Captain Garforth reports that

William Sloper A.B., came up to him on the ground, shot two Malays who were coming towards him, and stopped with him until Major Hawkins said "Save yourself; you can do me no good now."

Major Heathcote, who with Captain Badcock, Lieutenant Preston, and Major Twigge, had gone on in front of Major Hawkins towards the river, turned back with these officers and tried to move them, but they had to fall back to the river, before the superior numbers who were getting round them.

Surgeon Townsend was the first to be assailed, he being a little advanced; three Malays assailed him with spears, the centre one he shot with his pistol, and the man falling forward upon him knocked him down. The other two Malays were driving at him when Harry Bennett, A.B., and William Thompson, A.B., rushed forwardand killed them both.

The conduct of these three blue jackets above named has been specially brought to my notice, but all behaved admirably in a very difficult position, and very great credit is due to the three officers, Captain Garforth, Lieutenant Wood, and Sub-Lieutenant Poar, who directed and led them.

LONDON GAZETTE 10.3.1876

NOTES: Henry Thompson was also awarded the C.G.M. for his part in this action.

Harry Bennett's medals comprise C.G.M. and India General Service medal with clasp Perak.

BENNETT P/J.99941 Chief Petty Officer Percy Charles
H.M.S. Carnarvon Castle, Royal Navy

"For great courage and devotion to duty in action against an Armed Merchant Raider."

In this action Chief Petty Officer Bennett was wounded in six places, but gave no sign that he had been hit. He remained at his post until at last he was ordered below. His courage and fortitude were beyond all praise.

LONDON GAZETTE 6.6.1941

FOR CONSPICUOUS GALLANTRY

BENNISON O.N. 7495A Seaman William Henry
H.M.S. Dunraven, Royal Naval Reserve

" For services in action with enemy submarines."

From the official account published in the L.G. 19.11.1918:- On the 8th August, 1917, H.M.S. "Dunraven" under the command of Captain Gordon Campbell, V.C., D.S.O., R.N., sighted an enemy submarine on the horizon. In her role of armed British merchant ship, the "Dunraven" continued her zig-zag course, whereupon the submarine closed, remaining submerged to within 5,000 yards, and then, rising to the surface, opened fire. The "Dunraven" returned the fire with her merchant ship gun, at the same time reducing speed to enable the enemy to overtake her. Wireless signals were also sent out for the benefit of the submarine: "Help! Come quickly - submarine chasing and shelling me." Finally, when the shells began falling close, the "Dunraven" stopped and abandoned ship by the "panic party." The ship was then being heavily shelled, and on fire aft. In the meantime the submarine closed to 400 yards distant, partly obscured from view by the dense clouds of smoke issuing from the "Dunraven's" stern. Despite the knowledge that the after magazine must inevitably explode if he waited, and further, that a gun and gun's crew lay concealed over the magazine, Captain Campbell decided to reserve his fire until the submarine had passed clear of the smoke. A moment later, however a heavy explosion occurred aft, blowing the gun and gun's crew into the air, and accidentally starting fire-gongs at the remaining gun positions; screens were immediately dropped, and the only gun that would bear opened fire, but the submarine, apparently frightened by the explosion, had already commenced to submerge. Realising that a torpedo must inevitably follow, Captain Campbell ordered the surgeon to remove all wounded and conceal them in cabins; hoses were also turned on the poop, which was a mass of flames. A signal was sent out warning men-of-war to divert all traffic below the horizon in order that nothing should interrupt the final phase of the action. Twenty minutes later a torpedo again struck the ship abaft the engine-room. An additional party of men were again sent away as "panic party," and left the ship to outward appearances completely abandoned, with the White Ensign flying and guns unmasked. For the succeeding fifty minutes the submarine examined the ship through her periscope. During the period boxes of cordite and shells exploded every few minutes, and the fire on the poop still blazed furiously. Captain Campbell and the handful of officers and men who remained on board lay hidden during this ordeal. The submarine then rose to the surface astern, where no guns could bear and shelled the ship closely for twenty minutes. The enemy then submerged and steamed past the ship 150 yards off, examining her through the periscope. Captain Campbell decided then to fire one of his torpedoes, but missed by a few inches. The submarine crossed bows and came slowly down the other side, whereupon a second torpedo was fired and missed again. The enemy observed it and immediately submerged. Urgent signals for assistance were immediately sent out, but pending arrival of assistance Captain Campbell arranged for a third "panic party" to jump overboard if necessary and leave one gun's crew on board for a final attempt to destroy the enemy, should he again attack. Almost immediately afterwards, however, British and American destroyers arrived on the scene, the wounded were transferred, boats were recalled and the fire extinguished. The "Dunraven" although her stern was awash, was taken in tow, but the weather grew worse, and early the following morning she sank with colours flying.

LONDON GAZETTE 2.11.1917

NOTES: All of the gun's crew were put in a ballot for the V.C. this was awarded to P.O. Ernest Pitcher who commanded the gun, the remaining members of the gun crew Bennison, Martindale, Murphy, Sheppard and Thomson were all awarded the C.G.M. A ballot among the officers also awarded the V.C. to Lieut. Bonner D.S.C. In addition to these awards two further C.G.M.'s were awarded to crew of the Dunraven for the action, W/T Op. Fletcher and Seaman Morrison.

Mentioned in Despatches 21.4.1917.

Awarded French Medaille Militaire 28.8.1918.

Later Lieutenant. As Coxswain of the Hartlepool Lifeboat he was awarded the R.N.L.I.'s Gold Medal for rescuing five men from the London S.S. Hawkwood, 26 January 1942.

His medals comprising C.G.M., 1914-15 Star, British War Medal, Victory Medal (M.I.D.), R.N.R. Long Service Medal, French Medaille Militaire, appeared for sale at Spink on 23.9.1993.

FOR CONSPICUOUS GALLANTRY

BERNAYS A-321 Acting Chief Petty Officer Leopold
Royal Canadian Naval Reserve

"For services in action with enemy Submarines while serving in H.M. Canadian Ships."

LONDON GAZETTE 22.12.1942

BEVIS Assistant Sick Berth Attendant William
H.M.S. Boadicea, Royal Naval Brigade

Majuba Hill - South Africa : For having remained at his post in attendance upon the British wounded after our men had retired from that part of the field, and while the Boers were pouring in a hot fire on the wounded and the non-combatant officers and men attending upon them.

LONDON GAZETTE 3.5.1881

NOTES: A full report of the action, in which Bevis was shot twice through the helmet while waving a piece of lint attached to a bayonet, is given in the despatch of Surgeon Mahon, published in the London Gazette on 3.5.1881. This was the first of only two occasions where the C.G.M. was awarded for action in a campaign for which no campaign medal was issued. The other award being to John Bray.

Recommended for the Victoria Cross.

The CGM appeared for sale at Christies 14.3.1989.

BIRCHALL O.N. 271185 Chief Engine Room Artificer 2nd Class, Frederick Tinsley
H.M.S. Onslaught, Royal Navy

"For services rendered by Petty Officers and men of the Grand Fleet in the action in the North Sea on the 31st May - 1st June, 1916."

Chief Engine Room Artificer, Second Class, Birchall showed great coolness and resource in removing portions of shafting from forward to enable the after steering position to be successfully operated. His work was carried out under a heavy fire and he displayed a dexterity and calmness which did him the highest credit.

LONDON GAZETTE 15.9.1916

NOTES: With an annuity of £10.

Awarded French Medaille Militaire 17.3.1919.

Medals comprising C.G.M., 1914-15 Star, British War Medal, Victory Medal, Naval L.S.& G.C., French Medaille Militaire, offered for sale at Spink 8.11.1994.

BISHOP O.N. Ch. 201787 Chief Yeoman of Signals Albert Arthur
H.M.S. Agamemnon, Royal Navy

Showed great devotion to duty in action during the Dardanelles Operations. After his left leg had been shattered above the ankle, this man raised himself into a sitting position and continued performing his duties and passing reports to his Commanding Officer.

LONDON GAZETTE 21.4.1917

NOTES: With an annuity of £10.

Awarded French Medaille Militaire 28.8.1918. B.E.M. (Civil) 1.1.1954.

Medals comprising C.G.M., B.E.M. (Civil), 1914-15 Star, British War Medal, Victory Medal, Navy L.S. & G.C., French Medaille Militaire offered for sale at Spink on 28.3.1995.

BLORE London/3146 Leading Seaman Arthur Robert
Anson Battalion, Royal Naval Volunteer Reserve.

"For services in the Gallipoli Peninsula."

The battalion having occupied a portion of the enemy's fire trench on the 4th June, was engaged in digging communication trenches to a position in rear of it, on which they were consolidating the line. The officer being shot, Seaman Blore took charge of a party of 22 who advanced to cover the retirement. He shot two of the crew of a Turkish machine-gun enfilading the trench, and kept up a steady fire checking the enemy who were re-occupying it. He exhibited great bravery and power of leadership on a difficult occasion.

LONDON GAZETTE 13.9.1915

NOTES: Leading Seaman Blore is the only recipient to be awarded a bar to the C.G.M., see entry below.

BLORE London/3146 Acting Chief Petty Officer Arthur Robert, C.G.M.

Anson Battalion, Royal Naval Volunteer Reserve.

Bar to the Conspicuous Gallantry Medal

When all company officers had become casualties, and the company was held up by heavy machine-gun fire, this petty officer took command of the company. He reorganised and led the men forward by rushes to the enemy position. When about 100 yards from the position enemy fire became very heavy, and many casualties were caused to his command. Finding this, he went forward alone, and, single-handed, rushed the crew of a heavy machine gun, shooting the gunners. The enemy position was then turned, and thereby captured. By his initiative and personal courage a strong position was taken and many casualties avoided. Twenty-seven enemy machine guns, all of which were captured, were afterwards counted covering the ground over which this company advanced.

LONDON GAZETTE 29.10.1918

NOTES: With an annuity of £20.

Awarded M.M. as Chief Petty Officer with Anson Bn. 14.5.1919.

Chief Petty Officer Blore was born in 1890 and entered the Collingwood Battalion of the Royal Naval Division at the commencement of the Great War in 1914 and went immediately to France. He was transferred to the Anson Battalion and served at Cape Helles, Gallipoli in 1915 where he received his first C.G.M. He was promoted to Acting Petty Officer and returned to the Western Front and took part in the British offensive of 2nd September 1918 where he was awarded the bar to his C.G.M.

Medals comprising C.G.M. & Bar, M.M., 1914 Star and Bar, British War Medal and Victory Medal are now on display in the National Maritime Museum, Greenwich.

BOOKER P/JX.135773 Leading Seaman George Frederick

H.M.S. Ladybird, Royal Navy

"For courage and coolness when their ship was sunk by Enemy aircraft."

Who was in charge of one of the pom-poms when his ship was attacked. A bomb struck the ship, killing all the gun's crew but him, wrecking the gun and wounding many other men. He himself was badly wounded in both arms, but he at once set about rescuing the injured from a fire which had broken out near the magazine.

LONDON GAZETTE 7.10.1941

NOTES: Award presented 24.2.1942.

BOOTH C/JX186355 Acting Able Seaman Joseph
M.G.B. 8, Royal Navy

"For action with enemy ships off Boulogne."

Who, in his first action with the enemy, was hit in four places, but went on firing his gun until he ran out of ammunition, and then fell unconscious.

LONDON GAZETTE 3.3.1942

NOTES: The action took place on the night of 16/17th January 1942. Booth received his award at an investiture on 30th April 1943. The files relating to this award have now been destroyed and no further information is available from official sources.

BORROWMAN O.N. C/5/2407 Leading Seaman J.
Anson Battalion, Royal Naval Volunteer Reserve

"For services in the Gallipoli Peninsula."

For conspicuous gallantry on 4th June during operations at Cape Helles. During an assault a number of men had become separated from their units; Leading Seaman Borrowman gathered them together, re-organised them, and led them again to the assault, showing remarkable powers of leadership and command of men. He set a splendid example.

LONDON GAZETTE 19.11.1915

NOTES: Entitled to 1914 Star and bar, British War Medal and Victory Medal.

BRADDOCK R.F.R./B/Ch.2013 Private Charles
Chatham Battalion, Royal Marine Light Infantry

"For services with the Mediterranean Expeditionary Force."

Behaved with distinguished gallantry on May 1st during operations South of Achi Baba. When the enemy in greatly superior numbers attacked an outpost of 30 men he volunteered in company with Lieutenant Cheetham and one other man to counter-attack the enemy on a flank in the open under heavy fire, thus assisting to save the outpost line.

LONDON GAZETTE 3.6.1915

NOTES: Lt.Cheetham was awarded the D.S.C. for this action.

Entitled to 1914 Star and bar, British War Medal and Victory Medal.

BRAY Ships Corporal John
H.M.S. Griffon, Royal Navy

"Suppression of the slave trade, Indoni."

For gallantry during an anti-slavery patrol off Zanzibar on 27 October 1888.

NAVY LIST 1889

NOTES: With an annuity of £10.

This was one of only two instances of the C.G.M. being awarded for an action where no campaign medals were issued. The other being to William Bevis for the action at Majuba Hill in 1881.

BRENTNALL Gunner Alfred
H.M.S. Cleopatra, 12th Coy. Royal Marine Artillery

Awarded for action at Tamaai on 13th March 1884. No further information available.

NAVY LIST 1884

NOTES: Medals comprising C.G.M., Egypt 1883 with clasps Suakin 1884, El-Teb-Tamaai, Khedives Star 1882, appeared for sale at Spink on 8.12.1983.

BRIDGE C/SSX.28291 Able Seaman Rodney
H.M.S. Havock, Royal Navy

"For outstanding gallantry , fortitude and resolution during the battle of Crete."

Who stood to his gun, though grievously wounded by an enemy bomb, and went on firing without thought for his injury.

LONDON GAZETTE 8.1.1942

BRYANT O.N. Po./215297 Signalman Thomas Charles
Royal Navy

"In recognition of distinguished services during the operations against Zeebrugge and Ostend on the night of the 22nd-23rd April 1918."

This man, like all the crew of "Iris II.," behaved with great coolness and in a most exemplary manner under very heavy fire throughout the whole operation.

Shortly after leaving the mole at Zeebrugge the ship came under very heavy fire from the mole and shore batteries, being ten times hit by small shell and twice by large ones. The first large shell carried away the port side of the bridge on which Signalman Bryant was stationed, seriously wounding him and causing many other casualties.

Subsequently, being the only Signalman left in the ship, he was carried to the upper deck, and, although both his legs were shattered, he endeavoured to answer signals which were being made, behaving with great fortitude while in considerable pain.

LONDON GAZETTE 23.7.1918

NOTES: Awarded Croix de Guerre (France) 28.8.1918.

Entitled to 1914-15 Star, British War Medal and Victory Medal.

BUNCE FAA/SFX.631 Naval Airman First Class Donald Arthur
825 Squadron, Fleet Air Arm

Who was Air Gunner in the Swordfish aircraft piloted by Sub-Lieutenant Kingsmill. With his machine on fire, and the engine failing, he stayed steadfast at his gun, engaging the enemy fighters which beset his aircraft. He is believed to have shot one of them down. Throughout the action his coolness was unshaken.

LONDON GAZETTE 3.3.1942

NOTES: This action took place on the morning of Thursday, 12th February, 1942, when the Squadron, under the command of Lieutenant-Commander Esmonde D.S.O., were ordered to attack the German battle cruisers "Scharnhorst" and "Gneisenau" and the cruiser "Prinz Eugen" which, strongly escorted by thirty surface craft, were entering the Straits of Dover. The six planes of the Squadron which had been based at R.A.F. Manston in Kent, all failed to return from this action. Lieut-Commander Esmonde D.S.O. received the V.C. posthumously for his leadership in the attack Sub-Lt.Kingsmill and his Observer Sub-Lt Samples were awarded the D.S.O. for this action. In total the squadron earned one V.C., three D.S.O.'s one C.G.M. and twelve Posthumous M.I.D.'s.

Award presented April 1942.

BURGESS 251916 1st Sergeant Wilbur McC
United States Marine Corps

Awarded in connection with the conquest of Gilbert and Ellis Islands.

LONDON GAZETTE Not published in the gazette, award approved by H.M. King George VI 11.1.1945.

NOTES: Sergeant Burgess' medal was sent to him via the Foreign Office 19.11.1945.

BURKE CS.6600.A / O.N. 66729 Captain of the Maintop Henry
H.M.S. Rattlesnake, Royal Navy

ASHANTEE 1873-1874: Who, with Quarter Master William Holloway, behaved with the utmost coolness and intrepidity, and the latter was wounded on the occasion of the attack on our boats in the Prah (14th August 1873). Their services being however secondary to those of Godden and Sermon, but Burke and Holloway are most worthy of their Lordships' consideration.

NAVY LIST 1874

NOTES: William Burke, Henry Godden and William Sermon were all awarded the C.G.M. for this action.

Burkes medals comprise C.G.M., Ashantee War Medal and Navy L.S. & G.C.

BURNETT Po.412 Bugler George W.
38th Company Royal Marine Light Infantry

ASHANTEE 1873 - 1874: Was bugler of the 1st Company at the attack on Essaman and other hostile villages, 14th October 1873. Was in front from first to last. Showed coolness and courage in going from under cover and showing himself in the open to prevent our being fired into by the Houssas.

NAVY LIST 1874

C

CALDER CS.63617/23651.A Boatswain's Mate Alexander
H.M.S. Encounter, Royal Navy

ASHANTEE 1873-1874: At the battle of Amoaful, 31st January 1874, about noon, Ashantis in force came suddenly in sight, close to that portion of the line defended by the left of H.M.S. Encounter's (D) Company and right of the Royal Marines. Receiving a sharp fire, one of our men furthest in advance fell badly wounded and insensible.

The Ashantis continued to advance and would certainly have cut off the party taking the wounded man out of fire, had not a few men courageously stood their ground steadily and checked the rush of the enemy by a well defended fire.

The leader of this small party was a Boatswain's Mate of H.M.S. Encounter, by name Calder, and it was due to his distinguished gallantry and most admirable coolness, that the rest of the men held their position, and eventually caused the enemy to retreat.

NAVY LIST 1874

NOTES: With an annuity of £10.

CHAPMAN P/J.98330 Able Seaman Bennett
H.M.S. Aphis, Royal Navy

"For courage, skill and devotion to duty in operations off the Libyan coast."

Who, though badly wounded at his pom-pom, fought on until he could do no more, and then went to the bridge to report. On his way he passed the Sick Bay, but he did not go in until ordered to by the First Lieutenant.

LONDON GAZETTE 29.7.1941

NOTES: Award presented 24.3.1942.

FOR CONSPICUOUS GALLANTRY

CHEENEY P/MX.124844 Leading Motor Mechanic William Herbert

L.C.S. (L) 260, Royal Navy

"For gallantry, determination and devotion to duty in the assault and capture of the Island of Walcheren."

On 1st November, 1944, during the assault on Westkapelle L.C.S. (L) 260 received a direct shell hit in the wing petrol tank which penetrated to and caused a fire in the engine room. Leading Motor Mechanic Cheeney succeeded alone in getting the engine room fire under control with extinguishers, but could not get near the tank compartment hatch owing to the heat. When another craft came alongside to assist, Cheeney had a hose rigged from her, and sitting from outboard in the shell-hole in the ship's side, fought and put out the fire. Undeterred by the knowledge that petrol remained on board, he saved his ship by his very gallant action.

LONDON GAZETTE 22.12.1944

NOTES: Award presented 13.3.1945.

CHRISTMAS Petty Officer 2nd Class William John

Royal Navy

"In connection with the recent operations in China."

LONDON GAZETTE 14.5.1901

CLARK O.N.178489 Dev.B/1535 Petty Officer 1st Class Thomas James

Royal Fleet Reserve

"For services at Dar-es-Salaam, 28th November 1914."

Petty Officer Clark was Coxswain of H.M.S. "Goliath's" steam pinnace. He was wounded, but gallantly returned to the wheel, to which he stood until the boat was out of gunfire.

LONDON GAZETTE 10.4.1915

NOTES: With an annuity of £10.

Awarded French Medaille Militaire 28.8.1918.

Entitled to 1914-15 Star, British War Medal and Victory Medal.

CLEAVER O.N. Po./221196 Leading Seaman William Gladstone
H.M. Submarine C3, Royal Navy

"In recognition of distinguished services during the operations against Zeebrugge and Ostend on the night of the 22ⁿᵈ-23ʳᵈ April 1918."

Sto.1ˢᵗ Class Bindall, P.O. W.Harner, Ldg.Smn W.G.Cleaver and E.R.A. 3ʳᵈ Cl. A.G. Roxburgh.

The ratings above mentioned were members of the crew of Submarine C.3, which was skillfully placed between the piles of the Zeebrugge mole viaduct and there blown up, the fuse being lighted before the submarine was abandoned. They volunteered for and, under the command of an officer, eagerly undertook this hazardous enterprise, although they were well aware that if the means of rescue failed, and that if any of them were in the water at the time of the explosion, they would be killed outright.

LONDON GAZETTE 23.7.1918

NOTES: With an annuity of £10.

P.O Harner, Ldg Seaman Cleaver and E.R.A Roxburgh were also awarded the C.G.M. for this action. Lt. Howell-Price received the D.S.O. and Lt. Sandford the V.C.

Awarded D.S.M. 2.11.1917, Croix de Guerre (France) 28.8.1918.

Leading Seaman Cleavers medals comprising, C.G.M., D.S.M., 1914-15 Star, British War Medal, Victory Medal and Croix de Guerre are now on display at the Submarine Museum in Gosport.

COLE O.N. 110113 Chief Petty Officer William Stephen
Hood Battalion, Royal Naval Volunteer Reserve

"For services in the Gallipoli Peninsula."

For distinguished gallantry and meritorious work during operations at Cape Helles on 4ᵗʰ June. The advance had been checked and was hesitating; Cole rushed forward under heavy fire, rallied the men, and himself returned and got up the supports, and then again led the advance.

FOR CONSPICUOUS GALLANTRY

LONDON GAZETTE 19.11.1915

NOTES: With an annuity of £10.

Awarded D.S.M. LG 1.1.1915 for operations around Antwerp from 3rd to 9th October 1914. Mentioned in Despatches 22.9.1915, later commissioned as Sub.Lt.

Entitled to 1914 Star and bar, British War Medal and Victory Medal.

COONEY C/JX236141 Able Seaman Michael Stanley
M.L. 361, Royal Navy

"For gallantry and determination when heavily attacked from the air while serving in light craft."

Able Seaman Cooney was serving a gun and was severely wounded when aircraft attacked, and the sights of his gun were blown away. Nevertheless he kept up a continuous and accurate fire throughout the action, and even when attacking aircraft withdrew refused to leave his action station until his ship reached harbour. He was then discovered helping the other wounded until, on the point of collapse, he was himself ordered onto a stretcher.

His dauntless courage throughout this action was an inspiration to all who were present.

LONDON GAZETTE 2.11.1943

NOTES: The action took place during Operation Emolument.

Award presented 8.5.1945.

COXON O.N. K.X./265 Leading Seaman Thomas
Howe Battalion, Royal Naval Volunteer Reserve.

"For services in the Gallipoli Peninsula."

For great gallantry and meritorious work on the 4th June during operations at Cape Helles. All the officers and section commanders of his Company had been killed or wounded. Leading Seaman Coxon, with great presence of mind, grasped the situation, rallied his Company, and led them on to the enemy's trenches; a retirement might have had serious results. By his personality and example he saved the situation.

LONDON GAZETTE 19.11.1915

NOTES: With an annuity £10.

CREMER O.N. 214235 Able Seaman Ernest Randall
Submarine E6, Royal Navy

"Extract from Commodore (S) R.J.B. Keyes, C.B., M.V.O. despatch dated 17th October, 1914 and published in the London gazette on 23rd October, 1914."

On 25th September, Submarine "E6" (Lieutenant-Commander C.P.Talbot), while diving, fouled the moorings of a mine laid by the enemy. On rising to the surface she weighed the mine and sinker; the former was securely fixed between the hydroplane and its guard; fortunately, however, the horns of the mine were pointed outboard. The weight of the sinker made it a difficult and dangerous matter to lift the mine clear without exploding it. After half an hour's patient work this was effected by Lieutenant Frederick A.P. Williams-Freeman and Able Seaman Ernest Randall Cremer, Official Number 214235, and the released mine descended to it's original depth.

LONDON GAZETTE 23.10.1914

NOTES: Lt. F.A.P. Williams-Freeman was awarded the D.S.O. for his part in this action in the same gazette.

With an annuity of £10.

Awarded D.S.M. 2.11.1917, French Medaille Militaire 17.3.1919.

Entitled to 1914-15 Star, British War Medal and Victory Medal.

CROUCH Chief Gunners Mate Robert H.
Royal Navy

No information available on the circumstances surrounding this award.

NAVY LIST 1894

NOTES: With an annuity of £10.

D

DARROCK O.N. Ch./K5718 Stoker 1st Class John
H.M.S. Botha, Royal Navy

"For services in the action with enemy destroyers off the Belgian coast on the 21st March 1918."

For most conspicuous gallantry and devotion to duty. He entered the damaged boiler-room of H.M.S. "Botha," from which steam was still escaping, and assisted watchkeepers to get on deck under heavy fire.

LONDON GAZETTE 21.6.1918

NOTES: Awarded French Medaille Militaire 17.3.1919.

Entitled to 1914-15 Star, British War Medal and Victory Medal.

DAVIDSON O.N.K14753 Stoker 1st Class Thomas, D.S.M.
H.M.S. Indefatigable, Royal Navy

"For services when H.M.S. "Inflexible" was damaged by a mine on 18th March."

LONDON GAZETTE 16.8.1915

NOTES: Awarded Croix de Guerre (France) 19.12.1917, also entitled to 1914-15 Star, British War Medal and Victory Medal.

DAVIES O.N. Ch. 301312 Stoker 1st Class James
Royal Navy

For very gallant rescue work performed when the ship in which he was serving struck a mine.

LONDON GAZETTE 12.5.1917

NOTES: Entitled to 1914-15 Star, British War Medal and Victory Medal.

DAVIS O.N. Ch./189243 Leading Seaman Albert Oscar
Royal Navy

"In recognition of distinguished services during the operations against Zeebrugge and Ostend on the night of the 22nd-23rd April 1918."

Leading Seaman Davis remained at his station in "Iphigenia" after the mines had been fired and after the cutter had left, awaiting, in accordance with instructions previously given, orders to destroy his gun. The order was not received, and he stayed at his post until the ship sank under him, when he jumped into the water and swam to the boats.

LONDON GAZETTE 23.7.1918

NOTES: With an annuity of £10.

Awarded Croix de Guerre (France) 28.8.1918.

Entitled to 1914-15 Star, British War Medal and Victory Medal.

DAY O.N. 134670 Petty Officer Frederick Adolphus (alias Parsons)
H.M.S. Malaya, Royal Navy

"For services rendered by Petty Officers and men of the Grand Fleet in the action in the North Sea on the 31st May - 1st June, 1916."

When a shell exploded in the starboard battery of the ship in which Petty Officer Day and Leading Seaman Watson were serving, a considerable blast of flame and smoke caused a quantity of smouldering debris to fall among a hoist of cartridges in bags. Petty Officer Day showed great coolness and presence of mind in immediately jumping amongst the cartridges, removing the debris. In doing this he was assisted by Leading Seaman Watson; these two dealing with the dangerous situation promptly.

LONDON GAZETTE 15.9.1916

NOTES: Awarded Croix de Guerre (France) 19.12.1917. Entitled to 1914-15 Star, British War Medal and Victory Medal. The medal card for the first world war medals has the notation 'Alias Parsons'.

Leading Seaman Watson was also awarded the CGM for this action.

FOR CONSPICUOUS GALLANTRY

DEAN Plymouth/12447 Corporal Ernest Victor
Royal Marine Light Infantry

"From the despatch of Rear Admiral E.Charlton describing the later coastal operations by H.M. ships against German East Africa."

Showed great initiative at Bagamoyo. After Captain Thomas, R.M.L.I., had been killed he immediately informed the Commanding Officer of the situation, and then taking cover behind a tree shot one German and one Askari, and wounded a second Askari.

LONDON GAZETTE 15.6.1917

NOTES: Croix de Guerre (France) 14.9.1918.

Corporal Dean's medals comprising C.G.M., 1914-15 Star, British War Medal, Victory Medal (M.I.D.), Navy L.S.&G.C., Navy M.S.M. and Croix de Guerre are now on display at the Royal Marines Museum, Portsmouth.

DESRANGES Premier Maitre Andre Jules Marcel
French Navy

Awarded for great gallantry on special service.

LONDON GAZETTE Not published in the gazette, award approved by H.M. King George VI 24.1.1945.

NOTES: Presented by His Excellency the British Ambassador, Paris, 28.10.1947.

DEWAR Clyde Z/232 Acting Leading Seaman John
Royal Naval Volunteer Reserve

On the 20th November, 1915, in the Gallipoli Peninsula he threw away a live grenade, which had fallen in the trench, just in time to save a serious accident.

LONDON GAZETTE 31.5.1916

NOTES: Entitled to 1914-15 Star, British War Medal and Victory Medal.

FOR CONSPICUOUS GALLANTRY

DEWHURST RMA.3649 Gunner William
5th Company Royal Marine Artillery, H.M.S. Druid

ASHANTEE 1873 - 1874: For seizing a flag from the enemy at one of the actions around Elmina on 13th June 1873.

NAVY LIST 1874

DOE K.P. /61 Able Seaman George Henry
Howe battalion, Royal Naval Volunteer Reserve

"For services with the Mediterranean Expeditionary Force."

Displayed conspicuous gallantry on May 7th during operations South of Achi Baba in continuing to work his machine-gun after the remainder of the crew had been wounded; this resulted in the enemy's shrapnel being turned from the advancing infantry onto himself.

LONDON GAZETTE 3.6.1915

NOTES: Killed in action on 13.11.1916. He has no known grave and is commemorated on the Thiepval memorial.

Entitled to 1914-15 Star, British War Medal and Victory Medal.

DOLLAR O.N. 41560 Able Seaman Tom
H.M.S.Monarch, Royal Navy

ASHANTEE 1873 - 1874: When appointed to the command of the scouts in the second phase of the Ashantee Campaign of 1874, I asked for this man's service as a scout in consequence of the conspicuous gallantry I had personally seen him display at Abrakrampa on 5th November 1873.

He served throughout the remainder of the war as a scout, particularly distinguishing himself at Becquah and in the advance guard engagements near the river Ordah, where he was severely wounded whilst pluckily leading the scouts against an ambuscade. Although suffering from the wound received the day previous, he took part in the action before entering Coomassie until ordered to desist. In all the skirmishes the Scouts had, Dollar was the first man to volunteer to lead against the Ashanti fire.

29

NAVY LIST 1875

NOTES: The recommendation was written by Captain Lord Gifford V.C. Tom Dollar had been erroneously discharged in the Gold Coast and had served as one of Gifford's scouts during the Ashantee war. Interestingly the ship H.M.S. Monarch shown on his C.G.M. did not serve in the Ashantee war, indeed it lay unmanned in reserve at Portsmouth.

His medals comprise C.G.M., Ashantee Medal with clasp Coomassie.

DORAN Boatswain's Mate James
H.M.S. Agamemnon, Royal Navy

"17th October 1854, Fleet bombardment of Sebastopol and Fort Constantine."

No further information concerning the award of this medal have been found.

LONDON GAZETTE Award not published.

NOTES: With gratuity of £15.

Doran had applied, as was the practice at this time, for the V.C. Although his recommendation was endorsed by Admiral Lord Lyons, Commander in Chief in the Mediterranean, it did not reach the Admiralty until 11th January 1857, when disposed of on the following February 27th it was said to be "Too late for grant of the Victoria Cross".

DRADY Private Daniel
13th Company, H.M.S. Cleopatra, Royal Marine Light Infantry

Awarded on 13th March 1884 at Tamaai, Egypt.

NAVY LIST 1884

NOTES: C.G.M. offered for sale at Spink 10.12.1987.

DRISCOLL C.S. 67843 Able Seaman Dennis
H.M.S. Active, Royal Navy

ASHANTEE 1873 - 1874: Particularly mentioned by Lieutenant W.F.S. Mann R.N. for the good example he set during the battle of Amoaful, 31st

January, 1874, by his coolness and cheerfulness under a heavy fire. Was severely wounded and lost an eye.

NAVY LIST 1874

DUNN X.19116A Seaman Joseph
H.M.S. Cape Finisterre, Royal Naval Reserve

For bringing down an enemy aircraft and for returning to a sinking ship and searching in a steam-filled engine room for a missing shipmate.

LONDON GAZETTE 6.9.1940

NOTES: Award presented 1.3.1941.

E

ELTON LT/JX.180250 Seaman Cook Jesse Harry Herbert
H.M.Y. Bystander, Royal Navy

"For good services in the withdrawal of the Allied Armies from the beaches of Dunkirk."

LONDON GAZETTE 16.8.1940

EWING O.N. 2637 E.S. Engineman James
H.M. Drifter Violet May, Royal Naval Reserve

"For services in action on the occasion of the raid into the straits of Dover by enemy destroyers on the night of the 14th-15th February 1918."

For conspicuous gallantry and devotion to duty.

When their ship had been severely handled by the enemy, and was on fire forward, and all the rest of the crew had been killed with two exceptions, and those so badly wounded that they could render little or no assistance, Engmn. Ewing and Noble cleared the wreckage of the boom from the small boat, got out the boat, put their wounded shipmates into it, and then took to the boat. Finding the ship did not sink, they returned to her, attacked the fire with buckets, and got it out, small arm ammunition in the wheelhouse exploding as they worked. They then got their injured shipmates on board again and made them comfortable, afterwards burning flares of old clothes soaked in paraffin until picked up and towed in at 7 a.m.

LONDON GAZETTE 16.3.1918

NOTES: With an annuity of £10.

Awarded French Medaille Militaire 17.3.1919.

Engineman Noble was also awarded the C.G.M. The Vice Admiral, Dover Patrol reported - "The conduct of Noble and Ewing was altogether admirable. Their great gallantry and devotion to duty - and, I would add, their simple modesty - entitles them to very special consideration.

Entitled to 1914-15 Star, British War Medal and Victory Medal.

F

FERRIER C/JX.145141 Leading Seaman Alexander Mitchell
H.M.S. Talbot, Royal Navy

"For great gallantry in carrying out a daring attack by night, with "Human Torpedoes", on the strongly defended enemy base at Palermo. The operation was most hazardous. The defences of the harbour had to be penetrated and it's whole length crossed without detection, and the "Human Torpedoes" manoeuvred into position under the targets. An enemy cruiser was sunk and a transport much damaged."

This was the succesful attack on the Italian Cruiser Ulpio Traiano on 2nd January 1943.

LONDON GAZETTE 18.4.1944

NOTES: Award presented 25.7.1944.

Awarded Polish Cross of Valour (Krzyz Walecznych) for service in Polish ships 21.10.1941.

FLETCHER O.N. 404 W.T.S. W/T Op. 1st Class Thomas Ernest
H.M.S. Dunraven, Royal Naval Reserve

"For services in action with enemy submarines."

From the official account published in the L.G. 19.11.1918:- On the 8th August, 1917, H.M.S. "Dunraven" under the command of Captain Gordon Campbell, V.C., D.S.O., R.N., sighted an enemy submarine on the horizon. In her role of armed British merchant ship, the "Dunraven" continued her zig-zag course, whereupon the submarine closed, remaining submerged to within 5,000 yards, and then, rising to the surface, opened fire. The "Dunraven" returned the fire with her merchant ship gun, at the same time reducing speed to enable the enemy to overtake her. Wireless signals were also sent out for the benefit of the submarine: "Help! Come quickly - submarine chasing and shelling me." Finally, when the shells began falling close, the "Dunraven" stopped and abandoned ship by the "panic party." The ship was then being heavily shelled, and on fire aft. In the meantime the submarine closed to 400 yards distant, partly obscured from view by the dense clouds of smoke issuing from the "Dunraven's" stern. Despite the knowledge that the after magazine must inevitably explode if he waited, and further, that a gun and gun's crew lay concealed over the magazine, Captain Campbell decided to reserve his fire until the submarine had passed clear of the smoke. A moment later, however a heavy explosion occurred aft, blowing the gun and gun's crew into the air, and accidentally starting fire-gongs at the remaining gun positions; screens were immediately dropped, and the only gun that would bear opened fire, but the submarine, apparently frightened by the explosion, had already commenced to submerge. Realising that a torpedo must inevitably follow, Captain Campbell ordered the surgeon to remove all wounded and conceal them in cabins; hoses were also turned on the poop, which was a mass of flames. A signal was sent out warning men-of-war to divert all traffic below the horizon in order that nothing should interrupt the final phase of the action. Twenty minutes later a torpedo again struck the ship abaft the engine-room. An additional party of men were again sent away as "panic party," and left the ship to outward appearances completely abandoned, with the White Ensign flying and guns unmasked. For the succeeding fifty minutes the submarine examined the ship through her periscope. During the period boxes of cordite and shells exploded every few minutes, and the fire on the poop still blazed furiously. Captain Campbell and the handful of officers and men who remained on board lay hidden during this ordeal. The submarine then rose to the surface astern, where no guns could bear and shelled the ship closely for twenty minutes. The enemy then submerged and steamed past the ship 150 yards off, examining her through the periscope. Captain Campbell decided then to fire one of his torpedoes, but missed by a few inches. The submarine crossed bows and came slowly down the other side, whereupon a second torpedo was fired and missed again. The enemy observed it and immediately submerged. Urgent signals for assistance were immediately sent out, but pending arrival of assistance Captain Campbell arranged for a third "panic party" to jump overboard if necessary and leave one gun's crew on board for a final attempt to destroy the enemy, should he again attack. Almost immediately afterwards, however, British and American destroyers arrived on the scene, the wounded were transferred, boats were recalled and the fire extinguished. The "Dunraven" although her stern was awash, was taken

35

in tow, but the weather grew worse, and early the following morning she sank with colours flying.

LONDON GAZETTE 30.10.1917

NOTES: All of the gun's crew were put in a ballot for the V.C. this was awarded to P.O. Ernest Pitcher who commanded the gun, the remaining members of the gun crew Bennison, Martindale, Murphy Sheppard and Thomson were all awarded the C.G.M. A ballot among the officers also awarded the V.C. to Lieut. Bonner D.S.C. In addition to these awards two further C.G.M.'s were awarded to crew of the Dunraven for the action, W/T Op. Fletcher and Seaman Morrison.

LONDON GAZETTE 2.11.1917

NOTES: With annuity of £10.

Awarded D.S.M. 23.3.1917, French Medaille Militaire 28.8.1918.

Entitled to 1914-15 Star, British War Medal and Victory Medal.

FLOWERS Po/9146 Corporal John Edward
H.M.S. Fox, Royal Marine Light Infantry

"In recognition of gallantry at Illig, Somaliland on 21ˢᵗ April, 1904."
LONDON GAZETTE 6.9.1904

NOTES: With an annuity of £10.

FOX O.N. M.B.1872 Chief Motor Mechanic Sydney Harold
Royal Naval Volunteer Reserve

"In recognition of distinguished services during the operations against Zeebrugge and Ostend on the night of the 22ⁿᵈ-23ʳᵈ April 1918."
Leading Deckhand Weeks with Chief Motor Mechanic Attwood and Chief Motor Mechanic Fox. These three ratings were amongst those who volunteered to man the motor launches detailed to rescue the crews of the blockships, and it was largely due to the coolness and courage with which the crews of these motor launches carried out their duties that so many officers and men were rescued. These three men displayed most

conspicuous gallantry in the face of intense gun and machine-gun fire at short range.

LONDON GAZETTE 23.7.1918

NOTES: With an annuity of £10.

Leading Dockhand Weeks and Chief Motor Mechanic Attwood were also awarded the C.G.M. for this action.

Awarded Croix de Guerre (France) 28.8.1918.

Entitled to British War Medal and Victory Medal.

FREEL D/JX.149484 Acting Leading Seaman James Michael
Royal Navy

"For great gallantry in carrying out a daring attack by night, with "Human Torpedoes", on the strongly defended enemy base at Palermo. The operation was most hazardous. The defences of the harbour had to be penetrated and it's whole length crossed without detection, and the "Human Torpedoes" manoeuvred into position under the targets. An enemy cruiser was sunk and a transport much damaged."
The succesful sinking of the Italian SS Viminali on 2nd January 1943.

LONDON GAZETTE 18.4.1944

NOTES: Award presented 19.11.1946.

FULLER CJX 138699 Leading Seaman George Robert
H.M.S. Wryneck, Royal Navy

"For gallantry and distinguished services in operations in Greek waters."
Who, though badly wounded, fought his gun till the last, and when his ship was sunk, heartened the survivors by his courage and cheerfulness.

LONDON GAZETTE 11.11.1941

NOTES: Award presented 16.11.1943.

G

GALE O.N. Ch./272503 Chief Engine Room Artificer Frank Marsden
Royal Navy

"In recognition of distinguished services during the operations against Zeebrugge and Ostend on the night of the 22nd-23rd April 1918."

After both engines of "Thetis" had been disabled, and when the ship was in a sinking condition, this Chief Petty Officer returned to the engine-room, with an Engineer Officer, and succeeded in re-starting the starboard engine, thereby enabling the ship to be turned mote into the fairway before she sank..

LONDON GAZETTE 23.7.1918

NOTES: With an annuity of £10.

Awarded Croix de Guerre (France) 28.8.1918.

Entitled to 1914-15 Star, British War Medal and Victory Medal.

GALLAGHER O.N.(Dev.)222943 Leading Seaman Thomas Arthur
Royal Navy

"For services at Dar-es-Salaam, 28th November 1914."

Leading Seaman Gallagher was coxswain of H.M.S. "Fox's" steam cutter. When twice wounded, and under galling fire, he remained at the tiller, and with the utmost coolness steered his board through the danger zone.

LONDON GAZETTE 10.4.1915

NOTES: With an annuity of £10.

Awarded French Medaille Militaire 28.8.1918.

Killed by a mine explosion in the North Sea on 2.8.1918 whilst serving aboard H.M.S. Vehement. He is commemorated on the Plymouth memorial.

Entitled to 1914-15 Star, British War Medal and Victory Medal.

GARDNER Sick Berth Steward Thomas
Royal Navy

"In connection with the recent operations in China."
LONDON GAZETTE 14.5.1901

GAVAN Gunner Dominick
H.M.S. Active, 26th Company, Royal Marine Artillery

ASHANTEE 1873 - 1874: Was present in all engagements, was wounded in the face and chin at Amoaful, 31st January, 1874, remained in the field and was conspicuous by his bravery.

NAVY LIST 1874

GEORGE Leading Seaman Herbert Edward
Royal Navy

"For services in connection with the recent operations in China."
LONDON GAZETTE 22.3.1901

NOTES: With an annuity of £10.

GHOM O.N. 17113 Petty Officer 1st Class, Frederick
H.M.S. Ganges, Royal Navy

"In recognition of their services during the action between our cruisers and the enemy squadron which bombarded Lowestoft on the 25th April, 1916."
LONDON GAZETTE 22.6.1916

NOTES: With an annuity £10.

Awarded French Medaille Militaire 17.3.1919. His medals comprising C.G.M., 1914-15 Star, British War Medal, Victory Medal, Navy L.S. & G.C. and French Medaille Militaire are now held by the Imperial War Museum in London.

C.G.M. is inscribed with the date of action being 27th - 29th April 1916.

GIBSON O.N. Ch./191025 R.F.R. B.3829 Petty Officer 2nd Class Frederick

H.M.S. Albion, Royal Fleet Reserve

"Despatch of Vice Admiral John M. de Robeck reporting on the landing of the Army on the Gallipoli Peninsula 25th-26th April 1915."

Jumped overboard with a line and got his boat beached to complete bridge from "River Clyde" to shore. He then took wounded to "River Clyde" under heavy fire.

LONDON GAZETTE 16.8.1915

NOTES: See the account under Petty Officer J.H.Russell.

With an annuity £10.

Awarded French Medaille Militaire 28.8.1918.

Medals comprising C.G.M., 1914-15 Star, British War Medal, Victory Medal, Royal Fleet Reserve L.S. Medal, French Medaille Militaire, offered for sale at Spink 8.11.1994.

GODDARD P/MX.89069 Engine Room Artificer Fourth Class Edmund

H.M. Submarine X6, Royal Navy

"For gallantry, skill and daring during the successful attack by His Majesty's Midget Submarines X7 and X6 on the Tirpitz."

LONDON GAZETTE 22.12.1944

NOTES: Operation Source was the daring attack by H.M. Submarines X6 and X7 and their crews who penetrated the anti-torpedo nets which surrounded the Tirpitz in Kaafjord, Norway, and successfully laid their charges under the battleship.

Having been damaged it was impossible for X6 to escape and Lieut. Cameron destroyed most of the secret equipment and scuttled his craft. The crew, comprising Lieut. Cameron, Sub-Lieut Loriman, Sub-Lieut Kendall and E.R.A. Goddard were all taken prisoner and were being interrogated aboard the Tirpitz when their charges along with those laid by X7 exploded.

The X7 was also badly damaged, after surfacing several times, by gun-fire and Lieut Place decided to bring the craft to the surface to give the crew chance to escape before scuttling the craft. Lieut. Place and Sub-Lieut. Aitken were the only survivors from X7.

The V.C. was awarded to Lieutenants Cameron and Place and the D.S.O. to Sub Lieutenants Loriman, Kendall, and Aitken.

In March 1945 when POW's were being marched from their camp, Marlag und Milag Nord, near Bremen, to Lubeck, Goddard and two others took advantage of a bend in the road and a nearby wood to break away unseen. After surviving for more than a week on the run, Goddard passed through the German lines and was found by advancing British troops.

Edmund Goddard was born in 1921and after his education in Oxford started as an apprentice tool maker in Coventry. In 1941 he joined the Royal Navy and found instead of travelling the world by sea, he was firewatching on the roof of the Royal Naval Barracks in Portsmouth. He volunteered for 'special duties', not knowing what they were, and found himself on the early X-craft training programme.

Award presented 22.6.1945.

GODDEN CS10001.A Captain's Coxswain Henry
H.M.S. Rattlesnake, Royal Navy

ASHANTEE 1873 - 1874: With Able Seaman William Sermon. These men waded on shore through the surf at Chamah on 14th August 1873, and at the imminent risk to their lives, brought off the second cutter of the Rattlesnake, William Fryer A.B., who was seriously wounded and unable to make good his retreat to his own boat which was outside the surf. Both these men were mentioned in despatches by Captain Commerell.

NAVY LIST 1874

NOTES: With an annuity of £10.

Godden's medals comprising C.G.M., Ashantee War 1873, no bar, South Africa 1877-9 bar 1879, Naval L.S.& G.C. appeared for sale at Glendinings on 5.12.1990.

GOLDEN Able Seaman Patrick
Royal Navy

"In connection with the recent operations in China."
LONDON GAZETTE 14.5.1901

GOSS 019299 Marine Gunner Angus Robert
1st Marine Division, United States Marine Corps

Awarded for action on the Solomon Islands 10.8.1942

LONDON GAZETTE Not published in the gazette, award approved by H.M. King George VI 25.4.1943.

GREENFIELD O.N. (Po.)185253 Petty Officer George Robert
Royal Navy

"For action in the Heligoland Bight on the 17th November, 1917."
For conspicuous gallantry.

He set a fine example in continuing to serve and fire his gun single-handed, when all his crew had become casualties. Owing to his energy only one salvo was missed. He quickly reorganised the new crew, and kept his gun in action. During a lull he cleared away the casualties and steadied up his new crew.

LONDON GAZETTE 17.5.1918

NOTES: With an annuity of £10.

Awarded French Medaille Militaire 17.3.1919.

Entitled to 1914-15 Star, British War Medal and Victory Medal.

GREGG P/MX.51369 Engine Room Artificer Third Class Henry
Royal Navy

"For great gallantry in H.M.S. Glowworm's last action on 8th April, 1940. H.M.S. Glowworm attacked the German heavy cruiser Admiral Hipper and, after inflicting damage, was sunk with colours flying."

Lieutenant Commander Roope was awarded the Victoria Cross for this action, his citation, describing the action, is as follows: On the 8th April, 1940, H.M.S. Glowworm was proceeding alone in heavy weather towards a rendezvous in West Fjord, when she met and engaged two enemy destroyers, scoring at least one hit on them. The enemy broke off the action and headed North, to lead the Glowworm on to his supporting forces. The Commanding Officer, whilst correctly appreciating the intentions of the enemy, at once gave chase. The German heavy cruiser, Admiral Hipper, was sighted closing the Glowworm at high speed and an enemy report was sent which was received by H.M.S. Renown. Because of the heavy sea, the Glowworm could not shadow the enemy and the Commanding Officer therefore decided to attack with torpedoes and then to close in order to inflict as much damage as possible. Five torpedoes were fired and later the remaining five, but without success. The Glowworm was badly hit; one gun was out of action and her speed was much reduced, but with the other three guns still firing she closed and rammed the Admiral Hipper. As the Glowworm drew away, she opened fire again and scored one hit at a range of 400 yards. The Glowworm, badly stove in forward and riddled with enemy fire, heeled over to starboard, and the Commanding Officer gave the order to abandon her. Shortly afterwards she capsized and sank. The Admiral Hipper hove to for at least an hour picking up survivors but the loss of life was heavy, only 31 out of the Glowworm's compliment of 149 being saved.

LONDON GAZETTE 10.7.1945

NOTES: Petty Officer W. T. Scott and Able Seaman R. T. Merritt were also awarded the C.G.M. for this action and Lieut. R. A. Ramsay the D.S.O.

Award presented 30.10.1945.

FOR CONSPICUOUS GALLANTRY

GRINDEY Po./15585 Private Ernest Arnold
Portsmouth Battalion, Royal Marine Light Infantry

On the 25th November, 1915, at Cape Helles, he extinguished a fuse in a live grenade and threw it out of our trench, thereby avoiding a serious accident.

LONDON GAZETTE: 31.5.1916

NOTES: Awarded Croix de Guerre (France) 19.12.1917. also M.I.D.

Private Grindey joined the R.A.F. after the First World War. His medals comprising C.G.M., 1914 Star and Bar, British War Medal, Victory Medal (M.I.D.) and R.A.F. L.S. & G.C. are now on display in the Royal Marines Museum in Portsmouth.

GWILLIAM Able seaman William G.,
H.M.S. Exeter, Royal Navy

"In recognition of the gallant and successful action with the "Admiral Graf Spee" (to be dated the 13th of December, 1939)"

William G. Gwilliam, Able Seaman, H.M.S. Exeter, who helped Midshipman Cameron to smother the flames of a burning ammunition locker, and to throw hot shells, with their brass cases either missing or split open, over the side. He showed no regard for his own safety in putting out fires on the upper deck near the aircraft from which petrol was leaking.

LONDON GAZETTE 23.2.1940.

NOTES: The action became known as the battle of the River Plate, Gwilliams medals now held by the Royal Naval Museum in Portsmouth.

Award presented 23.2.1940.

H

HALCROW LT/JX.181736 Seaman Sidney
H.M.T. Lady Shirley, Royal Navy

"For daring and skill in a brilliant action against a U boat in which the Enemy was sunk and surrendered to H.M. Trawler Lady Shirley."

Who was so badly wounded that he was ordered to go below, but stood to his gun until the action was over, when he fainted.

LONDON GAZETTE 18.11.1941

NOTES: This action took place on 4th October 1941.

Award presented 28.4.1942.

HAMLIN O.N. 150438 Chief Sick Berth Steward Henry A.
H.M.S. Inflexible, Royal Navy

"For services when H.M.S. "Inflexible" was damaged by a mine on 18th March."

Though partially overcome by fumes he assisted Surgeon Langford while the Inflexible was proceeding to Tenedos'.

LONDON GAZETTE 16.8.1915

NOTES: With an annuity of £10.

Awarded French Medaille Militaire 17.3.1919

Medals comprising C.G.M., 1915-15 Star, British War Medal, Victory Medal, Naval L.S. & G.C. and French Medaille Militaire offered for sale at Spink on 8.11.1994.

HAMILTON Gunner Frederick
Royal Marine Artillery

Awarded for the Egypt campaign. No further details of the exact circumstances of the award are available.

FOR CONSPICUOUS GALLANTRY

NAVY LIST 1883

HAMMOND D138513P, Chief Petty Officer (Diver) Philip John
Royal Navy

"In recognition of brave and gallant service during the operations in the Gulf:"

During Operation Desert Slash, Hammond was the CPO of Fleet Diving Units (FDU) A and B, embarked in RFA Sir Galahad in the Northern Arabian Gulf. He acted as a supervisor of diving operations from Gemini craft in live minefields and of a helicopter-borne Explosive Ordnance Disposal (EOD) team. Not content to take a purely directing stance, he willingly put others' safety before his own by taking the leading role on many occasions in protracted night dives on live enemy ground mines to recover them for exploitation. At all times he displayed admirable calmness and great personal courage, working tirelessly to protect and direct his men, thereby instilling great confidence in their minds.

When FDUs A and B moved ashore on 5 March Hammond took a principal part in port recovery and EOD operations. He supervised and participated in the first searches of oil tankers, bunkers and buildings for booby traps, the gruesome task of recovering dead bodies, and the rendering safe of unstable live ordnance, beached mines and Improvised Explosive Devices. All this was done with his men's safety uppermost in his mind, often leading them through areas of anti-personnel mines and barbed wire to reach the objectives. Throughout this extremely dangerous operation he was a focal point of experience among the divers and his measured advice was highly prized by the Officers in Charge of the FDUs.

The conditions under which the Units operated were atrocious. With no infrastructure ashore the men subsisted in cargo containers on a jetty with no light, sanitation or potable water, in an atmosphere heavy with acrid smoke and toxic fumes from the oilfield fires burning inland, and diving in water with zero visibility due to thick oil pollution. All the time they were at risk from random gunfire from uncontrolled factions of the local population. Hammond's deep reserves of personal stamina, his ebullience and mature leadership gave much succour to the young divers in the FDUs.

46

LONDON GAZETTE 29.6.1991

NOTES: Chief Petty Officer Hammond was the last recipient of the Naval C.G.M.

HANLAN Able Seaman Peter
H.M.S. Curlew, Royal Navy

"4ᵗʰ-6ᵗʰ November 1855, Glofira & Gheisk, Sea of Azoff."

No precise details exist surrounding the act or act of bravery which resulted in this award of this medal which appeared in a list at the end of Captain Sherard Osborn's dispatch dated 7 November 1855, from H.M.S. Vesuvius off Gheisk when acting as Senior Officer in the Sea of Azoff. This list includes Thomas Kerr and David Barry who also received the C.G.M.

LONDON GAZETTE 8.12.1855

NOTES: Mentioned in Despatches, 8.12.1855.

HARMER P/JX.141086 Petty Officer Telegraphist Victor George
H.M.S. Shakespeare, Royal Navy

"For gallantry, seamanship and determination during patrols in one of H.M. Submarines."

When the pressure hull of the submarine was pierced by enemy gun-fire Petty Officer Harmer, under heavy fire, went down without any orders and tried to stem the flow of water with a blanket. Though a shell hit very close to him blowing off his boots and burning his feet he kept at his task, and so prevented a considerable quantity of water from entering. For the rest of the day from 9.30 till dusk he carried out the duty of air lookout with great courage, though receiving a further wound in the arm.

LONDON GAZETTE 10.4.1945

NOTES: Award presented 23.7.1946.

This action, which took place on the 3ʳᵈ January 1945, followed an attack by H.M.S. Shakespeare on an enemy merchant ship in the East Indies. The enemy returned fire and damaged the hull so that she could not dive.

They were subsequently attacked from the air but managed to return to harbour.

The crew received, in addition to this C.G.M., one D.S.O., two D.S.C.'s, seven D.S.M.'s and six M.I.D.'s for this engagement.

HARNER O.N. Dev./228795 Petty Officer Walter
H.M. Submarine C3, Royal Navy

"In recognition of distinguished services during the operations against Zeebrugge and Ostend on the night of the 22nd-23rd April 1918."

Sto.1st Class Bindall, P.O. W.Harner, Ldg.Smn W.G.Cleaver and E.R.A. 3rd Cl. A.G. Roxburgh.

The ratings above mentioned were members of the crew of Submarine C.3, which was skillfully placed between the piles of the Zeebrugge mole viaduct and there blown up, the fuse being lighted before the submarine was abandoned. They volunteered for and, under the command of an officer, eagerly undertook this hazardous enterprise, although they were well aware that if the means of rescue failed, and that if any of them were in the water at the time of the explosion, they would be killed outright.

LONDON GAZETTE 23.7.1918

NOTES: With an annuity of £10.

Sto. Bindall, Ldg Seaman Cleaver and E.R.A Roxburgh were also awarded the C.G.M. for this action. Lt. Howell-Price received the D.S.O. and Lt. Sandford the V.C.

Awarded Croix de Guerre (France) 28.8.1918.

Petty Officer Harners medals comprising C.G.M., 1914-15 Star, British War Medal, Victory Medal, Navy L.S. & G.C. and Croix de Guerre are on display at the Submarine Museum in Gosport.

HAWKSWORTH C/MX.50341 Engine Room Artificer Henry
H.M.S. Achates, Royal Navy

"For bravery in Northern Waters"

LONDON GAZETTE 27.4.1943

NOTES: This award was for service in Convoy JW51B on 31st December 1942.

Award presented 29.2.1944.

HENDRY O.N. 1959 SA 2nd Hand Jospeh
Royal Naval Reserve

"For services in the action in the Straits of Otranto on the 15th May, 1917."

His ship being in a sinking condition, the remainder of the crew left her in a small boat and were taken prisoners, but Hendry refused to leave. His ship eventually sank under him, and he was in the water for some hours until picked up by another drifter.

LONDON GAZETTE 28.8.1917

NOTES: With an annuity of £10.

Killed in action whilst serving on H.M.S. Venerable on 30.10.1918.

HENRY Corporal Harry
Royal Marine Light Infantry

Award for the Egypt campaign. No further details surrounding the award are available.

NAVY LIST 1883

HILL O.N. (Ch.)173927 Chief Petty Officer Henry
Royal Navy

"For services rendered by Petty Officers and men of the Eastern Mediterranean Squadron between the time of landing in the Gallipoli Peninsula in April, 1915, and the evacuation in December, 1915 - January 1916."

On 25th April, 1915, this Petty Officer whilst at the wheel during the landing operations at Anzac, under heavy fire, was struck in the mouth by a bullet, which removed all his front teeth. He was taken below, and after washing out his mouth he insisted on returning to his duty at the wheel, where he remained during the landing trips of 25th and 26th April, on both days under fire.

LONDON GAZETTE 15.5.1916

NOTES: With an annuity of £10.

Entitled to 1914-15 Star, British War Medal and Victory Medal.

Awarded French Medaille Militaire 28.8.1918.

HILLS C/JX 372402 Able seaman Thomas Henry Richard
L.C. G.12, Royal Navy

"For gallantry, leadership and undaunted devotion to duty under heavy and continuous fire from the enemy during landings on the Italian mainland."

Able Seaman Hills was serving in a Landing Craft which was heavily damaged by a shell which burst just over the bridge. All the Officers were killed or badly wounded and he was the only man left alive on the bridge. With complete coolness he took control and steered the craft through bursting shells and ammunition out of range of the enemy's guns and brought her to safety.

LONDON GAZETTE 25.1.1944

NOTES: Award presented 19.11.1946.

Action took place during Operation Baytown and Ferdy.

HOGAN O.N. 306261 Stoker Petty Officer Patrick James
Royal Navy

"For services rendered by Petty Officers and men of the Grand Fleet in the action in the North Sea on the 31st May - 1st June, 1916."

Stoker Petty Officer Hogan remained for over eighteen hours continuously at his station, where, during the action, the fans were broken down and the temperature became almost unbearable; in order to stop leaks in cover joints he had to take off his clothes. He showed great judgment in hurrying on salt water supply at a critical time.

LONDON GAZETTE 15.9.1916

NOTES: With an annuity of £10.

Awarded Croix de Guerre (France) LG 19.12.1917.

Entitled to 1914-15 Star, British War Medal and Victory Medal.

HOLDSTOCK Sergeant Thomas W.
Royal Marine Light Infantry

Award for the Egypt campaign. No further details surrounding the award are available.

NAVY LIST 1883

NOTES: With an annuity of £10.

HOLIGAN O.N. 343159 Shipwright First Class William
Royal Navy

"For services rendered by Petty Officers and men of the Grand Fleet in the action in the North Sea on the 31st May - 1st June, 1916."

Shipwright First Class, Holigan acted with great courage when a shell burst in the canteen flat of the ship in which he was serving, killing and wounding about twenty men. He was knocked down and scorched about the head, but immediately plugged leaking pipes which had been shot away.

LONDON GAZETTE 15.9.1916

NOTES: With an annuity of £10.

Entitled to 1914-15 Star, British War Medal and Victory Medal.

HOLLOWAY C.S. 37850 Quarter Master William
H.M.S. Rattlesnake, Royal Navy

ASHANTEE 1873 - 1874: Behaved with the utmost coolness and intrepidity. Holloway was wounded on the occasion of the attack on our boats in the Prah, 14th August, 1873. The services of Burke and Holloway being considered secondary to those of Godden and Sermon, but Burke and Holloway are most worthy of their Lordships' consideration.

NAVY LIST 1874

HOMER O.N. 160808 Chief Petty Officer Richard Henry
Howe Battalion, Royal Naval Volunteer Reserve

"For services in the Gallipoli Peninsula."

For great gallantry on the 4th June in advancing to a position, from which he could fire at an enemy machine-gun, which was commanding the ground held by our men. Exhibiting coolness and resource he was able to work his way to a spot whence he managed greatly to diminish the effect of the enemy's fire.

LONDON GAZETTE 13.9.1915

NOTES: With an annuity of £10.

Commissioned as Sub.Lt. 13.7.1915.

Medals comprising C.G.M., Queens South Africa Medal, no bar, Africa General Service Medal bar Aro 1901-1902, 1914 Star, British War Medal, Victory Medal, M.I.D., and Naval L.S. & G.C., were offered for sale at Spink on 22.6.1989.

HONER Po. 629 Private Richard
H.M.S. Active, Royal Marines

ASHANTEE 1873 - 1874: Was with the brigade from the first landing and never absent from duty. He was conspicuous alike for good conduct and bold gallantry, and whilst at Amoaful, 31st January, 1874, volunteered to enter the bush at a very critical moment to discover whether it was the Ashantis of Native allies who were firing on the advance.

NAVY LIST 1874

NOTES: Private Honers medals comprising C.G.M., Ashantee medal with clasp (Coomassie), Navy L.S. & G.C. are now on display at the Royal Marines Museum in Portsmouth.

FOR CONSPICUOUS GALLANTRY

HOPEWELL Ply./15995 Private William
Royal Marine Light Infantry

"In recognition of distinguished services during the operations against Zeebrugge and Ostend on the night of the 22nd-23rd April 1918."

After the No 1 and 2 of his Lewis gun section had become casualties in the ship in which Pte. Hopewell was serving, he took the Lewis gun ashore and brought it into action. He continued to fire the gun throughout the operation, and was almost the last man to retire, bringing his gun out of action with him, until it was rendered useless by a direct hit by a shell.

LONDON GAZETTE 23.7.1918

NOTES: Awarded Croix de Guerre (France) 28.8.1918.

Entitled to 1914-15 Star, British War Medal and Victory Medal.

HOSKINS Ch.12888 (R.F.R. B./1952) Private Thomas Henry
Chatham Battalion, Royal Marine Light Infantry

For conspicuous gallantry at Gaba Tepe, on the 30th April, 1915, when, after volunteering for the duty, he moved across the open under very heavy and very close range fire to another sector of the outpost line with an urgent message for ammunition and water. Having delivered the message he courageously attempted to return to his unit, and in doing so was twice wounded.

LONDON GAZETTE 6.9.1916

NOTES: Entitled to 1914 Star and bar, British War Medal and Victory Medal.

HUGHES O.N. 302261 Stoker First Class Jospeh Henry
H.M.S. Vivid, Royal Navy

"For services rendered by Petty Officers and men of the Grand Fleet in the action in the North Sea on the 31st May - 1st June, 1916."

Stoker, First Class, Hughes was one of the ratings on duty in a compartment immediately above that struck by a torpedo. The deck of this compartment was distorted, and all lights save one were extinguished, and water was coming into it. Stoker Hughes at once closed

53

a valve, and the last light going out, he proceeded on deck to obtain another, with which he returned , closing steam and exhaust valves, although there was then 5 feet of water in the compartment. The action taken by this stoker, who remained alone at his place of duty in spite of the shock and noise of the explosion, and took effective steps to ensure the continued operation of the machinery in it, exhibited great presence of mind and bravery.

LONDON GAZETTE 15.9.1916

NOTES: Awarded French Medaille Militaire 17.3.1919.

Entitled to 1914-15 Star, British War Medal and Victory Medal.

HUNT Ex.4905 Marine George Thomas
Royal Marines

"For gallantry in the face of heavy odds in landings near Tobruk."

Marine Hunt acted with courage and resource in getting his section ashore and overcoming enemy resistance.

When an order was given to clear enemy posts and his platoon Commander was killed, Marine Hunt advanced alone, and though he was almost immediately wounded, led his section forward and the enemy posts were cleared. He continued the attack at the head of his section until his arm became paralyzed and he could no longer hold his rifle.

By his presence of mind he also saved his Company Commander.

LONDON GAZETTE 3.8.1943

NOTES: Award presented 12.10.1943.

HUNTER Ply/X.111414 Marine/Acting Temporary Sergeant Cecil John
556th L.C.A. Flotilla, Royal Marines

"For gallantry, skill, determination and undaunted devotion to duty during the landing of Allied Forces on the coast of Normandy."

Sergeant Hunter who was in command of an L.C.A., negotiated three rows of obstacles successfully and disembarked his troops. On being lightened the craft swung round and detonated a mine which blew the bottom out. He ordered the crew ashore and they took shelter under the stern of a Sherman tank.

He then saw a Sergeant Major of the Canadian Forces trying to attract the attention of the Sherman tank. Realising that the Sergeant Major was not visible to the crew of the Sherman, he crawled across the intervening thirty yards under heavy fire to the Sergeant Major and returned with the message that its fire was being directed towards the Canadians, and orders to cease fire and advance ahead of the Canadians. When this proved to be impossible Sergeant Hunter again crossed the fire-swept thirty yards with the message and returned to rejoin his troops.

LONDON GAZETTE 14.11.1944

NOTES: Award presented 20.3.1945.

HYDE C/JX.151597 Petty Officer Ronald Herbert Frank
Royal Navy

"For outstanding bravery and enterprise in the action in the harbour at Oran in H.M. Ships Hartland and Walney."

LONDON GAZETTE 18.5.1943

NOTES: Award presented 28.3.1944.

I

INGOUVILLE Captain of the Mast George

H.M.S. Arrogant, Royal Navy

Baltic: On 13th July, 1855. Whilst the boats of H.M.S. Arrogant were engaged with the enemy's gunboats and batteries off Viborg, her second cutter, with Ingouville on board, was swamped by the blowing up of her magazine, and drifted under a battery. Not withstanding that he was wounded in the arm, and that the boat was under a very heavy fire, Ingouville, without any order to do so, jumped overboard, caught hold of her painter and saved her.

LONDON GAZETTE Not published in the London Gazette.

NOTES: Awarded the Victoria Cross 24.2.1857 for the same action, along with Lieut. George Dowell, R.M.A.

George Ingouville was presented with his V.C. by Queen Victoria at the first presentation of crosses in Hyde Park on 26th June 1857.

Died 13th January, 1869.

J

JOHNS O.N. 183788 Dev./B3019 A.B. Harry
Royal Fleet Reserve

"For services in action with enemy submarines."

For conspicuous gallantry during the combined naval and military operations in the neighbourhood of Lindi, East Africa, on the 10th and 11th June, 1917.

He showed exemplary conduct in at once going below into the after flat, when the ship was hit by an enemy 4.1 shell, in order to assist in extinguishing the fire, and by his coolness and judgment prevented the fire from spreading.

LONDON GAZETTE 19.12.1917

NOTES: Awarded French Medaille Militaire 28.8.1918.

Entitled to 1914-15 Star, British War Medal and Victory Medal.

JONES O.N. 350868 Sick Berth Steward Alfred Edward
Royal Navy

"For services rendered by Petty Officers and men of the Grand Fleet in the action in the North Sea on the 31st May - 1st June, 1916."

Sick Berth Steward Jones showed conspicuous gallantry in bringing hoses to bear on a cordite fire in the vicinity of the mid-ship ammunition lobby, when the supply parties had been driven away by the fumes. He performed his duties in an exemplary manner in very trying circumstances.

LONDON GAZETTE 15.9.1916

NOTES: With an annuity of £10.

Awarded French Medaille Militaire 17.3.1919.

Entitled to 1914-15 Star, British War Medal and Victory Medal.

FOR CONSPICUOUS GALLANTRY

JONES O.N.227970 Stoker Petty Officer Arthur
Royal Navy

"For services in the Shatt-el-Arab, 3rd to 9th December 1914."

Petty Officer Jones, after being severely wounded, kept the engines of the launch "Miner" going when water was pouring into the Engine Room, and undoubtedly by his action saved the "Miner" from disaster.

LONDON GAZETTE 10.4.1915

NOTES: With an annuity of £10.

Awarded French Medaille Militaire 17.3.1919.

Entitled to 1914-15 Star, British War Medal and Victory Medal.

**JUDGE Gunner John
Royal Marine Artillery**

For services at Kassassin.

Although wounded by a fragment of shell in his right leg, he returned to his post after having it dressed. When asked why he had not remained in hospital he replied that there were so many wounded there that they had better not be troubled with him also.

LONDON GAZETTE 28.8.1882

NOTES: Gunner Judges medals comprising C.G.M., Ashantee Campaign Medal (No Clasp), Egypt 1882 Campaign Medal (No Clasp) and the Khedives Egypt Star (1882) are on display at the Royal Marines Museum in Portsmouth.

K

KERR Gunner Thomas
Royal Marine Artillery, H.M.S. Vesuvius

"4ᵗʰ-6ᵗʰ November 1855, Glofira & Gheisk, Sea of Azoff."

No precise details exist surrounding the act or act of bravery which resulted in this award of this medal which appeared in a list at the end of Captain Sherard Osborn's dispatch dated 7 November 1855, from H.M.S. Vesuvius off Gheisk when acting as Senior Officer in the Sea of Azoff. This list includes Peter Hanlan and David Barry who also received the C.G.M.

LONDON GAZETTE 8.12.1855

NOTES: Mentioned in Despatches, 8.12.1855.

KERWIN V.32313 Able Seaman Michael Roderick
Royal Canadian Naval Volunteer Reserve

"For gallantry, skill, determination and undaunted devotion to duty during the landing of Allied Forces on the coast of Normandy."

During one action a fierce fire broke out at "Y" gun in H.M.C.S. Haida. Two of the crew were killed and a third seriously injured . Able Seaman Kerwin, although blinded and wounded by splinters, went into the blazing gun shield at great risk to his own life and dragged the injured man to safety. Both were badly burned, but Able Seaman Kerwin's prompt and gallant action saved the life of his shipmate.

LONDON GAZETTE 14.11.1944

FOR CONSPICUOUS GALLANTRY

KNILL RMA/12738 Sergeant Frank John
Royal Marine Artillery

"In recognition of distinguished services during the operations against Zeebrugge and Ostend on the night of the 22nd-23rd April 1918."

This non-commissioned officer was in charge of "Vindictive's" howitzer, which was fired continuously under the most difficult conditions during the whole period that the ship was alongside the mole at Zeebrugge. In spite of being semi-gassed, Sgt Knill did not leave his post, but remained in charge of his gun until it ceased firing.

LONDON GAZETTE 23.7.1918

NOTES: With an annuity of £10.

Awarded Croix de Guerre (France) 28.8.1918.

Sgt Knills medals comprising C.G.M., British War Medal, Victory Medal, Defence Medal, War Medal, Navy L.S. & G.C., Navy M.S.M. and Croix de Guerre are on display at the Royal Marines Museum in Portsmouth.

L

LAKE O.N. Po./J.22273 A.B. Ferdinand Eugene Minns
Royal Navy

"In recognition of distinguished services during the operations against Zeebrugge and Ostend on the night of the 22nd-23rd April 1918."

This Able Seaman formed one of the seaman storming party. His commanding officer reports that when "Iris II." was hit by several large shells, he found Able Seaman Lake extinguishing a fire under the fore-bridge with sand, under very heavy shrapnel fire. Regardless of his own safety, Able Seaman Lake assisted his commanding officer to throw overboard Stokes and Mills bombs, which were quite hot. He then took the wheel, and acted as quartermaster for six hours.

LONDON GAZETTE 23.7.1918

NOTES: Medals now held by the Royal Naval Museum in Portsmouth. Awarded Croix de Guerre (France) 28.8.1918.

Entitled to 1914-15 Star, British War Medal and Victory Medal.

LAMB O.N. 1491 TS. Deckhand Frederick Hawley
Royal Naval Reserve

"For services in the action in the Straits of Otranto on the 15th May, 1917."

Though severely wounded in the leg by the explosion of a box of ammunition on H.M. Drifter "Gowan Lea", he stuck to his gun endeavouring to make it work.

LONDON GAZETTE 28.8.1917

NOTES: Entitled to 1914-15 Star, British War Medal and Victory Medal.

LAMB P/JX.141113 Acting Petty Officer Leonard Sidney
M.L.160, Royal Navy

"For great gallantry, daring and skill in the attack on the German Naval Base at St. Nazaire."

For great bravery in rescuing many men from a blazing Motor Launch under intense fire at very short range, and for selfless devotion in tending the wounded on the way back from the raid.

LONDON GAZETTE 21.5.1942

NOTES: Award presented 21.7.1942.

LAMBERT C/JX.171403 Able Seaman Dennis Norman
M.L.160, Royal Navy

"For great gallantry, daring and skill in the attack on the German Naval Base at St. Nazaire."

Though himself wounded and under heavy fire from the enemy, this Able Seaman remained on board a blazing Motor Launch after the order to abandon ship had been given, and with great bravery helped to carry a wounded shipmate across to another Motor Launch.

LONDON GAZETTE 21.5.1942

NOTES: Award presented 13.4.1943.

LANFEAR P/JX.154702 Able Seaman Leslie Douglas
M.G.B. 43, Royal Navy

"For courage and skill in an attack on an Enemy Convoy in the English Channel in which one Supply Ship was sunk and three other Enemy Ships were damaged."

Able Seaman Lanfear during this attack was in charge of the gun which did most damage to the enemy. A few days later he was again in action and showed the same coolness and skill. This time he was very badly wounded, but, though in great pain and unable to stand, he seized a Lewis gun and turned a steady and accurate fire on the Enemy, until he fainted.

62

FOR CONSPICUOUS GALLANTRY

LONDON GAZETTE 21.10.1941

NOTES: Award presented 21.7.1942.

LARGE D/J.108351 Petty Officer Fred
H.M.S. Illustrious, Royal Navy

"For great courage and devotion to duty in the face of enemy air attack."

Whose courage and determination in the face of danger was an inspiration to his shipmates, and who, in a brave company, was yet remarkable for his bravery.

LONDON GAZETTE 17.6.1941

NOTES: Action took place on 10th January 1941.

Award presented 29.2.1944.

LARSEN S/Lt (Kuarter Mastre) Leif Andreas
Norwegian Navy

Awarded for an unsuccessful attempt on the Tirpitz by Chariots in Trondheimsfjord, supported by the fishing vessel Arthur, in October 1942. The recommendation no longer survives as it was destroyed following approval of the award.

LONDON GAZETTE Not published in the gazette, award approved by H.M. King George VI 28.1.1943.

NOTES: Award presented 8.6.1943.

Larsen was also awarded the D.S.O., D.S.C., and the D.S.M. and bar, a unique combination of naval gallantry awards.

LEACH O.N. K11874 (Po.) Leading Stoker James
Royal Fleet Reserve

"For services in action with enemy submarines."

For conspicuous gallantry during the combined naval and military operations in the neighbourhood of Lindi, East Africa, on the 10th and 11th June, 1917.

Though wounded in two places in the legs, he showed exemplary conduct in continuing to stand by the engines (the engine-room artificer in charge having been killed) until ordered on deck for medical treatment.

LONDON GAZETTE 19.12.1917

NOTES: Awarded French Medaille Militaire 28.8.1918.

Entitled to 1914-15 Star, British War Medal and Victory Medal.

LEAMAN D/J.90618 Chief Petty Officer William Arthur
H.M.S. Illustrious, Royal Navy

"For great courage and devotion to duty in the face of enemy air attack."

Who, while in charge of a repair party was wounded in the face and leg, and burnt, but carried on at his task and fought a fire on deck until he could no longer stand.

LONDON GAZETTE 17.6.1941

NOTES: Action took place on 10th January 1941.

Award presented 7.10.1941.

LEE C/JX.299940 Ordinary Seaman Thomas Albert
L.C.T. 127, Royal Navy

"For gallantry, daring and skill in the combined attack on Dieppe."

While the craft on which Ordinary Seaman Lee was serving was beached for some fifteen minutes landing tanks, under concentrated fire, her guns were kept in action against an enemy gun position and houses on the beach, until all the guns crew had been killed or wounded. Although gravely wounded himself, his cheerful courage and devotion to duty were an example to the rest. He carried on until the guns were silenced and then crawled away to report to his Skipper.

LONDON GAZETTE 2.10.1942

NOTES: Action was part of Operation Jubilee.

Award presented 18.5.1943.

LIVINGSTONE O.N. J.39103 (Dev.) A.B. Samuel James
Royal Navy

For services in action with enemy submarines."
LONDON GAZETTE 13.9.1918

NOTES: Awarded French Medaille Militaire 17.3.1919.

Entitled to 1914-15 Star, British war Medal and Victory Medal.

LUMSDEN O.N. 218195 Ch./B10894 A.B. Aaron
Royal Fleet Reserve

"For services in action with enemy submarines."
LONDON GAZETTE 7.6.1918

NOTES: Awarded D.S.M. 15.5.1916, French Medaille Militaire 17.3.1919.

Entitled to 1914-15 Star, British War Medal and Victory Medal.

LOVEGROVE P/MX.70809 Chief Motor Mechanic Forth Class William Henry
M.T.B. 74, Royal Navy

"For great gallantry and outstanding devotion to duty."
In the attack on St. Nazaire on 28th March, 1942, a shell passed through the engine-room of Motor Torpedo Boat 74 and Chief Motor Mechanic Lovegrove was wounded by splinters down the right leg. Disregarding his wounds he set to work to repair the centre engine, which had been put out of action, and although bleeding badly and in great pain he continued until he had repaired it, thus enabling the ship to set out on her return

65

voyage. After starting for home the ship was again hit and became one mass of flame. The crew abandoned ship, but Lovegrove seeing that the Commanding Officer was not with them, fought his way through the flames to look for him in the wheelhouse where he had been blown by the force of the explosion. He brought him on deck, pulled him into the water and swam with him to a Carley float, where he supported him for some twelve hours until they were picked up by the enemy.

But for Chief Motor Mechanic Lovegrove's resolute action and unselfish courage his Commanding Officer would not have survived.

LONDON GAZETTE 1.5.1945

NOTES: Award presented 22.6.1945.

LOVELOCK O.N.(Ch.)J.28798 Ordinary Seaman Jesse
H.M.S. Albion, Royal Navy

"Despatch of Vice Admiral John M. de Robeck reporting on the landing of the Army on the Gallipoli Peninsula 25th-26th April 1915."

Assisted in getting pontoon in position; also helped wounded on beach and in boats to reach "River Clyde", displaying great gallantry and coolness under fire.

LONDON GAZETTE 16.8.1915

NOTES: See the account under Petty Officer J.H.Russell.

Awarded French Medaille Militaire 28.8.1918.

Entitled to 1914-15 Star, British War Medal and Victory Medal.

M

McDANIEL Bugler Thomas F.
Royal Marine Light Infantry

For bravery during a reconnaissance on 5th August 1882 at Tel-El-Kebir.

LONDON GAZETTE 13.9.1882

NOTES: Bugler McDaniels medals comprising C.G.M., Egypt Campaign Medal with Clasp Tel-El-Kebir, and Khedives Egypt star (1882) are now on display in the Royal Marines Museum in Portsmouth.

McEVOY O.N. 173198 Chief Petty Officer Telegraphist Patrick
Royal Navy

"For services rendered by Petty Officers and men of the Grand Fleet in the action in the North Sea on the 31st May - 1st June, 1916."

Chief Petty Officer McEvoy was working on deck almost continuously throughout the action. Four times he repaired or cleared the Main Aerial under fire in a cool and efficient manner. The smoke on the Mess Deck was so intense that he had to feel his way up on deck.

LONDON GAZETTE 15.9.1916

NOTES: With an annuity of £10.

Awarded French Medaille Militaire 15.9.1916, also entitled to 1914-15 Star, British War Medal and Victory Medal.

Later commissioned.

McGOVERN O.N. K.5606 (Dev.) Leading Stoker Thomas
Royal Navy

"For service in the Battle of Jutland."

Showed much courage in extinguishing a large fire, which could only be reached through a shell hole surrounded by intense heat, fumes and smoke. His behaviour was highly commendable.

LONDON GAZETTE 1.1.1917

NOTES Awarded Croix de Guerre (France) LG 19.12.1917.

Entitled to 1914-15 Star, British War Medal and Victory Medal. Medal card states that a duplicate set were issued on 28.4.1961 to a private address.

McGRATH LT/JX.228057 Leading Seaman Owen Joseph
L.C.P. (L) 144, Royal Navy

"For gallantry, determination and devotion to duty in the assault and capture of the Island of Walcheren."

On 1st November, 1944, Leading Seaman McGrath was Coxswain in L.C.P. (L) 144 during the assault on Westkapelle, in which craft no Officer was embarked. Her duty was to make smoke on the Southern Flank.

Many craft were hit by the accurate enemy fire, and some blew up very close inshore under the enemy guns. L.C.P. (L) 144 was ordered to close, make smoke and pick up survivors. This was done at point blank range with an off-shore wind making effective smoke difficult. By his most courageous action Leading Seaman McGrath rescued over twenty survivors.

LONDON GAZETTE 22.1.1944

NOTES: This was Operation Infatuate.

Award presented in Canada 20.11.1946.

FOR CONSPICUOUS GALLANTRY

McKINLAY P/JX.245579 Petty Officer Ronald Harry George
Royal Naval Commando, Royal Navy

"For gallantry, skill and determination and undaunted devotion to duty during the initial landings of Allied Forces on the coast of Normandy."

Petty Officer McKinlay was put ashore between noon and 1400 hours on 6th June. Finding himself at some distance from his pre-arranged destination he made his way along the beach and took charge of a party of Naval ratings and Army ranks who were bound for the same point. Single-handed, he silenced two enemy strong points on the way with hand grenades. Later, on an open stretch of sand which was under fire from enemy snipers, disregarding his own safety, he went to the rescue of a wounded man and brought him safely to cover.

LONDON GAZETTE 29.8.1944

NOTES: Medals comprising C.G.M. 1939-45 Star, Atlantic Star (clasp France & Germany), Africa Star, Defence Medal, War Medal, Naval General Service Medal (clasp Palestine 1945-48) Navy L.S.& G.C., Queens Commendation for Brave Conduct, awarded to P.O. McKinlay appeared for sale at Christie's on 24.7.1990.

McLOUGHLIN Po. 8873 Sergeant James Francis
Royal Marine Light Infantry

For conspicuous gallantry at the capture of Salif on the 12th June, 1917. Just before the surrender he came across 11 unwounded and one wounded Turkish soldiers. Followed by one Petty Officer, Serjt McLoughlin jumped among them, shot one, and made seven surrender.

LONDON GAZETTE 11.8.1917

NOTES: With annuity of £10.

Awarded French Medaille Militaire 28.8.1918.

Entitled to 1914-15 Star, British War Medal and Victory Medal.

FOR CONSPICUOUS GALLANTRY

MALIA K.P.760 Leading Seaman James
Royal Navy

No citation was published with this award, however, the citation for the Victoria Cross awarded to Sub-Lieutenant Arthur Walden St.Clair Tisdall R.N.V.R. gives the background detail to the award.

During the landing from the S.S. "River Clyde" at V beach in the Gallipoli Peninsula on the 25th April, 1915, Sub-Lieutenant Tisdall, hearing wounded men on the beach calling for assistance, jumped into the water and, pushing a boat in front of him, went to their rescue. He was, however, obliged to obtain help, and took with him on two trips Leading Seaman Malia and on other trips Chief Petty Officer Perring and Leading Seamen Curtiss and Parkinson. In all Sub-Lieutenant Tisdall made four or five trips between the ship and the shore, and was thus responsible for rescuing several wounded men under heavy and accurate fire.

Owing to the fact that Sub-Lieutenant Tisdall and the platoon under his orders were on detached service at the time, and that this Officer was killed in action on the 6th May, it has only now been possible to obtain complete information as to the individuals who took part in this gallant act. Of these Leading Seaman Fred Curtiss, O.N. Dev. 1899, has been missing since the 4th June 1915.

LONDON GAZETTE 31.3.1916

NOTES: Chief Petty Officer Perring, and Leading Seamen Malia and Parkinson were all awarded the C.G.M. for this action.

MARTINDALE O.N.8556A Seaman John Stephen
Royal Naval Reserve

"For services in action with enemy submarines."

From the official account published in the L.G. 19.11.1918:- On the 8th August, 1917, H.M.S. "Dunraven" under the command of Captain Gordon Campbell, V.C., D.S.O., R.N., sighted an enemy submarine on the horizon. In her role of armed British merchant ship, the "Dunraven" continued her zig-zag course, whereupon the submarine closed, remaining submerged to within 5,000 yards, and then, rising to the surface, opened fire. The "Dunraven" returned the fire with her merchant ship gun, at the same time reducing speed to enable the enemy to overtake her. Wireless signals were also sent out for the benefit of the submarine: "Help! Come quickly - submarine chasing and shelling me." Finally, when the shells began falling close, the "Dunraven" stopped and abandoned ship by the "panic party." The ship was then being heavily shelled, and on fire aft. In the meantime the submarine closed to 400 yards distant, partly obscured from view by the dense clouds of smoke issuing from the "Dunraven's" stern. Despite the knowledge that the after magazine must inevitably explode if he waited, and further, that a gun and gun's crew lay concealed over the magazine, Captain Campbell decided to reserve his fire until the submarine had passed clear of the smoke. A moment later, however a heavy explosion occurred aft, blowing the gun and gun's crew into the air, and accidentally starting fire-gongs at the remaining gun positions; screens were immediately dropped, and the only gun that would bear opened fire, but the submarine, apparently frightened by the explosion, had already commenced to submerge. Realising that a torpedo must inevitably follow, Captain Campbell ordered the surgeon to remove all wounded and conceal them in cabins; hoses were also turned on the poop, which was a mass of flames. A signal was sent out warning men-of-war to divert all traffic below the horizon in order that nothing should interrupt the final phase of the action. Twenty minutes later a torpedo again struck the ship abaft the engine-room. An additional party of men were again sent away as "panic party," and left the ship to outward appearances completely abandoned, with the White Ensign flying and guns unmasked. For the succeeding fifty minutes the submarine examined the ship through her periscope. During the period boxes of cordite and shells exploded every few minutes, and the fire on the poop still blazed furiously. Captain Campbell and the handful of officers and men who remained on board lay hidden during this ordeal. The submarine then rose to the surface astern, where no guns could bear and shelled the ship closely for twenty minutes. The enemy then submerged and steamed past the ship 150 yards off, examining her through the periscope. Captain Campbell decided then to fire one of his torpedoes, but missed by a few inches. The submarine crossed bows and came slowly down the other side, whereupon a second torpedo was fired and missed again. The enemy observed it and immediately submerged. Urgent signals for assistance were immediately sent out, but pending arrival of assistance Captain Campbell arranged for a third "panic party" to jump overboard if necessary and leave one gun's crew on board for a final attempt to destroy the enemy, should he again attack. Almost immediately afterwards, however, British and American destroyers arrived on the scene, the wounded were transferred, boats were recalled and the fire extinguished. The "Dunraven" although her stern was awash, was taken in tow, but the weather grew worse, and early the following morning she sank with colours flying.

LONDON GAZETTE 30.10.1917

NOTES: All of the gun's crew were put in a ballot for the V.C. this was awarded to P.O. Ernest Pitcher who commanded the gun, the remaining members of the gun crew Bennison, Martindale, Murphy Sheppard and Thomson were all awarded the C.G.M. A ballot among the officers also awarded the V.C. to Lieut. Bonner D.S.C. In addition to these awards two further C.G.M.'s were awarded to crew of the Dunraven for the action, W/T Op. Fletcher and Seaman Morrison,

LONDON GAZETTE 2.11.1917

NOTES: Awarded D.S.M. 20.7.1917, French Medaille Militaire 28.8.1918.

Entitled to 1914-15 Star, British War Medal and Victory Medal.

MASTERS Ch. 8239 Colour Sergeant John C.

H.M.S. Barracouta, Royal Marine Light Infantry

ASHANTEE 1873 - 1874: Commanded marine detachment of Barracouta in the action at Elmina on 13th June 1873. Led the advance of the party under the Late Lieutenant Wells and was one of the first to get over the wall separating our men from the Ashantis, where he was wounded but continued to command his men till the action was over.

NAVY LIST 1874

MATHEWS Sussex 1/218 Leading Seaman George William

Royal Naval Volunteer Reserve

On the 31st October, 1915, during a bomb action he threw back the enemy's bombs, thereby saving many casualties among his comrades. During this action he was severely wounded.

LONDON GAZETTE 31.5.1916

MAXWELL CS.10713A 2ⁿᵈ Captain Quarter Deck John, H.M.S. Barracouta, Royal Navy

ASHANTEE 1873 - 1874: It was his duty to fire the rockets at Essaman on the 14th October 1873, and whilst placing the rocket trough in such a position as to command the village by the retreat of the Houssas covering our front, the rocket party were necessarily much exposed to a hot fire from the bush at a few yards distance both in front and on the right flank.

Under these circumstances the coolness and deliberation with which Maxwell dropped rocket after rocket into the houses till the whole village was in flames, elicited the warm admiration of the Major General Commanding and Captain Freemantle.

NAVY LIST 1874

NOTES: M.I.D. 18.11.1873 together with Henry Ransome as deserving special mention for the manner in which they directed the fire of the gun and rockets at the village of Essaman with a precision worthy of parade practice.

MAYES B./3307, Sergeant Charles Portsmouth R.F.R., H.M.S. Kent, Royal Marines

"For action off the Falkland Islands on Tuesday the 8th of December 1914."

A shell burst and ignited some cordite charges in the casemate; a flash of flame went down the hoist into the ammunition passage. Sergeant Mayes picked up a charge of cordite and threw it away. He then got hold of a fire hose and flooded the compartment, extinguishing the fire in some empty shell bags which were burning. The extinction of this fire saved a disaster which might have led to the loss of the ship.

LONDON GAZETTE 3.3.1915

NOTES: With an annuity of £20.

Awarded the French Medaille Militaire 17.3.1919.

Sergeant Mayes medals consisting of C.G.M., 1914-15 Star, British War Medal, Victory Medal (M.I.D.), and, French Medaille Militaire are now on display in the Royal Marines Museum in Portsmouth.

MERRITT P/JX.154145 Able Seaman Reginald Thomas
H.M.S. Glowworm, Royal Navy

"For great gallantry in H.M.S. Glowworm's last action on 8th April, 1940. H.M.S. Glowworm attacked the German heavy cruiser Admiral Hipper and, after inflicting damage, was sunk with colours flying."

Lieutenant Commander Roope was awarded the Victoria Cross for this action, his citation, describing the action, is as follows: On the 8th April, 1940, H.M.S. Glowworm was proceeding alone in heavy weather towards a rendezvous in West Fjord, when she met and engaged two enemy destroyers, scoring at least one hit on them. The enemy broke off the action and headed North, to lead the Glowworm on to his supporting forces. The Commanding Officer, whilst correctly appreciating the intentions of the enemy, at once gave chase. The German heavy cruiser, Admiral Hipper, was sighted closing the Glowworm at high speed and an enemy report was sent which was received by H.M.S. Renown. Because of the heavy sea, the Glowworm could not shadow the enemy and the Commanding Officer therefore decided to attack with torpedoes and then to close in order to inflict as much damage as possible. Five torpedoes were fired and later the remaining five, but without success. The Glowworm was badly hit; one gun was out of action and her speed was much reduced, but with the other three guns still firing she closed and rammed the Admiral Hipper. As the Glowworm drew away, she opened fire again and scored one hit at a range of 400 yards. The Glowworm, badly stove in forward and riddled with enemy fire, heeled over to starboard, and the Commanding Officer gave the order to abandon her. Shortly afterwards she capsized and sank. The Admiral Hipper hove to for at least an hour picking up survivors but the loss of life was heavy, only 31 out of the Glowworm's compliment of 149 being saved.

LONDON GAZETTE 10.7.1945

NOTES: Petty Officer W. T. Scott and Engine Room Artificer H. Gregg were also awarded the C.G.M. for this action and Lieut. R. A. Ramsay the D.S.O.

74

FOR CONSPICUOUS GALLANTRY

Award presented 30.10.1945.

MITCHELL Ch.X.934 Sergeant Peter Mitchell
Royal Marines

"For courage and devotion to duty during the withdrawals from Boulogne and Calais."

Who, under intense machine-gun fire and many dive-bombing attacks, brought many wounded comrades to a pinnace in Calais Harbour, until he himself could do no more.

LONDON GAZETTE 6.9.1940

NOTES: Presented 1.3.1941.

MOBBS O.N. 1760 ES Engineman Charles
Royal Naval Reserve

"For services in the action in the Straits of Otranto on the 15th May, 1917."

He remained at his post until the main steam pipe was shot away, when he was forced to leave the engine-room, but as soon as possible he returned and put out the fires. He also went in a small boat and assisted to plug holes in the ship's side, thus enabling her to reach port safely.

LONDON GAZETTE 28.8.1917

NOTES: With an annuity of £10.

Entitled to 1914-15 Star, British War Medal and Victory Medal.

MOORE O.N. 200003 Dev./B.685 Edward James
Royal Fleet Reserve

"For services in action with enemy submarines."

LONDON GAZETTE 7.6.1918

NOTES: Awarded French Medaille Militaire 17.3.1919

Died of wound received whilst serving on SS Minnekahda 26.11.1918. He is buried in Tottenham and Wood Green cemetery.

Entitled to 1914-15 Star, British War Medal, Victory Medal.

MORRISON O.N. 5848A Seaman Alexander Salisbury
Royal Naval Reserve

"For services in action with enemy submarines."

From the official account published in the L.G. 19.11.1918:- On the 8th August, 1917, H.M.S. "Dunraven" under the command of Captain Gordon Campbell, V.C., D.S.O., R.N., sighted an enemy submarine on the horizon. In her role of armed British merchant ship, the "Dunraven" continued her zig-zag course, whereupon the submarine closed, remaining submerged to within 5,000 yards, and then, rising to the surface, opened fire. The "Dunraven" returned the fire with her merchant ship gun, at the same time reducing speed to enable the enemy to overtake her. Wireless signals were also sent out for the benefit of the submarine: "Help! Come quickly - submarine chasing and shelling me." Finally, when the shells began falling close, the "Dunraven" stopped and abandoned ship by the "panic party." The ship was then being heavily shelled, and on fire aft. In the meantime the submarine closed to 400 yards distant, partly obscured from view by the dense clouds of smoke issuing from the "Dunraven's" stern. Despite the knowledge that the after magazine must inevitably explode if he waited, and further, that a gun and gun's crew lay concealed over the magazine, Captain Campbell decided to reserve his fire until the submarine had passed clear of the smoke. A moment later, however a heavy explosion occurred aft, blowing the gun and gun's crew into the air, and accidentally starting fire-gongs at the remaining gun positions; screens were immediately dropped, and the only gun that would bear opened fire, but the submarine, apparently frightened by the explosion, had already commenced to submerge. Realising that a torpedo must inevitably follow, Captain Campbell ordered the surgeon to remove all wounded and conceal them in cabins; hoses were also turned on the poop, which was a mass of flames. A signal was sent out warning men-of-war to divert all traffic below the horizon in order that nothing should interrupt the final phase of the action. Twenty minutes later a torpedo again struck the ship abaft the engine-room. An additional party of men were again sent away as "panic party," and left the ship to outward appearances completely abandoned, with the White Ensign flying and guns unmasked. For the succeeding fifty minutes the submarine examined the ship through her periscope. During the period boxes of cordite and shells exploded every few minutes, and the fire on the poop still blazed furiously. Captain Campbell and the handful of officers and men who remained on board lay hidden during this ordeal. The submarine then rose to the surface astern, where no guns could bear and shelled the ship closely for twenty minutes. The enemy then submerged and steamed past the ship 150 yards off, examining her through the periscope. Captain Campbell decided then to fire one of his torpedoes, but missed by a few inches. The submarine crossed bows and came slowly down the other side, whereupon a second torpedo was fired and missed again. The enemy observed it and immediately submerged. Urgent signals for assistance were immediately sent out, but pending arrival of assistance Captain Campbell arranged for a third "panic party" to jump overboard if necessary and leave one gun's crew on board for a final attempt to destroy the enemy, should he again attack. Almost immediately afterwards, however, British and American destroyers arrived on the scene, the wounded were transferred, boats were recalled and the fire extinguished. The "Dunraven" although her stern was awash, was taken in tow, but the weather grew worse, and early the following morning she sank with colours flying. Seaman Morrison was in charge of depth charges on the Dunraven and on one occasion was blown away from his post when one of the charges exploded. Although severely wounded by the explosion he crawled back to his post where he remained throughout the action.

LONDON GAZETTE 30.10.1917

NOTES: All of the gun's crew were put in a ballot for the V.C. this was awarded to P.O. Ernest Pitcher who commanded the gun, the remaining members of the gun crew Bennison, Martindale, Murphy Sheppard and Thomson were all awarded the C.G.M. A ballot among the officers also awarded the V.C. to Lieut. Bonner D.S.C. In addition to these awards two further C.G.M.'s were awarded to crew of the Dunraven for the action, W/T Op. Fletcher and Seaman Morrison,

LONDON GAZETTE 2.11.1917

NOTES: Awarded D.S.M. 23.3.1917.

Entitled to 1914-15 Star, British War Medal and Victory Medal.

Died of wounds received 19.11.1917. He is buried in Wallasey cemetery, Cheshire.

MURPHY O.N. (Mersey) Z3/182 Engine Room Artificer 2nd Class Alexander
Royal Naval Volunteer Reserve

For most conspicuous gallantry as a volunteer in H.M.S. "Julnar" on the 24th April, 1916, when that vessel attempted to reach Kut-El-Amarah with stores for the besieged garrison.

LONDON GAZETTE 11.11.1919

NOTES: Medal card shows 1914 Star, Britsh War Medal and Victory medal with a note that the 1914 star was returned to the mint.

MURPHY O.N. Dev. J.25416 A.B. Dennis
Royal Navy

"For services in action with enemy submarines."

From the official account published in the L.G. 19.11.1918:- On the 8th August, 1917, H.M.S. "Dunraven" under the command of Captain Gordon Campbell, V.C., D.S.O., R.N., sighted an enemy submarine on the horizon. In her role of armed British merchant ship, the "Dunraven" continued her zig-zag course, whereupon the submarine closed, remaining submerged to within 5,000 yards, and then, rising to the surface, opened fire. The "Dunraven" returned the fire with her merchant ship gun, at the same time reducing speed to enable the enemy to overtake her. Wireless signals were also sent out for the benefit of the submarine: "Help! Come quickly - submarine chasing and shelling me." Finally, when the shells began falling close, the "Dunraven" stopped and abandoned ship by the "panic party." The ship was then being heavily shelled, and on fire aft. In the meantime the submarine closed to 400 yards distant, partly obscured from view by the dense clouds of smoke issuing from the "Dunraven's" stern. Despite the knowledge that the after magazine must inevitably explode if he waited, and further, that a gun and gun's crew lay concealed over the magazine, Captain Campbell decided to reserve his fire until the submarine had passed clear of the smoke. A moment later, however a heavy explosion occurred aft, blowing the gun and gun's crew into the air, and accidentally starting fire-gongs at the remaining gun positions; screens were immediately dropped, and the only gun that would bear opened fire, but the submarine, apparently frightened by the explosion, had already commenced to submerge. Realising that a torpedo must inevitably follow, Captain Campbell ordered the surgeon to remove all wounded and conceal them in cabins; hoses were also turned on the poop, which was a mass of flames. A signal was sent out warning men-of-war to divert all traffic below the horizon in order that nothing should interrupt the final phase of the action. Twenty minutes later a torpedo again struck the ship abaft the engine-room. An additional party of men were again sent away as "panic party," and left the ship to outward appearances completely abandoned, with the White Ensign flying and guns unmasked. For the succeeding fifty minutes the submarine examined the ship through her periscope. During the period boxes of cordite and shells exploded every few minutes, and the fire on the poop still blazed furiously. Captain Campbell and the handful of officers and men who remained on board lay hidden during this ordeal. The submarine then rose to the surface astern, where no guns could bear and shelled the ship closely for twenty minutes. The enemy then submerged and steamed past the ship 150 yards off, examining her through the periscope. Captain Campbell decided then to fire one of his torpedoes, but missed by a few inches. The submarine crossed bows and came slowly down the other side, whereupon a second torpedo was fired and missed again. The enemy observed it and immediately submerged. Urgent signals for assistance were immediately sent out, but pending arrival of assistance Captain Campbell arranged for a third "panic party" to jump overboard if necessary and leave one gun's crew on board for a final attempt to destroy the enemy, should he again attack. Almost immediately afterwards, however, British and American destroyers arrived on the scene, the wounded were transferred, boats were recalled and the fire extinguished. The "Dunraven" although her stern was awash, was taken in tow, but the weather grew worse, and early the following morning she sank with colours flying.

LONDON GAZETTE 30.10.1917

NOTES: All of the gun's crew were put in a ballot for the V.C. this was awarded to P.O. Ernest Pitcher who commanded the gun, the remaining members of the gun crew Bennison, Martindale, Murphy Sheppard and Thomson were all awarded the C.G.M. A ballot among the officers also awarded the V.C. to Lieut. Bonner D.S.C. In addition to these awards two further C.G.M.'s were awarded to crew of the Dunraven for the action, W/T Op. Fletcher and Seaman Morrison.

FOR CONSPICUOUS GALLANTRY

LONDON GAZETTE 2.11.1917

NOTES: Awarded French Medaille Militaire 28.8.1918.

Entitled to 1914-15 Star, British War Medal and Victory Medal.

MURPHY Petty Officer 1ˢᵗ Class John
Royal Navy

"In recognition of gallantry at Illig, Somaliland on 21ˢᵗ April, 1904."
LONDON GAZETTE 6.9.1904

NOTES: With an annuity of £10.

N

NEW P/KX.65752 Acting Stoker Petty Officer Thomas Edward
H.M.S. Atherstone, Royal Navy

"For bravery in defence of a Channel Convoy."

Who, on 11th September, when a bomb exploded in the boiler room of his ship, at once went below and made his way through fumes, steam, oil fuel and salt water to save a wounded shipmate. He then tried to go down again, but found the boiler room flooded.

LONDON GAZETTE 20.12.1940

NOTES: Award presented 18.3.1941.

NOBLE O.N. 2651 E.S. Engineman Alexander
H.M. Drifter Violet May, Royal Naval Reserve

"For services in action on the occasion of the raid into the straits of Dover by enemy destroyers on the night of the 14th-15th February 1918."

For conspicuous gallantry and devotion to duty.

When their ship had been severely handled by the enemy, and was on fire forward, and all the rest of the crew had been killed with two exceptions, and those so badly wounded that they could render little or no assistance, Engineman. Ewing and Noble cleared the wreckage of the boom from the small boat, got out the boat, put their wounded shipmates into it, and then took to the boat. Finding the ship did not sink, they returned to her, attacked the fire with buckets, and got it out, small arm ammunition in the wheelhouse exploding as they worked. They then got their injured shipmates on board again and made them comfortable, afterwards burning flares of old clothes soaked in paraffin until picked up and towed in at 7 a.m.

LONDON GAZETTE 16.3.1918

NOTES: With an annuity of £10.

Awarded French Medaille Militaire 17.3.1919.

Engineman Ewing was also awarded the C.G.M. The Vice Admiral, Dover Patrol reported - "The conduct of Noble and Ewing was altogether admirable. Their great gallantry and devotion to duty - and, I would add, their simple modesty - entitles them to very special consideration.

NOBLE O.N. Po. 205234 A.B. Francis George
H.M.S. Topaze, Royal Navy

For conspicuous gallantry at the capture of Salif on 12th June, 1917. When a Private of Marines was fatally wounded, and was lying in an exposed position, Noble went out from cover and brought him in. His behaviour throughout was most praiseworthy.

LONDON GAZETTE 11.8.1917

NOTES: Awarded French Medaille Militaire 17.3.1919.

His medals comprising C.G.M., 1914-15 Star, British War Medal, Victory Medal, Navy L.S.&G.C. (awarded on H.M.S. Excellent), and the French Medaille Militaire were offered for sale at Sotheby's on 8.2.1990.

NORTH C/M 11514 Chief Engine Room Artificer 2nd Class Frank
H.M.S. Vimiera, Royal Navy

For good services in operations off the Dutch, Belgian and French coasts."

When the engine room of H.M.S. Vimiera was damaged, Chief Engine Room Artificer North remained with Mr Blofield at his post. They searched the Engine Room in reeking darkness with steam escaping, at grave and increasing risk, until they found the cause of the damage. Both showed fine courage and great devotion to duty.

LONDON GAZETTE 27.8.1940

NOTES: He was also awarded the D.S.M. 10.11.42 for service in Operation Pedestal (Malta Convoy) serving on H.M.S. Penn.

Award presented 13.3.1941.

O

O'BRIEN Stoker First Class Patrick
H.M.S. Exeter, Royal Navy

"In recognition of the gallant and successful action with the "Admiral Graf Spee" (to be dated the 13th of December, 1939)."

Who, when ordered from the Damage Control Headquarters to make contact with the main switchboard, found his way through the Chief Petty Officer's flat where an 11-inch shell had just burst. Through the dense and deadly smoke, escaping steam and high explosive fumes, he made contact with the main switchboard and so with the Engine Room Artificer in the Forward Dynamo Room. From there he returned by way of the Upper Deck and let his party into the reeking Flat.

LONDON GAZETTE 23.2.1940

NOTES: Award presented 23.2.1940.

OBREE C/SSX.14027 Leading Seaman John Edward Victor
L.C.F. (L) 2, Royal Navy

"For gallantry, daring and skill in the combined attack on Dieppe."

For great bravery when the engines of his craft were put out of action during an engagement with the shore defences, for an hour and a half she was drifting under heavy fire from the cliffs. Leading Seaman Obree kept her guns in action until the order was given to abandon ship. Then he helped the wounded into the water and returned to his gun, keeping it in action for some time to draw the enemy fire from the survivors. When at length his craft sank he was taken to a Destroyer where he at once went to a gun and served it until the operation was over.

LONDON GAZETTE 20.10.1942

NOTES: Award presented 27.9.1945.

FOR CONSPICUOUS GALLANTRY

OLDEN Boatswains Mate Henry

Royal Navy

No information concerning the background of this award are available.

NAVY LIST 1885

P

PARKINSON K.P.982 Leading Seaman James
Royal Naval Volunteer Reserve

No citation was published with this award, however, the citation for the Victoria Cross awarded to Sub-Lieutenant Arthur Walden St.Clair Tisdall R.N.V.R. gives the background detail to the award.

During the landing from the S.S. "River Clyde" at V beach in the Gallipoli Peninsula on the 25th April, 1915, Sub-Lieutenant Tisdall, hearing wounded men on the beach calling for assistance, jumped into the water and, pushing a boat in front of him, went to their rescue. He was, however, obliged to obtain help, and took with him on two trips Leading Seaman Malia and on other trips Chief Petty Officer Perring and Leading Seamen Curtiss and Parkinson. In all Sub-Lieutenant Tisdall made four or five trips between the ship and the shore, and was thus responsible for rescuing several wounded men under heavy and accurate fire.

Owing to the fact that Sub-Lieutenant Tisdall and the platoon under his orders were on detached service at the time, and that this Officer was killed in action on the 6th May, it has only now been possible to obtain complete information as to the individuals who took part in this gallant act. Of these Leading Seaman Fred Curtiss, O.N. Dev. 1899, has been missing since the 4th June 1915.

LONDON GAZETTE 31.3.1916

NOTES: Chief Petty Officer Perring, and Leading Seamen Malia and Parkinson were all awarded the C.G.M. for this action.

Entitled to 1914-15 Star, British War Medal and Victory Medal.

PARSONAGE Able Seaman William
Royal Navy

"In connection with the recent operations in China."
LONDON GAZETTE 14.5.1901

PASCALL O.N. 221595 Dev. /B4016 Leading Stoker George Horrocks

H.M.S. Thistle, Royal Fleet Reserve

"For services in action with enemy submarines."

For conspicuous gallantry during the combined naval and military operations in the neighbourhood of Lindi, East Africa, on the 10th and 11th June, 1917.

He showed exemplary conduct in at once going below into the after flat, when the ship was hit by an enemy 4.1 shell, in order to assist in extinguishing the fire, and by his coolness and judgment prevented the fire from spreading.

LONDON GAZETTE 19.12.1917

NOTES: Awarded French Medaille Militaire 28.8.1918, French Croix de Guerre 14.9.1918.

Entitled to 1914-15 Star, British War Medal and Victory Medal.

Medals comprising C.G.M., 1914-15 Star, British War Medal, 1939-45 Star, War Medal, Africa Service Medal, French Medaille Militaire and French Croix de Guerre were offered for sale at Sotheby's on 12.9.1989.

PATTERSON Private Stephen

Royal Marine Light Infantry

Awarded for the Egypt campaign. No further details on the actual details of the award are available.

NAVY LIST 1884

PERKINS Leading Stoker 1st Class Joseph

Royal Navy

No details on the background to this award are available.

NAVY LIST 1894

NOTES: With an annuity of £20.

PERRING Chief Petty Officer Wlliam Henry
Royal Naval Volunteer Reserve

No citation was published with this award, however, the citation for the Victoria Cross awarded to Sub-Lieutenant Arthur Walden St.Clair Tisdall R.N.V.R. gives the background detail to the award.

During the landing from the S.S. "River Clyde" at V beach in the Gallipoli Peninsula on the 25th April, 1915, Sub-Lieutenant Tisdall, hearing wounded men on the beach calling for assistance, jumped into the water and, pushing a boat in front of him, went to their rescue. He was, however, obliged to obtain help, and took with him on two trips Leading Seaman Malia and on other trips Chief Petty Officer Perring and Leading Seamen Curtiss and Parkinson. In all Sub-Lieutenant Tisdall made four or five trips between the ship and the shore, and was thus responsible for rescuing several wounded men under heavy and accurate fire.

Owing to the fact that Sub-Lieutenant Tisdall and the platoon under his orders were on detached service at the time, and that this Officer was killed in action on the 6th May, it has only now been possible to obtain complete information as to the individuals who took part in this gallant act. Of these Leading Seaman Fred Curtiss, O.N. Dev. 1899, has been missing since the 4th June 1915.

LONDON GAZETTE 31.3.1916

NOTES: Chief Petty Officer Perring, and Leading Seamen Malia and Parkinson were all awarded the C.G.M. for this action.

With an annuity of £10.

Entitled to the 1914 Star and bar, British War Medal and Victory Medal. Later commissioned as Sub-Lieutenant.

PETRIE 335730 Sergeant Clarence E.
United States Marine Corps

Awarded in connection with the conquest of Gilbert and Ellice Islands.

LONDON GAZETTE Not published in the gazette, award approved by H.M. King George VI 11.1.1945.

NOTES: Sergeant Burgess' medal was sent to him via the Foreign Office 19.11.1945.

PIERCE 3/226 Able Seaman William James
Howe Battalion, Royal Naval Volunteer Reserve

"For services in the Gallipoli Peninsula."

Showed great gallantry on the 4th June in remaining in the enemy's trench and continuing firing, although wounded, to cover the retirement of other wounded men, and finally in carrying in a wounded man under heavy fire.

LONDON GAZETTE 13.9.1915

NOTES: Entitled to 1914 Star, British War Medal and Victory Medal.

PILGRIM Po./846 (S) Acting Corporal Frank
Royal Marine Light Infantry

On the 20th November, 1915, at Cape Helles, he threw a live Turkish grenade out of a trench and thereby avoided a dangerous accident.

LONDON GAZETTE 31.5.1916

NOTES: Awarded Croix de Guerre (France) 19.12.1917, also entitled to 1914-15 Star, British War Medal and Victory Medal.

Commissioned as 2nd Lieutenant 27.3.1918.

PLENDERLEITH P/X.10109B Petty Officer George Hood
M.G.B. 335, Royal Naval Reserve

"For bravery in action against the enemy, while serving in H.M. Motor Gun Boats."

For great bravery and fortitude when wounded in action. He rigged hand steering when the gear broke down. He was hit a second time, but tackled a fire which had broken out in the engine room, and then helped to carry the wounded. He then went to a gun and fought it although wounded a third time.

LONDON GAZETTE 10.11.1942

NOTES: Award presented 23.2.1943.

POITRAS Petty Officer Edwin W.
United States Navy

Awarded for services after being parachuted into occupied France 1.5.1944.

LONDON GAZETTE Not published in the gazette, award approved by H.M. King George VI 27.9.1945.

NOTES: Medal presented in Washington 11.7.1946.

POORE P/J.111056 Acting Petty Officer Leslie Roy
H.M.S. Aphis, Royal Navy

"For courage, skill and devotion to duty in operations off the Libyan coast."

Who, as a Beechworker in charge of one of the guns in his ship, when two of the guns crew were killed and one wounded, though cut off from the rest of the ship, fought his gun until the Enemy were out of range.

LONDON GAZETTE 29.7.1941.

NOTES: Award presented 21.7.1942.

Action took place on 3rd January 1941.

POVALL Po.X.122 Corporal (Temporary) John
Royal Marines

"For gallantry in the face of heavy odds in landings near Tobruk."

Corporal Povall was among the first in a party to land, under heavy fire from the enemy, at Tobruk.

On getting ashore, he rallied his platoon, proceeded to attack at the head of his men, and was largely responsible for establishing a bridgehead among the enemy. Hand to hand fighting followed in which Corporal Povall's skillful use of his bayonet and rifle were an example which instilled in his men the dash and offensive spirit which enabled them to sweep aside several machine-gun nests and a considerable number of the enemy. His gallantry and outstanding leadership were worthy of the high tradition of the Royal Marines.

LONDON GAZETTE 3.8.1943.

NOTES: Award presented 2.11.1943.

Action took place during Operation Agreement.

PRESCOTT 23834301 Staff Sergeant James
Corps of Royal Engineers

"In recognition of brave and gallant service during the operations in the South Atlantic."

On 22nd May 1982 Staff Sergeant Prescott under the command of another N.C.O. of 49 Engineer Explosives Disposal Squadron Royal Engineers were carrying out explosive ordnance disposal duties in the Falkland Islands. They were tasked to deal with an unexploded bomb in the boiler room of H.M.S. Argonaut. Another unexploded bomb lay in a flooded missile magazine nearby. Working in extraordinarily cramped conditions and in very unfamiliar surroundings Staff Sergeant Prescott and the other N.C.O. successfully remotely rendered safe the bomb which was later removed from the ship. This action enabled the damage to the boiler room to be repaired, so that H.M.S. Argonaut regained propulsion and was able to manoeuvre defensively in further air attacks .

On 23rd May 1982. Staff Sergeant Prescott and the N.C.O. were tasked to neutralise two unexploded bombs in H.M.S. Antelope. The first bomb examined could not be approached until extensive clearance of debris had taken place. They therefore set about rendering safe the second bomb which was situated near the centre of the ship. The bomb had been slightly damaged and was assessed as being in a dangerous condition. They tried three times to render the bomb safe using a remote method. having to approach the bomb after each attempt to adjust the equipment, but on each occasion, the fuse could not be withdrawn. After a fourth attempt which involved using a small charge, the bomb unexpectedly exploded. The blast was considerable. Despite a blast route of open doors and hatches up through the ship, the fully clipped steel door at the forward end of the passageway, where the bomb disposal team was standing, was completely blown off and nearly bent double. Staff Sergeant Prescott died instantly.

Staff Sergeant Prescott displayed courage of the highest order in persevering with attempts to defuse the bomb in H.M.S. Antelope, fully aware that the condition was particularly dangerous.

LONDON GAZETTE 6.1982

NOTES: This is the only instance of the C.G.M. being awarded posthumously and the only occasion the Naval award has been made to the Army.

The N.C.O. in charge of this operation was W.O.2 John Henry Phillips who was awarded the D.S.C. for his part in neutralising the bombs.

PRESS Po./15394 Private John Denis Lyons
Royal Marine Light Infantry

"In recognition of distinguished services during the operations against Zeebrugge and Ostend on the night of the 22nd-23rd April 1918."

Private Press landed on the mole at Zeebrugge as runner to an officer of the Royal Marines. When his officer was seriously wounded in the head and rendered unconscious, Pte Press remained with him, and, although himself wounded, eventually succeeded in carrying him back on board "Vindictive".

LONDON GAZETTE 23.7.1918

NOTES: Awarded Croix de Guerre (France) 28.8.1918.

Private Press' medals consisting of C.G.M., 1914-15 Star, British War Medal, Victory Medal, 1939-1945 Star, Africa Star, War Medal, Navy L.S. & G.C., Navy M.S.M. are now on display in the Royal Marines museum in Portsmouth.

PRESTON Po/7358 L/Sgt James E.
Royal Marine Light Infantry, Legation Guard China

"For Defence of Legations, China 1900".

LONDON GAZETTE Not published, award was for action on 13.7.1900. Award granted in 1901.

NOTES: With an annuity of £10.

Awarded D.C.M. , London Gazette 25.7.1901, initials given as T.E. This award was made for Defence of Legations in the China war of 1900.

A force of just over 400 Allied officers and men of the Legations settlement defended against a force of superior numbers of Chinese regular and irregular forces.

The British Legation Guard arrived in Peking on the night of 31ˢᵗ May, 1900, and comprised three officers, seventy-five N.C.O.'s and men including Preston and one bugler, all from the Royal Marine light Infantry along with three Naval ratings, under the command of Captain M.B. Strouts, R.M.

On 13ᵗʰ June some three hundred Boxers entered the City near the Legations Settlement and from this date on the detachment was continuously in a state of readiness. On the 19ᵗʰ the Chinese issued an ultimatum for all ministers and foreigners to leave the City within twenty-four hours. This ultimatum was rejected and the decision taken to stay and defend the Legations. All women and children were brought into the British compound, which was to be the last line of defence.

Hostilities began on the night of the 20ᵗʰ June and except for a period for communication between the two sides between the 17ᵗʰ of July and 5ᵗʰ August was to continue until relived by the allied army on 14ᵗʰ August.

Medals comprising D.C.M., C.G.M., China Medal 1900 with clasp Defence of Legations, 1914-15 Star, British War Medal, Victory Medal and Navy L.S. & G.C. now reside in the Royal Marines Museum, Portsmouth. This is the only instance of a man being awarded both the D.C.M. and C.G.M.

Later Commissioned as Lieutenant.

PRING O.N. 161176 Chief Stoker William George
Royal Navy

"For services rendered by Petty Officers and men of the Grand Fleet in the action in the North Sea on the 31ˢᵗ May - 1ˢᵗ June, 1916."

Although severely wounded early in the action, Chief Stoker Pring continued to carry out important duties with repair parties until the action was finished.

FOR CONSPICUOUS GALLANTRY

LONDON GAZETTE 15.9.1916

NOTES: With annuity of £10.

Awarded Croix de Guerre (France) LG 19.12.1917.

Entitled to 1914-15 Star, British War Medal and Victory Medal.

R

RANSOME CS 51773 / 25963 A. Leading Seaman Henry
H.M.S. Barracouta, Royal Navy

ASHANTEE 1873 - 1874: On 14th October, 1873 at Essaman, Leading Seaman Ransome acted as Captain of the 7 pounder gun and with equal coolness as that shown by John Maxwell, deliberately fought his gun making capital practice till the advance of the Marines in support.

NAVY LIST 1874

NOTES: M.I.D. 18.11.1873 together with John Maxwell as deserving special mention for the manner in which they directed the fire of the gun and rockets at the village of Essaman with a precision worthy of parade practice.

RAWLES O.N. Po. 201767 A.B. William George
H.M.S. Broke, Royal Navy

"In recognition of their services in H.M.S. "Swift" and H.M.S. "Broke" on the night of the 20th to 21st April, 1917, when they successfully engaged a flotilla of five or six German destroyers, of which two were sunk"

Although he had four bad wounds in his legs, in addition to other injuries, he continued to steer H.M.S. "Broke" in action - until the enemy destroyer had been rammed.

LONDON GAZETTE 10.5.1917

NOTES: Awarded French Medaille Militaire 28.8.1918.

Entitled to 1914-15 Star, British War Medal and Victory Medal.

RAYSBROOK 277812 Sergeant Robert David
United States Marine Corps

Awarded for action in the Solomon Islands 27.9.1942.

FOR CONSPICUOUS GALLANTRY

LONDON GAZETTE Not published in the gazette, award approved by H.M. King George VI 25.4.1943.

READ Able Seaman Ernest John
Royal Navy

"For services in connection with the operations in South Africa."

No further information surrounding this award is available.

LONDON GAZETTE 22.3.1901

NOTES: With an annuity of £10.

REID C/MX.58457 Engine Room Artificer Third Class Charles Alfred
H.M.S. Bonaventure, Royal Navy

"For gallantry endurance and great devotion to duty."

Engine Room Artificer Reid was the operational Engine Room Artificer of XE-3 for her successful attack on a heavy Japanese cruiser of the Atago class in Johore Strait. He was at the wheel continuously for the 16½ hours that XE-3 was submerged, a fine feat of endurance. He shared, with the other three of XE-3's crew, the hazards of an 80 mile trip through closely protected enemy waters and like them cheerfully volunteered to carry out a repeat mission if required.

LONDON GAZETTE 13.11.1945

NOTES: This attack, code named Operation Struggle, was made by the midget submarines XE-1 and XE-3 on the Japanese heavy cruisers Myoko and Takao and resulted in awards to the crew of XE-3 of the V.C. to Lieutenant Ian Fraser R.N.R. and Leading Seaman James Magennis, and the D.S.O to Sub/Lt Smith.

The operation took place over 30/31st July 1945, XE-1 had been assigned to attack the Myoko and XE-3 the Takao. XE-3 successfully laid her charges but XE-1 was unable to make a successful attack on her target and so added her payload to that already laid under the Takao by XE-3. The charges detonated at approximately 21.30 on the 31st July and tore a hole in the bottom of the Takao some 60 feet by thirty feet.

Award presented 26.2.1946.

REED O.N. (Ch.).230360 Petty Officer Joseph James, D.S.M.
H.M.S. Vindictive, Royal Navy

"For distinguished service in the second blocking operation against Ostend on the night of 9ᵗʰ/10ᵗʰ May, 1918."

This Petty Officer was in "Brilliant" in the previous attempt to block Ostend. He immediately volunteered to accompany his officers in a second operation. On the night of 9ᵗʰ/10ᵗʰ May he steered "Vindictive" into Ostend harbour and, when the charges were fired and the ship abandoned, he picked up Lieut. Sir John Alleyne, who was lying unconscious in the conning tower, carried him to the gangway, and lowered him over the side. This very gallant Petty Officer then assisted others to escape, and on board M.L. 254 was of the greatest assistance in keeping that vessel afloat until she was picked up.

LONDON GAZETTE 28.8.1918

NOTES: With an annuity of £10.

Awarded D.S.M 23.7.1918.

Medals comprising C.G.M., D.S.M., 1914-15 Star, British War Medal, Victory Medal appeared for sale at Spink on 17.7.1997. The catalogue states that he was also M.I.D. twice, one certificate for the M.I.D. sold with the lot was dated 28.8.1918, the same date his C.G.M. was published in the gazette!

REES O.N. 3146S.D. Leading Deckhand, David George
M.L. 254, Royal Naval Reserve

For his conspicuous gallantry as coxswain of M.L. 254, remaining at the wheel after being wounded. He assisted Lieut.-Cdr. Drummond - also seriously wounded - to put the motor launch alongside "Vindictive" in Ostend harbour and carried on until he was relieved by one of the rescued crew.

LONDON GAZETTE 28.8.1918

NOTES: Entitled to British War Medal and Victory Medal.

FOR CONSPICUOUS GALLANTRY

RHODES Ordinary Seaman Ian Dennis
H.M.S. Kashmir, Royal Australian Naval Volunteer Reserve

"For outstanding gallantry , fortitude and resolution during the battle of Crete."

Who, when his ship was hit by a bomb and sinking rapidly, left the port gun, of which he was gunlayer, and which was going under water, and climbed to the starboard gun. This he turned on an aircraft which was machine-gunning his shipmates, and brought it down in flames into the sea.

LONDON GAZETTE 8.1.1942

NOTES: Award presented 24.2.1942.

RICKARD Quartermaster William
H.M. Steam Gun Vessel. Weser, Royal Navy

Azoff: When commanding the Weser in the Sea of Azoff, crossed the Isthmus of Arabat and destroyed large quantities of forage on the Crimean shore of the sivash. This enterprise was performed by Captain Commerell at night, accompanied by William Rickard, Quartermaster, and George Milestone, Able Seaman. Having hauled their small boat across the spit of Arabat, they traversed the sivash to the Crimean shore of the Putrid Sea. The magazine of corn of which they were in search lay about two miles and a half off, and to reach it, they had to ford two rivers, the Kara-su and the Salghir. The forage and corn, amounting to 400 tons, were stacked on the banks of the latter river, in the vicinity of a guard house and close to from 20 to 30 Cossacks, who were encamped in the neighbouring village. Commander Commerell and his two companions contrived to ignite the stacks, the rapid blazing of which alarmed the guard, who pursued them to the shore with a very heavy fire of musketry, and very nearly succeeded in taking them prisoners.

LONDON GAZETTE 20.11.1855

NOTES: Mentioned in Despatches 20.11.1855.

Awarded the Victoria Cross 24.2.1857. Rickard was also awarded the French Legion d'Honneur for this action.

William Rickard died on 21st February 1905.

RIVETT O.N. 5727 D.A. 2nd Hand George Bertie
H.M. Drifter Kosmos, Royal Naval Reserve

"For services in action on the occasion of the raid into the straits of Dover by enemy destroyers on the night of the 14th-15th February 1918."

For conspicuous gallantry and devotion to duty.

He displayed great courage and presence of mind when, first, his own ship having sunk, he went overboard after the small boat which was adrift. Later, he put his lifebelt on a severely wounded engineman of another ship. Finally, he assisted in saving the life of Engmn. Wakerley when the later became unconscious. He was in the water for over two hours.

LONDON GAZETTE: 16.3.1918

NOTES: With an annuity of £10.

Engineman Wakerley was awarded the D.S.M. in the same gazette.

Entitled to 1914-15 Star, British War Medal and Victory Medal.

ROBB D/KX.83589 Leading Stoker Ronald Keith
H.M.S. Pangbourne, Royal Navy

"For good services in the withdrawal of the Allied Armies from the French Coast."

Who, when badly wounded in both arms stood by, without cover, to slip the cable. Later, though he could use only one damaged arm, he helped repair parties.

LONDON GAZETTE: 25.10.1940

NOTES: Award presented 1.3.1941.

ROLFE Chief Gunners Mate William
Royal Navy

No details surrounding this award are available.

NAVY LIST 1884

NOTES: With an annuity of £10.

ROWBOTTOM O.N. (Ch.) J2953 Petty Officer 1st Class William
H.M.S. Julnar, Royal Navy

For most conspicuous gallantry as a volunteer in H.M.S. "Julnar" on the 24th April, 1916, when that vessel attempted to reach Kut-El-Amarah with stores for the besieged garrison.

LONDON GAZETTE 11.11.1919

NOTES: Entitled to 1914-15 Star, British War Medal and Victory Medal. Medal card shows name and Rowbotham.

ROWLINSON P/MX.49217 Chief Engine Room Artificer Geoffrey
Royal Navy

"For resolution, enterprise and fine leadership in a successful encounter with enemy forces in the Mediterranean."

After shells had burst inside the engine room of his ship, severing the steam pipes and making it uninhabitable, Chief Engine Room Artificer Rowlinson was escaping by a ladder when he saw a stoker fall back into the worst part of the steam from another ladder. he immediately went down again into the steam-filled engine room and hauled him up to safety, himself being badly burnt in this gallant action.

LONDON GAZETTE 27.7.1943

NOTES: Award presented 18.7.1945.

Mentioned in Despatches 2.6.1943, whilst serving in H.M.S. Pakenham.

ROXBURGH O.N. Ch./272442 Engine Room Artificer 3rd Class,
Allan Gordon
Royal Navy

"In recognition of distinguished services during the operations against Zeebrugge and Ostend on the night of the 22nd-23rd April 1918."

Sto.1st Class Bindall, P.O. W.Harner, Ldg.Smn W.G.Cleaver and E.R.A. 3rd Cl. A.G. Roxburgh.

The ratings above mentioned were members of the crew of Submarine C.3, which was skillfully placed between the piles of the Zeebrugge mole viaduct and there blown up, the fuse being lighted before the submarine was abandoned. They volunteered for and, under the command of an officer, eagerly undertook this hazardous enterprise, although they were well aware that if the means of rescue failed, and that if any of them were in the water at the time of the explosion, they would be killed outright.

LONDON GAZETTE 23.7.1918

NOTES: With an annuity of £10.

P.O Harner, Ldg Seaman Cleaver and Sto Bindall were also awarded the C.G.M. for this action. Lt. Howell-Price received the D.S.O. and Lt. Sandford the V.C.

Awarded Croix de Guerre (France) 28.8.1918.

Entitled to 1914-15 Star, British War Medal and Victory Medal.

RUMMING O.N. F813 Petty Officer Mechanic Geoffrey Charlton Paine

Royal Naval Air Service

"Despatch of Vice Admiral John M. de Robeck reporting on the landing of the Army on the Gallipoli Peninsula 25th-26th April 1915."

Assisted Commander Unwin in rescuing wounded men.

LONDON GAZETTE 16.8.1915

NOTES: See the account under Petty Officer J.H. Russell. Awarded with an annuity of £10.

Awarded French Medaille Militaire 28.8.1918.

Entitled to 1914-15 Star, British War Medal and Victory Medal.

RUNALLS O.N. 272059 Engine Room Artificer 2nd Class, Joseph J. Fielding
H.M.S. Inflexible, Royal Navy

"For services when H.M.S. "Inflexible" was damaged by a mine on 18th March.."

Engine Room Artificer Second Class Joseph J. Fielding Runalls escaped up the trunk from the fore air compressor room with difficulty, helped up his stoker and closed the W.T. door of the trunk before he fell insensible.

LONDON GAZETTE 16.8.1915

NOTES: With an annuity of £10.

Awarded Croix de Guerre (France) LG 19.12.1917.

Medals comprising C.G.M., 1914-15 Star, British War Medal, Victory Medal, Navy L.S. & G.C., French Croix de Guerre, appeared for sale at Spink on 28.3.1995.

RUSSELL O.N.F839 Petty Officer Mechanic John Hepburn
Royal Naval Air Service

"Despatch of Vice Admiral John M. de Robeck reporting on the landing of the Army on the Gallipoli Peninsula 25th-26th April 1915."

Wounded in gallantly going to Commander Unwin's assistance.

LONDON GAZETTE 16.8.1915

NOTES: Commander Unwin was awarded the V.C. for this action, the extract from the same despatch is as follows - " While in the "River Clyde", observing that the lighters which were to form the bridge to the shore had broken adrift, Commander Unwin left the ship and under a murderous fire attempted to get the lighters into position. He worked on until, suffering from the effects of cold and immersion, he was obliged to return to the ship, where he was wrapped in blankets. Having in some degree recovered, he returned to his work against the doctor's order and completed it. He was later again attended by the doctor for three abrasions caused by bullets, after which he once more left the ship, this time in a lifeboat, to save some wounded men who were lying in shallow water near the beach. He continued at this heroic labour under continuous fire, until forced to stop through pure physical exhaustion.

With an annuity of £10.

Awarded French Medaille Militaire 28.8.1918.

Entitled to 1914-15 Star, British war Medal and Victory Medal.

RUSSELL Ply/X214 Sergeant Wilfred A.
H.M.S. Exeter Royal Marines

"In recognition of the gallant and successful action with the "Admiral Graf Spee" (to be dated the 13th of December, 1939)."

Wilfred A. Russell, Royal Marines, H.M.S. Exeter who, having his left forearm blown away and his right arm shattered when a turret was put out of action by a direct hit from an 11 inch shell, refused all but first aid, remaining on deck and went about cheering on his shipmates and putting courage into them by his great fortitude; and did not give in until the heat of battle was over. He has since died of wounds.

LONDON GAZETTE 23.2.1940

NOTES: Died of Wounds. Medal presented to next of Kin 23.2.1940.

S

SANDFORD D/JX.133162 Able Seaman Guy Aundrie
M.L. 139, Royal Navy

"For Gallantry, resolution and seamanship when H.M. Air/Sea Rescue Craft were heavily attacked by enemy aircraft in the straits of Dover."

For great bravery when a fire broke out in one of H.M. Motor Launches. These two ratings, in the face of the greatest danger, entered a compartment and put out a fire. This action saved the ship.

LONDON GAZETTE 29.9.1942

NOTES: Acting Chief Motor Mechanic Leslie Charles Thomas Adams was also awarded the CGM for this action which took place on 15.7.1942.

Award presented 24.11.1942.

SAYER O.N. 170698 Petty Officer George Arthur
Royal Navy

"For services rendered by Petty Officers and men of the Grand Fleet in the action in the North Sea on the 31st May - 1st June, 1916."

Petty Officer Sayer's leg was shot away when the turret in which he was stationed was disabled, and he thereafter set a fine example by remaining at his post and trying to get his gun into action again.

LONDON GAZETTE 15.9.1916

NOTES: With an annuity of £20.

Awarded Croix de Guerre (France) 19.12.1917.

Entitled to 1914-15 Star, British War Medal and Victory Medal.

FOR CONSPICUOUS GALLANTRY

SCOTT P/J.113793 Petty Officer Walter Thomas William
Royal Navy

"For great gallantry in H.M.S. Glowworm's last action on 8th April, 1940. H.M.S. Glowworm attacked the German heavy cruiser Admiral Hipper and, after inflicting damage, was sunk with colours flying."

Lieutenant Commander Roope was awarded the Victoria Cross for this action, the first V.C. of the war, his citation, describing events, is as follows: On the 8th April, 1940, H.M.S. Glowworm was proceeding alone in heavy weather towards a rendezvous in West Fjord, when she met and engaged two enemy destroyers, scoring at least one hit on them. The enemy broke off the action and headed North, to lead the Glowworm on to his supporting forces. The Commanding Officer, whilst correctly appreciating the intentions of the enemy, at once gave chase. The German heavy cruiser, Admiral Hipper, was sighted closing the Glowworm at high speed and an enemy report was sent which was received by H.M.S. Renown. Because of the heavy sea, the Glowworm could not shadow the enemy and the Commanding Officer therefore decided to attack with torpedoes and then to close in order to inflict as much damage as possible. Five torpedoes were fired and later the remaining five, but without success. The Glowworm was badly hit; one gun was out of action and her speed was much reduced, but with the other three guns still firing she closed and rammed the Admiral Hipper. As the Glowworm drew away, she opened fire again and scored one hit at a range of 400 yards. The Glowworm, badly stove in forward and riddled with enemy fire, heeled over to starboard, and the Commanding Officer gave the order to abandon her. Shortly afterwards she capsized and sank. The Admiral Hipper hove to for at least an hour picking up survivors but the loss of life was heavy, only 31 out of the Glowworm's compliment of 149 being saved.

LONDON GAZETTE 10.7.1945

NOTES: Engine Room Artificer H. Gregg and Able Seaman R. T. Merritt were also awarded the C.G.M. for this action and Lieut. R. A. Ramsay the D.S.O.

Petty Officer Scott was repatriated from Marlag und Milag Nord, Westertimke (Tarnstedt) in 1945. Following the release of the P.O.W.'s the events surrounding the sinking of the Glowworm came to light and on 18th July he received the following communication from the Admiralty;

"Sir, I am commanded by My Lords Commissioners of the Admiralty to inform you that they have learned with great pleasure that, on the advice of the First Sea Lord, the King has been graciously pleased to award you the Conspicuous Gallantry Medal for great bravery in charge of two guns of H.M.S. Glowworm, during a very gallant action with the German Heavy Cruiser Hipper fought on 8th April 1940 against overwhelming odds. After your ship had rammed the enemy and was about to sink from the damage she received in the action, your guns re-opened fire and scored a hit at close range.

Petty Officer Scott received his medal at an Investiture at Buckingham Palace on 30th October 1945.

SCREECH C.S. 52343 Gunners Mate Joseph
H.M.S. Amethyst, Royal Navy

ASHANTEE 1873 - 1874: At Amoaful on 31st January 1874 commanded a detachment to cover Bush Cutting party with much coolness; this service was performed under a heavy fire.

NAVY LIST 1874

SERMON C.S. 6667 Able Seaman William
H.M.S. Rattlesnake, Royal Navy

ASHANTEE 1873 - 1874: Who with Henry Godden waded on shore through the surf at Chamah on 14th August 1873, and at the imminent risk to their lives, brought off the 2nd cutter of the Rattlesnake, William Fryer A.B., who was seriously wounded and unable to make good his retreat to his own boat which was outside the surf.

NAVY LIST 1874

SETHREN S.D.F. 71240 Stoker First Class Réné
H.M.S.A.S. Southern Isles, South African Navy

"For courage and devotion to duty while serving in the Mediterranean."

For his steadfast bearing when his ship was attacked by an Enemy aircraft which machine-gunned the deck. Though eleven times wounded, he stood to his gun and turned a steady fire on the aircraft until it fell in flames in the sea.

LONDON GAZETTE 25.11.1941

NOTES: The only award of the C.G.M. to the South African Navy.

Memories of war by Captain C.J.Jarris states " P/O Sethren was serving on a converted whaler, the HMSAS Southern Isles, in the Mediterranean on June 29 1941 when the ship was attacked by a German Junkers-88.

In the words of Lieutenant Louis Ribbink, who was serving on the same vessel: " I saw Sethren go down in a welter of blood and shouted to him: 'Get up and fight your gun.'

Somehow Sethren dragged himself up to his gun and went on firing.

We fired the four-inch at the last minute and scored a lucky hit on his port engine.

Suddenly the attack was over and the skies were clear."

P/O Sethren was later treated in a hospital in Alexandria for his 11 bullet wounds, but never fully recovered. He was released from the service in 1943.

SHEPHERD Boatswain's Mate John
H.M.S. St. Jean d'Acre, Royal Navy

Sebastopol Harbour: On 15th July, 1855, proceeding in a punt with an exploding apparatus into the harbour of Sebastopol, to endeavour to blow up one of the Russian line-of-battle ships. This service, which was attempted twice, is described by Lord Lyons as 'a bold one and gallantly executed'. On the first occasion Shepheard proceeded past the enemy's steamboats at the entrance of Careening bay; but was prevented penetrating further by the long string of boats that were carrying troops from the south to the north side of Sebastopol. The second attempt was made on 16th August, 1855, from the side of Careening Bay in the possession of the French.

LONDON GAZETTE Not published in the gazette

NOTES: Awarded the Victoria Cross 24.2.1857 for the same incident..

This was the first attempt to place what was to become know as the limpet mine. The idea had been Shepherds own and the design of the canoe in which he entered the harbour also was down to him. The British Commanders in the Crimea had the idea demonstrated to them when Shepheard succeeded, undetected, to attach a dummy explosive to the British Admirals flagship, despite being warned about the attempt and the fact that a very sharp lookout was posted. The Admiral and Lord Raglan however did not approve his plan to attack the Russian Fleet using his canoe, which floated a mere three inches above the water, as it was considered to be an un-gentlemanly way to conduct war. The French Commanders however did not have the same concerns and requested permission from the British to make an attempt, this they did using Shepheard and his canoe. Although he was unable to place the explosive because of the traffic in the harbour, he brought back a considerable amount of intelligence.

SHEPPARD O.N. Ch. J.25419 A.B. Richard Walter
Royal Navy

"For services in action with enemy submarines."

From the official account published in the L.G. 19.11.1918:- On the 8th August, 1917, H.M.S. "Dunraven" under the command of Captain Gordon Campbell, V.C., D.S.O., R.N., sighted an enemy submarine on the horizon. In her role of armed British merchant ship, the "Dunraven" continued her zig-zag course, whereupon the submarine closed, remaining submerged to within 5,000 yards, and then, rising to the surface, opened fire. The "Dunraven" returned the fire with her merchant ship gun, at the same time reducing speed to enable the enemy to overtake her. Wireless signals were also sent out for the benefit of the submarine: "Help! Come quickly - submarine chasing and shelling me." Finally, when the shells began falling close, the "Dunraven" stopped and abandoned ship by the "panic party." The ship was then being heavily shelled, and on fire aft. In the meantime the submarine closed to 400 yards distant, partly obscured from view by the dense clouds of smoke issuing from the "Dunraven's" stern. Despite the knowledge that the after magazine must inevitably explode if he waited, and further, that a gun and gun's crew lay concealed over the magazine, Captain Campbell decided to reserve his fire until the submarine had passed clear of the smoke. A moment later, however a heavy explosion occurred aft, blowing the gun and gun's crew into the air, and accidentally starting fire-gongs at the remaining gun positions; screens were immediately dropped, and the only gun that would bear opened fire, but the submarine, apparently frightened by the explosion, had already commenced to submerge. Realising that a torpedo must inevitably follow, Captain Campbell ordered the surgeon to remove all wounded and conceal them in cabins; hoses were also turned on the poop, which was a mass of flames. A signal was sent out warning men-of-war to divert all traffic below the horizon in order that nothing should interrupt the final phase of the action. Twenty minutes later a torpedo again struck the ship abaft the engine-room. An additional party of men were again sent away as "panic party," and left the ship to outward appearances completely abandoned, with the White Ensign flying and guns unmasked. For the succeeding fifty minutes the submarine examined the ship through her periscope. During the period boxes of cordite and shells exploded every few minutes, and the fire on the poop still blazed furiously. Captain Campbell and the handful of officers and men who remained on board lay hidden during this ordeal. The submarine then rose to the surface astern, where no guns could bear and shelled the ship closely for twenty minutes. The enemy then submerged and steamed past the ship 150 yards off, examining her through the periscope. Captain Campbell decided then to fire one of his torpedoes, but missed by a few inches. The submarine crossed bows and came slowly down the other side, whereupon a second torpedo was fired and missed again. The enemy observed it and immediately submerged. Urgent signals for assistance were immediately sent out, but pending arrival of assistance Captain Campbell arranged for a third "panic party" to jump overboard if necessary and leave one gun's crew on board for a final attempt to destroy the enemy, should he again attack. Almost immediately afterwards, however, British and American destroyers arrived on the scene, the wounded were transferred, boats were recalled and the fire extinguished. The "Dunraven" although her stern was awash, was taken in tow, but the weather grew worse, and early the following morning she sank with colours flying.

LONDON GAZETTE 30.10.1917

NOTES: All of the gun's crew were put in a ballot for the V.C. this was awarded to P.O. Ernest Pitcher who commanded the gun, the remaining members of the gun crew Bennison, Martindale, Murphy Sheppard and Thomson were all awarded the C.G.M. A ballot among the officers also awarded the V.C. to Lieut. Bonner D.S.C. In addition to these awards two further C.G.M.'s were awarded to crew of the Dunraven for the action, W/T Op. Fletcher and Seaman Morrison.

LONDON GAZETTE 2.11.1917

NOTES: Awarded French Medaille Militaire 28.8.1918.

Entitled to 1914-15 Star, British War Medal and Victory Medal. The medal card states that a duplicate set of first world war medals was issued to a private address on 1.5.1958.

SHERRINGTON D/J.113712 Able Seaman David Colin
H.M.S. Broke, Royal Navy

"For bravery and skill in hazardous operations in which the Allied Forces were landed in North Africa."

For gallantry at the wheel of H.M.S. Broke when she left the harbour of Algiers under heavy fire. A shell killed all in the wheel house save himself and one other; but though blinded by smoke and choked by fumes he steered his ship with unerring skill through the gap in the boom. Any deviation from his course would have endangered his ship and her company.

LONDON GAZETTE 16.3.1943

NOTES: Award presented 26.2.1946.

SHIPLIE R.M.A. 4407 Gunner William

H.M.S. Active, 26ᵗʰ Company Royal Marine Artillery

ASHANTEE 1873 - 1874: Was with the brigade from the first landing, and in each engagement distinguished himself by his good conduct, great coolness and personal bravery.

NAVY LIST 1874

SILLENCE Ch./15575 Bugler Ernest

Chatham Battalion, Royal Marine Light Infantry

"For services with the Mediterranean Expeditionary Force."

Behaved with distinguished gallantry on May 4ᵗʰ during operations South of Achi Baba in volunteering to throw back enemy bombs into enemy lines at great personal risk, thereby saving the lives of many of his comrades.

LONDON GAZETTE3.6.1915

NOTES: Entitled to the 1914 Star and bar, British War Medal and Victory Medal.

SKENE LT/KX.106765 Engineman George Campbell

S.S. Bodin, Royal Navy

"For services in and near Narvik."

Who, on 30ᵗʰ May, 1940, when his ship had been severely damaged by bombs, kept her engines running, and under fire brought many Norwegian troops to safety. When the vessel ran ashore the rescue of all on board was in great part due to him.

LONDON GAZETTE: 26.9.1940

NOTES: Awarded the Norwegian War Cross with sword 13.10.1942.

Award presented 24.2.1942.

SLOPER Able Seaman David
Royal Navy

"For services rendered during recent operations against Malays in the Straits of Malacca."

For standing by the body of Major Hawkins (Brigade Major) after he had been speared, shooting down two of the enemy and only retreating when obliged to do so.

LONDON GAZETTE 10.3.1876

NOTES: for full details of the action, see entry under A.B. Harry Bennett.

SMEDLEY O.N. 13729 Able Seaman Walter Samuel
Royal Navy

"For services when H.M.S. "Inflexible" was damaged by a mine on 18th March."

LONDON GAZETTE 16.8.1915

NOTES: Awarded Croix de Guerre (France) LG 19.12.1917, also entitled to 1914-15 Star, British War Medal and Victory Medal.

SMITH O.N. (Po.) 225904 Petty Officer David Percy
Iris II, Royal Navy

"In recognition of distinguished services during the operations against Zeebrugge and Ostend on the night of the 22nd-23rd April 1918."

Petty Officer Smith acted as quartermaster of "Iris II.," and carried out his duties with great coolness throughout. On leaving the mole at Zeebrugge, the bridge of his ship was partially shot away, the captain and the navigator being severely wounded. Petty Officer Smith remained at his exposed post under heavy fire, steering the ship to safety with one hand while lighting the compass with a torch held in the other.

LONDON GAZETTE 23.7.1918

NOTES: With an annuity of £10.

Awarded D.S.M. 29.8.1917, awarded for service in action with enemy submarines whilst serving on the 'Q' ship Cullist., Croix de Guerre (France) 28.8.1918.

Medals C.G.M., D.S.M., 1914-15 Star, British War Medal, Victory Medal (M.I.D.), Defence Medal, War Medal, Naval L.S. & G.C. French Croix de Guerre with palm, offered for sale at Spink on 18.7.1995.

SMITH D/JX.368318 Able Seaman Harry
Charioteers, Royal Navy

"For great gallantry as the crew of a "Human Torpedo" which on the night of 21st June, 1944, penetrated the heavily defended harbour of Spezia and sank the Italian Cruiser Bolzano."
LONDON GAZETTE 28.11.1944

NOTES: In June, 1944, while based at San Vito near Taranto, Sub. Lieutenant Malcolm Causer and Able Seaman Smith were put in touch with Sub. Lieutenant Carminati, an Italian Motor Torpedo boat officer who before his country's surrender had been based at Spezia where intelligence now reported the presence of two formidable 10,00 ton cruisers, the Bolzano and Gorizia. Causer and Smith were hastily assigned to attack the German controlled Bolzano, the last of the 8 inch gun cruisers with which Italy had entered the war. A plan was agreed with Carminati to drop Causer and Smith, and two other Charioteers, Petty Officer Cook Berry and Stoker Ken Lawrence, who were to attack the Gorizia, from his M.T.B., M.S. 74 at a position within two miles of the harbour entrance. The Charioteers would then proceed through the boom defences at the mouth of the heavily defended harbour, attack their respective targets, get ashore and make their way down the coats and swim out to a small island from which they would be picked up the following night. During the attack on the cruisers, a Gamma team of Italian Navy frogmen, under the direction of Count Luigi de la Pene, who in September 1941 had severely damaged H.M.S. Valiant at Alexandria, would make a separate attack, operating from two fast M.T.S.M.'s

The raiding force sailed from Naples to Corsica, then held by Allied troops, and on the evening of the 21st sailed in the direction of Spezia harbour in the Italian destroyer Greacle with M.S. 74 in attendance. At 20.30 hours Greacle arrived in position and stopped to lower the Gamma team's M.T.S.M's, M.S.74 came alongside Greacle and the Chariot crews together with their dressers and the Senior British Naval Officer, Commander P.E.H.Heathfield, transferred aboard her. M.S. 74 and the M.T.S.M's. then set course for Spezia, while Greacle commenced an East West patrol at a suitable distance.

Proceeding inshore, Causer and Smith travelled on the surface for the first hour, until the sound of an approaching engine made then submerge while it passed directly overhead. On resurfacing they found the sky swept by searchlights and tracers from two shore based guns firing out to sea. Shortly afterwards they sighted the harbour mouth to the right of the breakwater, and dived once more to nose their way towards the entrance. On the sea bed they cut an opening through the half dozen anti-submarine nets which made up the harbour defences. The breaching of the defences took considerably longer than they had envisaged and with daylight fast approaching, they surfaced and immediately sighted the Bolzano in the centre of the harbour. They then submerged to twenty feet.

They came up beneath the Bolzano and pulled themselves alongside until they were just forward of mid-ships. They then placed four magnets on the bottom of the ship, released the war head of the torpedo and lashed it to the magnets. Lt. Causer set the time fuse for two hours to give them time to get clear of the area. They then mouthed the torpedo and dropped to thirty feet. They now discovered that the batteries that operated the torpedo were very low due to the increased time it had taken to carry out the mission. Originally they had planned to sink the machine in deep water, get ashore, hide their diving gear and lay low for a while. The discovery about the batteries meant a change of plan. The made their way to the breakwater where they scuttled the craft. They then surfaced near some rocks which they climbed onto and removed their diving gear. At this point they had been in the water for seven and a half hours and being completely exhausted they slept on the rocks for around an hour and a half being woken at around 06.30 by the explosion in the harbour. The Bolzano rolled over onto her starboard side and sank in a quarter of an hour leaving her port side showing above the water.

Lt. Causer and Smith were on the rocks approximately half a mile from shore, it was however impossible to swim because of the activity in the harbour so they decided to stay where they were. Later that day an Italian fisherman spotted them and agreed to get another boat. He returned later with another small rowing boat which they got into. They spent the rest of the day mingling with the Italian fishermen in the harbour and on the night set out in the rowing boat with the intention of reaching Corsica some ninety miles away. The next day they made land, only to discover that they were twenty miles further down the coast, still in Italy. After hiding and wandering in the direction of the Allied lines, they were put in touch with a local Partisan unit which besides sheltering P.O. Cook Berey and Stoker Lawrence, whose attack on the Gorizia had been unsuccessful, contained several ex-members of the Decimo Flottiglia Mas who informed them that their chariot and net-cutters had been found alongside the breakwater by the Germans who made it known that those responsible for attacking the Bolzano had been killed.

Causer, Smith, Berey and Lawrence lived and fought with the Partisans for six weeks, but, after a skirmish in which a number of Partisans were killed, the Charioteers decided to try to make their way back to the British lines. Berey and Lawrence made the first attempt, Berey got through but Lawrence was wounded by a hand grenade and taken prisoner. Causer and Smith tried the next day but were both taken prisoner in "forbidden territory" and were immediately suspected of having been involved in sinking the Bolzano. They both claimed to be members of a conventional submarine and were sent North to P.o.W. camps in Germany, where further attempts were made to extract a confession from Smith. In spite of poor treatment in the camp, Maralg und Milag, Westertimke (Tarnstetd), he maintained his silence until the camp was liberated at the end of the war.

On the 8th July, 1944, Commander Heathfield put forward the recommendation for Smith's C.G.M. stating that, "it should be borne in mind that this act was not carried out in the heat of battle, but was the result of previous careful planning, and was therefore carried out in cold blood against what was known to be an extremely well defended harbour'.

Award presented 26.2.1946.

SNEFJELLA AB Ole Hoff
Norwegian Navy

Awarded for special services.

LONDON GAZETTE Not published in the gazette, award presented by H.M. King George VI 14.3.1944.

NOTES: The medal was sent via the Senior British Naval Officer, Norway, 7.12.1945.

SNOWDON O.N. 270654 Chief Engine Room Artificer, 2nd Class, Robert
H.M.S. Inflexible, Royal Navy

"For services when H.M.S. "Inflexible" was damaged by a mine on 18th March."

LONDON GAZETTE 16.8.1915

NOTES: With an annuity of £10.

Awarded D.S.M. 3.3.1915.

Entitled to 1914-15 Star, British War Medal and Victory Medal.

SPINDLER X.1075.B Second Hand David George.
H.M.S. Arab, Royal Naval Reserve

"For daring, resource and devotion to duty while serving in H.M.S. Arab at Namsos."

LONDON GAZETTE 16.8.1940

NOTES: Awarded the Norwegian War Cross with sword 21.8.1942.

Award presented 16.8.1940.

SPINKS D/KX.102770 Stoker First Class Robert Jenkins
M.T.B. 201, Royal Navy

"For courage and skill while serving in H.M.Motor Gun Boats and Motor Torpedo Boats in action against the Enemy in the Channel."

In action against the enemy all the engine-room staff were killed or seriously wounded save Stoker Spinks, whose leg was broken. A fire started in the engine-room but he put it out. Later he was wounded in the other leg, but insisted on being lowered into the engine-room, now in darkness and full of fumes. Here he gave orders to other members of the crew and got the boat under way, but at length fainted from exhaustion. By his great devotion to duty the ship's company were saved.

LONDON GAZETTE 25.8.1942

NOTES: 15.12.1942.

SPOONER R.M.A. /4980 Colour Sergeant Abraham
Royal Marine Artillery

"For service at the Battle of Jutland."

Second in command of the Marine detachment of H.M.S. "Warrior". After his guns were no longer required he showed the greatest gallantry and initiative in rescuing wounded in dense smoke and gas fumes from Marines' mess deck.

LONDON GAZETTE 1.1.1917

NOTES: With an annuity of £10.

Awarded French Medaille Militaire 17.3.1919.

Colour Sergeant Spooner's medals comprising C.G.M., 1914-15 Star, British War Medal, Victory medal (M.I.D.), Navy L.S.& G.C., and, French Medaille Militaire are now on display in the Royal Marines museum in Portsmouth.

116

STARLING O.N. L0627(Dev.) Officer's Steward 2ⁿᵈ Class Reginald John
Royal Navy

For services in action with enemy submarines."

LONDON GAZETTE 13.9.1918

NOTES: Awarded French Medaille Militaire 17.3.1919.

Entitled to the British War Medal and Victory Medal.

STEAR O.N. 173071 Chief Petty Officer Frederick Wilton
Anson Battalion, Royal Naval Volunteer Reserve

"For services in the Gallipoli Peninsula."

Showed great gallantry and did meritorious work on the 4ᵗʰ June in rallying the men of the support line of the Collingwood Battalion, which had lost most of the officers, and in leading them to the assault of the enemy's trenches.

LONDON GAZETTE 13.9.1915

NOTES: With an annuity of £10.

Commissioned as Sub.Lt. 13.7.1915.

Entitled to the 1914 Star and bar, British War Medal and Victory medal, later awarded the Military Cross as a Lieutenant.

SULLIVAN Boatswain's Mate John
H.M.S.Rodney, Royal Navy

Sebastopol: Recommended by Sir Stephen Lushington, for having on or about 10ᵗʰ April, 1855, deliberately placed a flag on a mound, in a most exposed position, under a heavy fire, to enable Battery 5 to open fire upon a concealed Russian battery that was doing great execution on one of our advanced works. This was reported by Commander Kennedy, commanding the battery. Commander Kennedy speaks of this act in high terms of praise, and observes that John Sullivan's gallantry was always conspicuous.

LONDON GAZETTE Not published in the gazette

NOTES: Awarded the Victoria Cross 24.2.1857 for the same action.

John Sullivan later became a boatswain in Portsmouth Dockyard.

His group of medals consists of V.C., C.G.M., Crimean War Medal with clasps Inkerman and Sebastopol, Turkish Crimean War Medal, French Legion d'Honneur, Sardinian Medal and the Royal Humane Society Medal.

SWANNELL Leading Signalman Harry
H.M.S. Orlando, Royal Navy

"In connection with the recent operations in China."

The following is extracted from the enclosure by Captain Poole to the main despatch by Captain Wray, R.M.L.I. published in the London Gazette 11th December 1900. Sir I have the honour to bring to your notice particularly the conduct of Leading Signalman H. Swannell, Her majesty's ship Orlando. On the 5th instant being in command of the Hanlin outposts, at 10.30 am I heard that Mr Oliphant, her Brittanic Majesty's Consular Service had just been wounded. I ran out to the spot and found Leading Signalman Swannell attending to Mr. Oliphant, who was mortally wounded, under the close and accurate fire of the enemy. He remained with Mr Oliphant until he was brought into a place of safety.

LONDON GAZETTE 14.5.1901

NOTES: The award was made for the historic defence of the Legations in Peking during the Boxer rebellion of 1900. A force of just over 400 Allied officers and men of the Legations settlement defended against a force of superior numbers of Chinese regular and irregular forces.

The British Legation Guard arrived in Peking on the night of 31st May, 1900, and comprised three officers, seventy-five N.C.O.'s and men and one bugler, all from the Royal Marine light Infantry along with three Naval ratings, including Swannell, under the command of Captain M. B. Strouts, R.M.

On 13th June some three hundred Boxers entered the City near the Legations Settlement and from this date on the detachment was continuously in a state of readiness. On the 19th the Chinese issued an ultimatum for all ministers and foreigners to leave the City within twenty-four hours. This ultimatum was rejected and the decision taken to stay and defend the Legations. All women and children were brought into the British compound, which was to be the last line of defence.

Hostilities began on the night of the 20th June and was to continue until relived by the allied army on 14th August. On 5th July Swannell distinguished himself when the enemy had mounted four smooth bore M.L. guns and were firing round shot on the Imperial City wall, and on a working party, which, with its covering force of British Marines in the Hanlin was forced to retire into the Legation.

Harry Swannell went on to serve in the First World War as a Signals Boatswain. His medal entitlement at the end of this period was C.G.M., China War Medal 1900 clasp Defence of Legations, 1914-15 Star, British War Medal and Victory Medal. These medals appeared for sale at Christie's on 3.4.1984.

T

TADMAN O.N. 271984 (Ch.) Chief Petty Officer (Mech.), 2nd Grade, John Frederick
Royal Navy

" For services in action with enemy submarines."

For conspicuous gallantry in climbing out on the wing of an aeroplane to plug a leak in the radiator. He remained in this position for a period of twenty minutes, thus enabling the aeroplane to return safely to her base.

LONDON GAZETTE 20.7.1917

NOTES: With an annuity of £10.

The pilot of this aeroplane, Flight Sub-Lieutenant J.E.A. Hoare, R.N.A.S. was awarded the D.S.C. in the same gazette.

TAYLOR R.M.A. 3073 Sergeant George
5th Company, Royal Marine Artillery

ASHANTEE 1873 - 1874: For standing to Rocket Trough and firing rockets at an imminent time, when the Houssa gunners had forsaken him near Dunquah on 3rd November 1873. Severely wounded.

Also for gallantry at the battle of Amoaful on 31st January 1874, and engagements during four following days whilst attached to the Native Artillery. Very severely wounded.

NAVY LIST 1874

NOTES: With an annuity of £20.

TAYLOR Captain of the Forecastle John
H.M.S. London, Royal Navy

Sebastopol: Henry James Raby, Commander, Royal Navy; John Taylor, Captain of the forecastle, Royal Navy; Henry Curtis, Boatswain's Mate, Royal Navy. On 18th June, 1855, immediately after the assault on

Sebastopol, a soldier of the 57th Regiment, who had been shot through both legs, was observed sitting up and calling for assistance. Climbing over the breastwork of the advanced sap, Commander Raby and the two seamen proceeded upwards of seventy yards across the open space towards the salient angle of the Redan, and is spite of a heavy fire which was still continuing, succeeded in conveying the wounded soldier to a place of safety, at the imminent risk of their own lives.

LONDON GAZETTE Not published in the gazette.

NOTES: Awarded the Victoria Cross 24.2.1857 for the same incident.

Commander Raby and Boatswains Mate Henry Curtis also received the V.C. for their part in the action.

John Taylor never lived to receive his V.C., he died on 24th February 1857, the day it was published in the gazette.

TAYLOR R.M.A. 183 Gunner William

H.M.S. Encounter, 12th Company, Royal Marine Artillery

ASHANTEE 1873 - 1874: For steady conduct under fire whilst leading the right section of his Company in advance through the bush at Amoaful on 31st January 1874, when the right flank was seriously threatened.

NAVY LIST 1874

TEW D/JX.303154 Ordinary Seaman Albert Walter

M.L. 446, Royal Navy

"For great gallantry, daring and skill in the attack on the German Naval Base at St. Nazaire."

For great gallantry and in standing by his gun, though badly wounded, and in continuing to lay it, in an exposed position and under heavy fire from the enemy, until it was silenced by a direct hit.

LONDON GAZETTE 21.5.1942

NOTES: Award presented 16.3.1943.

THIRLWALL C/JX 139421 Acting Leading Seaman Ronald
H.M.S. Mosquito, Royal Navy

"For good services in the withdrawal of the Allied Armies from the beaches of Dunkirk."

LONDON GAZETTE 16.8.1940

NOTES: Award presented 1.3.1941.

THOMAS Px.1730 Corporal Frank
H.M.S. Coventry, Royal Marines

"For courage, resolution and devotion to duty in operations in the Mediterranean."

Who was badly hurt while serving his gun, but stood to it until the action was over. Even then he would not go below until ordered to, for he feared that another attack might start before he could be back at his post.

LONDON GAZETTE 2.12.1941

NOTES: Award presented 24.2.1942.

THOMPSON D/JX 129888 Acting Petty Officer Arthur William
H.M.S. Li-Wo, Royal Navy

Acting Petty Officer Arthur William Thompson, D/JX 129888 who when his commanding officer's decision was made to fight the ship to the last, volunteered to serve as gun layer to the 4-inch gun, and laid this weapon with coolness and effect, showing the utmost skill, courage and resource throughout the action. In a brave company, his conduct was outstanding.

LONDON GAZETTE 17.12.1946

NOTES: Li-Wo's Commanding Officer Lieutenant Thomas Wilkinson R.N.R. was awarded the V.C. and the first Lieutenant Ronald George Gladstone Stanton, R.N.R. the D.S.O. for this action.

Award presented 20.5.1947.

THOMPSON Able Seaman Henry
H.M.S. Philomel, Naval Brigade

"For services rendered during recent operations against Malays in the Straits of Malacca."

On 4th January 1876 during the attack made by the Malays at Kotalama on Brigadier J.Ross Indian General Service. Perak 1875-1876 Henry Thompson and Harry Bennett saved the life of Doctor Townsend attached to the Buffs, by cutting down the Malays who were about to spear him when he was on the ground in a helpless condition, these seaman at the time being separated from the main body, caused through the thickness of the bush.

LONDON GAZETTE 10.3.1876

NOTES: Harry Bennett was also awarded the C.G.M. for his part in this action.

THOMSON O.N. 6029A Seaman James
Royal Naval Reserve

"For services in action with enemy submarines."

From the official account published in the L.G. 19.11.1918:- On the 8th August, 1917, H.M.S. "Dunraven" under the command of Captain Gordon Campbell, V.C., D.S.O., R.N., sighted an enemy submarine on the horizon. In her role of armed British merchant ship, the "Dunraven" continued her zig-zag course, whereupon the submarine closed, remaining submerged to within 5,000 yards, and then, rising to the surface, opened fire. The "Dunraven" returned the fire with her merchant ship gun, at the same time reducing speed to enable the enemy to overtake her. Wireless signals were also sent out for the benefit of the submarine: "Help! Come quickly - submarine chasing and shelling me." Finally, when the shells began falling close, the "Dunraven" stopped and abandoned ship by the "panic party." The ship was then being heavily shelled, and on fire aft. In the meantime the submarine closed to 400 yards distant, partly obscured from view by the dense clouds of smoke issuing from the "Dunraven's" stern. Despite the knowledge that the after magazine must inevitably explode if he waited, and further, that a gun and gun's crew lay concealed over the magazine, Captain Campbell decided to reserve his fire until the submarine had passed clear of the smoke. A moment later, however a heavy explosion occurred aft, blowing the gun and gun's crew into the air, and accidentally starting fire-gongs at the remaining gun positions; screens were immediately dropped, and the only gun that would bear opened fire, but the submarine, apparently frightened by the explosion, had already commenced to submerge. Realising that a torpedo must inevitably follow, Captain Campbell ordered the surgeon to remove all wounded and conceal them in cabins; hoses were also turned on the poop, which was a mass of flames. A signal was sent out warning men-of-war to divert all traffic below the horizon in order that nothing should interrupt the final phase of the action. Twenty minutes later a torpedo again struck the ship abaft the engine-room. An additional party of men were again sent away as "panic party," and left the ship to outward appearances completely abandoned, with the White Ensign flying and guns unmasked. For the succeeding fifty minutes the submarine examined the ship through her periscope. During the period boxes of cordite and shells exploded every few minutes, and the fire on the poop still blazed furiously. Captain Campbell and the handful of officers and men who remained on board lay hidden during this ordeal. The submarine then rose to the surface astern, where no guns could bear and shelled the ship closely for twenty minutes. The enemy then submerged and steamed past the ship 150 yards off, examining her through the periscope. Captain Campbell decided then to fire one of his torpedoes, but missed by a few inches. The submarine crossed bows and came slowly down the other side, whereupon a second torpedo was fired and missed again. The enemy observed it and immediately submerged. Urgent signals for assistance were immediately sent out, but pending arrival of assistance Captain Campbell arranged for a third "panic party" to jump overboard if necessary and leave one gun's crew on board for a final attempt to destroy the enemy, should he again attack. Almost immediately afterwards, however, British and American destroyers arrived on the scene, the wounded were transferred, boats were recalled and the fire extinguished. The "Dunraven" although her stern was awash, was taken in tow, but the weather grew worse, and early the following morning she sank with colours flying.

LONDON GAZETTE 30.10.1917

NOTES: All of the gun's crew were put in a ballot for the V.C. this was awarded to P.O. Ernest Pitcher who commanded the gun, the remaining members of the gun crew Bennison, Martindale, Murphy Sheppard and

Thomson were all awarded the C.G.M. A ballot among the officers also awarded the V.C. to Lieut. Bonner D.S.C. In addition to these awards two further C.G.M.'s were awarded to crew of the Dunraven for the action, W/T Op. Fletcher and Seaman Morrison.

LONDON GAZETTE 2.11.1917

NOTES: Awarded D.S.M. 20.7.1917, French Medaille Militaire 28.8.1918.

Entitled to 1914-15 Star, British War Medal and Victory Medal.

THORNTON-ALLEN C/J.105524 Chief Petty Officer Albert William, D.S.M.

H.M.S. Ladybird, Royal Navy

"For courage and coolness when their ship was sunk by Enemy aircraft."

Who was in charge of a gun when his ship was attacked by dive-bombers. A bomb falling on the after-deck wounded him and blew him from the gun. Fires were burning fore and aft of him, but he went back to his gun, opened fire and shot down an enemy aircraft.

LONDON GAZETTE 7.10.1941

NOTES: Awarded D.S.M. 12.8.1941.

Award presented 28.10.1941.

TOWNSEND Ply. 463Private Richard

H.M.S. Decoy, 8th Company, Royal Marine Light Infantry

ASHANTEE 1873 - 1874: He was never absent from his duty and frequently when under fire rendered assistance to the wounded at considerable risk. This man was attached to the Medical Staff and his excellent conduct has already been reported in my despatch No. 135 of 6th May last. (Commodore Hewitt).

NAVY LIST 1874

FOR CONSPICUOUS GALLANTRY

TOY Dev/.189327 Chief Petty Officer Richard Farley
Howe battalion, Royal Navy

"For services with the Mediterranean Expeditionary Force."

Behaved with conspicuous gallantry on May 6th ng operations South of Achi Baba, leading his platoon after his Company Commander had been wounded, and bringing in Lieutenant Commander Ford (wounded) under heavy fire.

LONDON GAZETTE 3.6.1915

NOTES: Killed in action 6.6.1915 he is commemorated on the Helles Memorial, Gallipoli.

Entitle to 1914 Star and bar, British War Medal and Victory Medal.

TREWAVAS Ordinary Seaman, Joseph
H.M.S. Agamemnon (lent to Beagle), Royal Navy

Azoff: Joseph Trewavas, Seaman, Royal Navy. Particularly mentioned as having cut the hawsers of the floating bridge in the straits of Genitchi, under a heavy fire of musketry, on which occasion he was wounded. This service was performed by the crews of the Captain's gig and of one of the paddle-box boats of the Beagle , under a heavy fire of musketry, at about a distance of 80 yards; the beach was completely lined with troops, and the adjacent houses filled with riflemen. Joseph Trewavas is especially mentioned as having been the person who cut the hawser.

For cutting adrift a Russian floating bridge under fire.

LONDON GAZETTE Not published in the gazette.

NOTES: Mentioned in Despatches, 23.7.1855.

Awarded the Victoria Cross 24.2.1857 for the same incident.

Trewavas was made a Knight of the Legion d'Honneur for the action · above. He also received the Crimean War medal with clasps for Inkerman and Sebastopol and the Turkish Crimean Medal.

Seaman Trewavas, although not having had to return the C.G.M. should not have worn both. However from contemporary photographs this seems to have been ignored!

Jospeh Trewavas was born on 14th December 1835, at Mousehole in Cornwall. He joined H.M.S. Agamemnon at Devonport on 15th October 1853, and it was on this ship that he sailed to the Crimea, taking part in the bombardment of Sebastopol on 17th October 1854. He was then landed ashore on 23rd October and served with the Naval Brigade. He was serving with the Naval Brigade when he performed the act detailed above for which he was awarded the C.G.M. with an annuity of £5 and subsequently the V.C.

He left the Navy as Leading Seaman on 22nd May 1857. He married Margaret Harry on 15th January 1866 and together they had three children.

Joseph Trewavas died at Mousehole in Cornwall on 20th July 1905.

TRIMBLE Po/22169 Sergeant Samuel John
H.M.S. Achilles, Royal Marines

"In recognition of the gallant and successful action with the "Admiral Graf Spee" (to be dated the 13th of December, 1939)."

Samuel John Trimble, Sgt Royal Marines, H.M.S. Achilles who, earlier in the action, when several splinters struck the Gun Director, at once killing three men and wounding two others inside the tower, was severely wounded; but stood fast without flinching or complaint throughout the hour of action that followed, bearing his wounds with great fortitude. When the medical party came he helped them to move the wounded and then made his own way to the sick bay with little aid.

LONDON GAZETTE 23.2.1940

NOTES: Award presented in New Zealand 15.6.1940.

TURNER Petty Officer 1st Class Edward
Royal Navy

"For services in connection with the recent operations in China."
LONDON GAZETTE 22.3.1901

NOTES: Medals C.G.M, China 1900, Navy L.S.& G.C. now in the National Maritime Museum.

TURNER O.N. 5098 DA 2nd Hand John
Royal Naval Volunteer Reserve

"For services in the action in the Straits of Otranto on the 15th May, 1917."

He displayed great coolness whilst under fire. Seeing that the enemy were endeavouring to destroy the W/T apparatus, Turner went aloft to strike the topmast, quite regardless of the fact that shells were passing between the mast and funnel.

LONDON GAZETTE 28.8.1917

NOTES: With an annuity of £10.

Entitled to 1914-15 Star, British War Medal and Victory Medal.

TURNER Po./343(S) Private Mark
Royal Marine Light Infantry

On the 31st October, 1915, at Cape Helles, he picked up and threw a live bomb out of our barricade, thereby avoiding a serious accident.

LONDON GAZETTE 31.5.1916

NOTES: Private Turner was killed in action on 13.11.1916. He has no known grave and is commemorated on the Thiepval memorial. He was entitled to the 1914-15 Star, British War Medal and Victory Medal. The medal roll shows him with a rank of Lance Corporal although all other references including the Thiepval memorial list him as Private.

V

VEAL D/J.53109 Chief Petty Officer Alfred Henry
H.M.S. Broke, Royal Navy

"For bravery and skill in hazardous operations in which the Allied Forces were landed in North Africa."

For great bravery at the wheel of H.M.S. Broke in the assault on the harbour of Algiers. Although wounded in the face, he stayed at his post until he had brought his ship alongside the harbour.

LONDON GAZETTE 16.3.1943

NOTES: Award presented 18.5.1943.

Also awarded Polish Cross of Valour (Krzyz Walecznya) 21.10.1941.

WALSH O.N. 2131A Seaman Lawrence J.
Royal Naval Reserve

In recognition of his services in one of the whalers which entered Sudi Harbour on the 11th April, 1916. He continued to steer the whaler after being seriously wounded, his leg being badly shattered, until out of range of gun fire, when it was possible to remove the conning tower plates and relieve him.

LONDON GAZETTE 14.7.1916

NOTES: Awarded French Medaille Militaire 28.8.1918.

Entitled to 1914-15 Star, British War Medal and Victory Medal.

WARBURTON O.N. 239084 (Po.) Petty Officer Frederick William
H.M.S. Kiawo, Royal Navy

"In recognition of their services at Wanhsien, Yangtse River, China, on the 5th September, 1926 , and connected events."

Showed conspicuous courage and fearlessness and took command of the boarding party after Lieutenant A.R.Higgins, R.N., was killed.

LONDON GAZETTE 6.5.1927

NOTES: Entitled to 1914-15 Star, British War Medal and Victory Medal.

WATERS Sergeant Timothy
H.M.S. Active, 8th Company, Royal Marine Light Infantry

ASHANTEE 1873 - 1874: For distinguished conduct generally throughout the campaign and especially at Amoaful 31st January, 1874, where, although very severely wounded himself, he volunteered to remain in the bush to take charge of and assist others who were also wounded.

NAVY LIST 1874

NOTES: With an annuity of £10.

WATSON O.N. 178876 (R.F.R., Po./B1329) Leading Seaman James Simpson
H.M.S. Malaya, Royal Fleet Reserve

"For services rendered by Petty Officers and men of the Grand Fleet in the action in the North Sea on the 31st May - 1st June, 1916"

When a shell exploded in the starboard battery of the ship in which Petty Officer Day and Leading Seaman Watson were serving, a considerable blast of flame and smoke caused a quantity of smouldering debris to fall among a hoist of cartridges in bags. Petty Officer Day showed great coolness and presence of mind in immediately jumping amongst the cartridges, removing the debris. In doing this he was assisted by Leading Seaman Watson; these two dealing with the dangerous situation promptly.

LONDON GAZETTE 15.9.1916

NOTES: Petty Officer Day was also awarded the C.G.M. for this action.

Awarded Croix de Guerre (France) 19.12.1917.

Commissioned as Sub.Lt.

Entitled to 1914 Star and bar, British War Medal and Victory Medal.

WATT O.N. 2089 TS Engineman Walter
Royal Naval Reserve

"For services in the action in the Straits of Otranto on the 15th May, 1917."

The crew ere taken prisoners, but on their way to the Austrian cruiser Watt jumped overboard. He was recaptured, and when alongside the cruiser he again jumped overboard and escaped. He was picked up by another drifter 1 ½ hours later.

LONDON GAZETTE 28.8.1917

NOTES: Entitled to 1914-15 Star, British War Medal and Victory Medal. Medal card shows surname as Wait.

FOR CONSPICUOUS GALLANTRY

WAY Po./4356/R.F.R./B./487 Lance Corporal John Gibson
Portsmouth Battalion, Royal Marine Light Infantry

"For services in the Gallipoli Peninsula"

For his services on the 13th July, when he exhibited great courage, presence of mind and powers of personal leadership in a moment of crisis in assisting Major Sketchley to turn a retreat into a successful advance.

LONDON GAZETTE 13.9.1915

NOTES: With an annuity £10.

Major Sketchley was awarded the D.S.O. for the same action.

Entitled to 1914 Star and Bar, British War Medal, Victory Medal. The bar to the 1914 Star was issued to him on H.M. Island Ascension on 4.3.1919.

WEEKS O.N. 13682 D.A. Leading Deckhand William George
Royal Naval Reserve

"In recognition of distinguished services during the operations against Zeebrugge and Ostend on the night of the 22nd-23rd April 1918."

Leading Deckhand Weeks with Chief Motor Mechanic Attwood and Chief Motor Mechanic Fox. These three ratings were amongst those who volunteered to man the motor launches detailed to rescue the crews of the blockships, and it was largely due to the coolness and courage with which the crews of these motor launches carried out their duties that so many officers and men were rescued. These three men displayed most conspicuous gallantry in the face of intense gun and machine-gun fire at short range.

LONDON GAZETTE 23.7.1918

NOTES: Ch. Motor Mechanics Attwood and Fox were also awarded the C.G.M. for this action.

Awarded Croix de Guerre (France) 28.8.1918.

Entitled to British War Medal and Victory Medal.

FOR CONSPICUOUS GALLANTRY

WELLARD C/SSX.22441 Able Seaman Ronald Harry
H.M.S. Pelican, Royal Navy

"For courage and resource in operations on the Norwegian Coast."
LONDON GAZETTE 26.6.1940

NOTES: Award presented 18.3.1941.

WHERRY O.N. K.5157 Acting Stoker Petty Officer Frederick John Henry
Royal Navy

"For services rendered by Petty Officers and men of the Grand Fleet in the action in the North Sea on the 31ˢᵗ May - 1ˢᵗ June, 1916"

Acting Stoker Petty Officer Wherry, at great risk, flooded the 6-inch magazine of the ship in which he was serving, and then, until gassed, assisted to extinguish a fire in close proximity to the magazine. Subsequently, while still suffering from the effect of the fumes, he left the dressing station to unlock the secondary position for 13.5 inch flooding valves, showing great devotion to duty.

LONDON GAZETTE 15.9.1916

NOTES: With an annuity of £20.

Awarded French Medaille Militaire 17.3.1919.

Entitled to 1914-15 Star, British War Medal and Victory Medal.

WHIBLEY Ordinary Seaman Ernest
Royal Navy

"In connection with the recent operations in China."
No further information is available concerning this award.

LONDON GAZETTE 14.5.1901

WHITE Colour Sergeant Benjamin

Royal Marine Artillery

Award for the Egypt campaign. No further details surrounding the award are available.

NAVY LIST 1883

NOTES: With an annuity of £10.

WILKES D/J.111017 Petty Officer Frederick William John

H.M.S. Saumarez, Royal Navy

"For gallantry, distinguished service and devotion to duty on the staff of the Commander-in0Chief, Home Fleet, and in H.M. ships Duke of York, Belfast, Norfolk, Sheffield, Jamaica, Savage, Saumarez, Scorpion, Musketeer, Matchless, Virago and Opportune during the action in which the Scharnhorst was engaged and sunk."

On the 26th December, 1943, when his ship, H.M.S. Saumarez, was being heavily engaged by the Scharnhorst, sprayed by splinters, and members of his torpedo tubes crew were killed or wounded, Petty Officer Wilkes, Torpedo Gunners Mate, by his leadership, coolness and splendid example ensured the firing of his torpedoes.

LONDON GAZETTE 7.3.1944

NOTES: Awarded M.I.D. 18.9.1945.

Award presented 9.7.1946.

WILLIS O.N. J.11010 Petty Officer John Adlam

Royal Navy

"For services rendered by Petty Officers and men of the Grand Fleet in the action in the North Sea on the 31st May - 1st June, 1916"

Petty Officer Willis brought his gun into action after he himself and the whole of his gun's crew had been wounded.

LONDON GAZETTE 15.9.1916

NOTES: With an annuity of £10.

Awarded French Medaille Militaire 17.3.1919.

WILSON C.S. 55105 Boatswain's Mate James
H.M.S. Active, Royal Navy

ASHANTEE 1873 - 1874: Particularly distinguished himself both at the capture of Boorbrassie, 29ᵗʰ January, 1874, and battle of Amoaful, 31ˢᵗ January, 1874, by the manner in which he led a section of his company. Was wounded on both occasions.

NAVY LIST 1874

NOTES: With an annuity of £10.

WOOD C/JX.134126 Leading Seaman James Harold
Royal Navy

"For courage and devotion to duty when H.M.S. Jervis Bay, defending a large convoy, was sunk by a powerful German Warship."
LONDON GAZETTE 23.1.1941

NOTES: Award presented 5.4.1941.

WRIGHT D/J111032 Able Seaman George Henry
H.M.S. Hastings, Royal Navy

"For great gallantry and devotion to duty."
When H.M.S. Hastings was attacked by enemy aircraft with machine gun fire Able Seaman Wright, the Director Trainer, was dangerously wounded. Though in great pain he kept his courage and carried on with his duties until the cease-fire, when he could hold out no longer. Even then his cheerfulness did not fail.

LONDON GAZETTE 8.4.1941

NOTES: Award presented 28.10.1941.

Y

YATES P/KX.95334 Stoker Petty Officer Jack
H.M.S. Saumarez, Royal Navy

"For great gallantry and outstanding devotion to duty."

Malacca Straits: No.1 Boiler Room of H.M.S. Saumarez was hit by an enemy shell. Stoker P.O. Yates, the sole survivor from the boiler room though badly burnt and in great pain at once shut the steam off from the oil fuel pump and heaters, and would not allow himself to be treated for his hurts until he had reported the damage. This most gallant action did much to limit the damage to his ship.

LONDON GAZETTE 18.9.1945

NOTES: M.I.D. 1.1.1943 serving on H.M.S. Halcyon.

Medals comprising C.G.M., 1939-35 Star, Atlantic Star (clasp France & Germany), Burma Star, War Medal (M.I.D.) appeared for sale at Buckland, Dix and Wood 7.4.1994.

YEARMOUTH C.S. 55062/13218B. Captain of the Forecastle
William L.
H.M.S. Encounter, Royal Navy

ASHANTEE 1873 - 1874: For invariably being the leading man of his company when in action. At Amoaful, 31st January, 1874, distinguished himself with a section of his company by effecting a junction with a body of Native troops, our allies, who were firing in the direction of the Naval Brigade, at the same time being exposed to a heavy cross fire from the enemy.

NAVY LIST 1874

NOTES: Medals comprising C.G.M., Ashantee 1973 bar Coomassie appeared for sale at Spink 6.7.1988

FOR CONSPICUOUS GALLANTRY

YOULTON O.N.(Po.)183625 Petty Officer 1ˢᵗ Class Edwin George
H.M.S. Vindictive, Royal Navy

"In recognition of distinguished services during the operations against Zeebrugge and Ostend on the night of the 22ⁿᵈ-23ʳᵈ April 1918."

This Petty Officer steered "Vindictive" when going alongside the mole at Zeebrugge, after which he remained with his commanding officer throughout, and gave a fine example of courage when standing in a most exposed position.

When a bursting shell caused a fire in a pile of boxes containing fused Stokes bombs, he averted catastrophe by stamping without the slightest hesitation on the burning parts. This brave action was repeated shortly afterwards, when the fire restarted, just before he was struck down and severely wounded by a shell.

LONDON GAZETTE 23.7.1918

NOTES: Recommended for the Victoria Cross. Awarded with an annuity of £10. Awarded Croix de Guerre (France) 28.8.1918.

Medals comprising C.G.M., 1914-15 Star, British War Medal, Victory Medal, Navy L.S. & G.C., French Croix de Guerre, offered for sale at Sotheby's 12.9.1989.

Section II

The Conspicuous Gallantry Medal (Flying)

1942 - 1993

A

AIREY 1112525 Sergeant Leslie
101 Squadron, Royal Air Force

"In recognition of gallantry displayed in flying operations against the enemy."

On the night of 14th February, 1943, Pilot Officer Gates, Flight Sergeant Dove and Sergeants Williams, Bain and Airey were members of the crew of an aircraft captained by Sergeant Hazard, which was detailed to attack Milan. Whilst over the target area, the aircraft was attacked by an enemy fighter from close range. It's gunfire exploded some incendiary bombs which had failed to release and a fire quickly developed in the bomber. The fuselage became a mass Of flames reaching through the mid-upper turret manned by Flight Sergeant Dove. Ammunition in the turret boxes and ducts commenced to explode in all directions. In the face of an appalling situation, Flight Sergeant Dove coolly remained at his post Although he was burned about the hands and face, he manned his guns with grim resolution skill, and accuracy. He delivered a devastating burst at the attacker which had already been engaged and hit by the rear gunner and succeeded in destroying it. Disregarding the roaring flames, he then descended from his turret and went to the assistance of Sergeant Airey the rear gunner, who had been wounded and extricated him from the rear turret. The situation had become extremely critical and Sergeant Hazard ordered the crew to prepare to abandon aircraft. When informed that one of his comrades was helpless be decided, in spite of the grave risk entailed, to attempt a forced landing. Meanwhile, Pilot Officer Gates, assisted by Sergeants Williams and Bain bravely tackled the fire with extinguishers and succeeded in getting it under control. The aircraft was now down to 8oo feet but, as the fire had subsided Sergeant Hazard quickly decided to attempt to fly the badly damaged bomber home. He regained height and displaying fine airmanship crossed the Alps in safety, although one engine failed whilst so doing.

On the remainder of the journey Pilot Officer Gates rendered valuable assistance to his captain and frequently ministered to his wounded comrade, although this necessitated clambering over a hole in the floor of the aircraft in darkness Aided by the skilful navigation of Sergeant Williams and good work by Sergeant Bain, the flight engineer, Sergeant Hazard succeeded in flying the seriously damaged aircraft back to this country In circumstances of the greatest danger, this aircraft crew displayed courage fortitude and devotion to duty In keeping with the highest traditions of the Royal Air Force.

LONDON GAZETTE 23.3.1943

NOTES: Pilot Officer Gates was awarded the D.S.O. and Flight Sergeant Dove, Sergeants Williams, Bain and Hazard the C.G.M. for this action.

Award presented by H.M. King George VI 12.10.1943.

ALEXANDER 745637 Warrant Officer James Michie
7 Squadron, Royal Air Force Volunteer Reserve

"In recognition of gallantry and devotion to duty in the execution of air operations."

LONDON GAZETTE 18.1.1944

NOTES: Killed in action 15/16th February 1944, buried in Skaro cemetery on the Isle of Skaro, Denmark.

Award presented by H.M. King George VI to next of kin 17.7.1945.

ALLEN 1880966 Sergeant Derrick John
467 (R.A.A.F.) Squadron, Royal Air Force Volunteer Reserve

"In recognition of gallantry and devotion to duty in the execution of air operations."

This airman was the mid-upper gunner in an aircraft detailed to attack Dusseldorf one night in November, 1944. During the operation the aircraft was attacked by a fighter. Sergeant Allen opened fire but the enemy aircraft closed in and the bomber was struck by a burst of machine-gun fire which caused much damage. A second attack followed and again the aircraft was hit. the port outer engine was hit and caught fire. All efforts to extinguish the flames were unavailing. Later, the aircraft lost height and then dived out of control. The position became hopeless and the captain ordered his crew to abandon aircraft. The rear gunner was unable to open his turret doors and was trapped. With complete disregard for his own safety, Sergeant Allen promptly went to the assistance of his comrade. The aircraft was now on fire and falling rapidly. Nevertheless, this gallant airman hacked away at the turret doors with an axe and finally succeeded in freeing his comrade. Just as Sergeant Allen got ready to jump, the aircraft broke in two. He fell clear, however, pulled the rip cord of his parachute and descended safely. In the face of extreme danger this airman displayed conduct in keeping with the best traditions of the Royal Air Force.

LONDON GAZETTE 6.3.1945

NOTES: Award presented by H.M. King George VI at Buckingham Palace 12.3.1946.

ANDREW Flight Sergeant Solomon Joseph Harold, D.F.M.
35 Squadron, Royal Air Force Volunteer Reserve

Awarded on the completion of eighty nine operations, many of which were with the pathfinder squadrons. He had been awarded the D.F.M. in 1944 on the completion of fifty four ops.

LONDON GAZETTE 26.10.1945

NOTES: Awarded D.F.M. 8.12.1945.

Award presented by H.M. King George VI 4.12.1945.

ASHPLANT 1382143 Flight Sergeant George
166 Squadron, Royal Air Force

"In recognition of gallantry displayed in flying operations against the enemy."

One night in February 1943, Flight Sergeant Ashplant, after successfully completing an operational sortie on Lorient, was returning to base when, while over this country, his aircraft came into collision with a Halifax bomber. As a result his aircraft was severely damaged. Both engines were torn from their bearers, the front and underside of the nose were completely ripped off, the bomb aimers parachute stowage and parachute were carried away and both propellers were missing. The aircraft went out of control into a spin. Regaining control, however, Flight Sergeant Ashplant gave his parachute to the bomb aimer and ordered the crew to abandon the aircraft. By a fine display of airmanship and determination he managed to make a crash landing with the remains of his bomber, without personal injury. Flight Sergeant Ashplant, in an appalling situation, displayed the utmost courage and devotion to duty and acted in accordance with the highest traditions of the Royal Air Force.

LONDON GAZETTE 30.3.1943

NOTES: Recommended for the Victoria Cross.

Killed in a raid over Hamburg on the night of 24/25th July 1943, buried in Hamburg cemetery.

Award presented by H.M. King George VI to next of kin 18.12.1945.

B

BAILEY Can/R.1077483 Sergeant John Calder
622 Squadron, Royal Canadian Air Force

"In recognition of gallantry displayed in flying operations against the enemy."

This airman was the bomb aimer of an aircraft which attacked Berlin one night in August, 1943. When leaving the target area a fighter was encountered and, in the subsequent action, the bomber sustained much damage and its pilot was seriously wounded. He endeavoured to regain control but slumped over the control column and had to be assisted from his seat. The aircraft lost considerable height and one of its engines was put out of action. Displaying rare coolness, Sergeant Bailey took over the controls and flew the aircraft to an airfield in this country. Although he had never attempted to land a heavy bomber before he succeeded in making a masterly landing. This airman displayed great skill and resource and was undoubtedly responsible for the safe return of the aircraft and its crew.

LONDON GAZETTE 17.9.1943

NOTES: Enlisted 1941. Incident occurred on the night of 23/24th August, 1943.

BAILEY 1571262 Sergeant William James
78 Squadron, Royal Air Force Volunteer Reserve

One night in July, 1944, this officer, Flying Officer Buchanan, and airman were captain and flight engineer respectively of an aircraft detailed to attack a target in North France. After the target had been bombed, the bomber was attacked by an enemy fighter and sustained severe damage. A fire broke out within the aircraft and an explosion occurred in Sergeant Bailey's compartment wounding him in both legs. Disregarding his injuries, this airman fought the fire until the flames were quelled. Meanwhile Flying Officer Buchanan, who had been severely burnt about the face, flew the aircraft on a level course. This officer and airman have completed many sorties and have at all times displayed courage, fortitude and determination of a high order.

LONDON GAZETTE 22.9.1944

NOTES: Flying Officer Buchanan was awarded the D.F.C. for this action.

The target on this occasion was a V1 site at Acquet, France.

Award presented 20.11.1945.

BAIN 654077 Sergeant James Fortune
101 Squadron, Royal Air Force

"In recognition of gallantry displayed in flying operations against the enemy."

On the night of 14th February, 1943, Pilot Officer Gates, Flight Sergeant Dove and Sergeants Williams, Bain and Airey were members of the crew of an aircraft captained by Sergeant Hazard, which was detailed to attack Milan. Whilst over the target area, the aircraft was attacked by an enemy fighter from close range. It's gunfire exploded some incendiary bombs which had failed to release and a fire quickly developed in the bomber. The fuselage became a mass Of flames reaching through the mid-upper turret manned by Flight Sergeant Dove. Ammunition in the turret boxes and ducts commenced to explode in all directions. In the face of an appalling situation, Flight Sergeant Dove coolly remained at his post Although he was burned about the hands and face, he manned his guns with grim resolution skill, and accuracy. He delivered a devastating burst at the attacker which had already been engaged and hit by the rear gunner and succeeded in destroying it. Disregarding the roaring flames, he then descended from his turret and went to the assistance of Sergeant Airey the rear gunner, who had been wounded and extricated him from the rear turret. The situation had become extremely critical and Sergeant Hazard ordered the crew to prepare to abandon aircraft. When informed that one of his comrades was helpless be decided, in spite of the grave risk entailed, to attempt a forced landing. Meanwhile, Pilot Officer Gates, assisted by Sergeants Williams and Bain bravely tackled the fire with extinguishers and succeeded in getting it under control. The aircraft was now down to 8oo feet but, as the fire had subsided Sergeant Hazard quickly decided to attempt to fly the badly damaged bomber home. He regained height and displaying fine airmanship crossed the Alps in safety, although one engine failed whilst so doing.

On the remainder of the journey Pilot Officer Gates rendered valuable assistance to his captain and frequently ministered to his wounded comrade, although this necessitated clambering over a hole in the floor of the aircraft in darkness Aided by the skilful navigation of Sergeant Williams and good work by Sergeant Bain, the flight engineer, Sergeant Hazard succeeded in flying the seriously damaged aircraft back to this country In circumstances of the greatest danger, this aircraft crew displayed courage fortitude and devotion to duty In keeping with the highest traditions of the Royal Air Force.

LONDON GAZETTE 23.3.1943

NOTES: Pilot Officer Gates was awarded the D.S.O. and Flight Sergeant Dove, Sergeants Williams, Hazard and Airey the C.G.M. for this action.

Killed along with Sergeant Williams C.G.M. and Sergeant Hazard C.G.M while taking a new bomber on a test flight, over Hornsea 20th March, 1943. Buried in Wolvercote Cemetary, Oxford.

Award presented to Next of Kin 13.6.1944.

BENNETT 1384134 Sergeant Bertram Gordon
623 Squadron, Royal Air Force Reserve

"In recognition of gallantry displayed in flying operations against the enemy."

Sergeant Bennett was the wireless operator of an aircraft detailed to attack Berlin one night in August, 1943. During the bombing run the aircraft was attacked by a fighter. Sergeant Bennett was badly wounded in the chest but, in spite of this, gallantly attempted to quell a fire which had broken out in the structure. With his bare hands he kept the flames under control until an extinguisher was obtained with which the fire was put out. Not until the aircraft was clear of the target did Sergeant Bennett disclose that he had been hit. His prompt and courageous action contributed materially to the safe return of the aircraft.

LONDON GAZETTE 17.9.1943

NOTES: Born 1913 Chiswick, Middlesex. Enlisted in the R.A.F., 1941.

Bennett was taken to Ely Hospital on landing. On leaving the hospital he was declared unfit by a medical board and so re-mustered to flying control duties. Left the R.A.F. in February 1946.

Award presented 29.2.1944.

BETTANY 1147696 Flight Sergeant John
625 Squadron, Royal Air Force Volunteer Reserve

"In recognition of gallantry and devotion to duty in the execution of air operations."

This airman was the wireless operator in an aircraft detailed to attack Pforzheim one night in February, 1945. Soon after the target had been bombed the aircraft sustained serious damage. Several small fires commenced but Flight Sergeant Bettany, displaying great promptitude and bravery, dealt with most of them effectively. Some few minutes later, one of the starboard tanks exploded and set the starboard outer engine on fire. The pilot gave the order to abandon the aircraft. The intercommunication system was out of action so he requested Flight Sergeant Bettany to give the message verbally to the mid-upper and rear gunners. As he made his way along the fuselage, this airman's parachute caught on some wreckage and opened. Undaunted, Flight Sergeant Bettany completed his errand and ensured that his comrades were clear before he, himself, donned the spare parachute and jumped. His coolness, bravery and resolution in a critical situation set an example of the highest standard.

LONDON GAZETTE 24.4.1945

NOTES: Award presented by H.M. King George VI at an investiture 12.3.1946.

BICKLEY 530493 Warrant Officer Wilfred George
617 Squadron, Royal Air Force

As air gunner, Warrant Officer Bickley has completed a very large number of sorties, many of them calling for a high degree of courage and resolution. His appreciation of the responsibilities entrusted to him and his determination to achieve success have been a notable feature of his service. His great gallantry and fine fighting qualities have set an example in keeping with the best traditions of the Royal Air Force.

LONDON GAZETTE 26.5.1944

NOTES: When recommended for the C.G.M., Bickley had completed seventy-one operations and was at the time front gunner with the CO of the squadron, Wing Commander Leonard Cheshire V.C., D.S.O., D.F.C.

Commissioned in July 1944 and left the R.A.F. in 1946.

Award presented 24.7.1945.

Medals comprising C.G.M. (Flying), 1939-45 Star, Air Crew Europe Star (clasp France & Germany), Defence Medal, War Medal, offered for sale at Sotheby's 19.9.1992.

BISBY 1127605 Sergeant Thomas Ernest
10 Squadron, Royal Air Force Volunteer Reserve

One night in November, 1943, Flight Sergeant Mowatt and Sergeants Bisby and Bridge were mid upper gunner, wireless operator and flight engineer respectively in an aircraft piloted by Flight Lieutenant Trobe and detailed to attack Dusseldorf. During the operation the aircraft was subjected to a series of attacks by 4 fighters. In the actions the bomber was repeatedly hit. The rear turret, the hydraulic gear, the inter-communication system, the wireless apparatus and other important equipment were rendered unserviceable. Flight Sergeant Mowatt and Sergeants Bisby and Bridge were wounded .In spite of this, Flight Lieutenant Trobe succeeded in flying clear. Two of the bomber's engines had failed but Sergeant Bridge succeeded in re-starting one of them . He afterwards extinguished a fire which had started near one of the turrets and later assisted Flight Sergeant Mowatt to quell another fire which had commenced in the fuselage. Meanwhile, Sergeant Bisby although in considerable pain, had remained at his post throughout the encounters, and worked unremittingly to effect a temporary repair to his wireless apparatus. He succeeded in obtaining a fix which proved of material help in enabling his pilot to set course for home. Later on, his wireless apparatus again failed but, although on the point of collapse Sergeant Bisby continued his task of repairing it. By a superb effort, Flight Lieutenant Trobe succeeded in reaching base and, in difficult circumstances, effected a masterly landing. In the face of a perilous situation this officer displayed outstanding skill and courage and his valiant efforts were well supported by his comrades, whose courage, fortitude and devotion to duty were of a high order.

LONDON GAZETTE 3.12.1943

NOTES: Flight Lieutenant Trope was awarded the D.F.C., Flight Sergeant Mowatt and Sergeant Bridge the D.F.M. for this action.

Commissioned October 1944, promoted Flight Lieutenant 1948.

Award presented 6.6.1944.

BLACKWELL Aus.403980 Sergeant Arthur Frederick
500 Squadron, Royal Australian Air Force

"In recognition of gallantry displayed in flying operations against the enemy."

In April, 1943, at night, these airmen were navigator and wireless operator/air gunner respectively of an aircraft the pilot of which was killed by anti-aircraft fire. Displaying great promptitude and resource Flight Sergeant Kempster pulled back the control column, while other members of the crew were removing the pilot from his seat, and succeeded in regaining height. His immediate action undoubtedly saved the aircraft from crashing. Sergeant Blackwell then took over the controls and flew the aircraft to base where the remaining members of the crew were enabled to leave the aircraft by parachute. All landed safely. During the return flight Sergeant Blackwell displayed exceptional leadership and captaincy which inspired his comrades in trying circumstances.

LONDON GAZETTE 1.6.1943

NOTES: The wireless operator/air gunner, F/Sgt. Kempster, was awarded the D.F.M. for his part in this action.

Enlisted in R.A.A.F. in 1941. After completing his training in Canada and England he joined 500 Squadron, Coastal Command, in July 1942. The Squadron was based in Gibraltar with a detachment in Blida, North Africa. Their duties were anti-submarine patrols in the Mediterranean.

Award presented 20.3.1945.

BROOK 1213186 Acting Warrant Officer George Wilfred
550 Squadron, Royal Air Force Volunteer Reserve

"In recognition of gallantry and devotion to duty in the execution of air operations."

This officer has completed a successful tour of operations during which he has attacked Berlin on ten occasions. He has at all times displayed praiseworthy determination in the execution of his tasks, many of which were undertaken in adverse weather. He is a most efficient Captain, whose example of courage and devotion to duty has proved inspiring.

LONDON GAZETTE 31.3.1944

NOTES: Later commissioned. After the war he became a pilot with B.O.A.C.

Award presented 26.6.1945

BROWN Can./R.94567 Flight Sergeant Kenneth William
617 Squadron, Royal Canadian Air Force

"On the night of 16th May, 1943, a force of Lancaster bombers was detailed to attack the Möehne, Eder and Sorpe dams in Germany. The operation was one of great difficulty and hazard, demanding a high degree of skill and courage and close co-operation between the crews of the aircraft engaged. Nevertheless, a telling blow was struck at the enemy by the successful breaching of the Möehne, and Eder dams. This outstanding success reflects the greatest credit on the efforts of the following personnel who participated in the operation in various capacities as members of aircraft crew."

LONDON GAZETTE 28.5.1943

NOTES: The was the famous dam-buster raid led by Wing Commander Guy Gibson, a number of awards were made for this raid including the C.G.M.'s to F/Sgt. Williams and F/Sgt. Townsend, D.F.M. and the Victoria Cross to Guy Gibson.

The BBC broadcast the following announcement on the 17th May 1943, "The Air Ministry has just issued the following communique: In the early hours of this morning a force of Lancasters of Bomber Command led by Wing Commander G.P.Gibson, D.S.O., D.F.C. attacked with mines the dams of the Möehne, and Sorpe reservoir. These control two thirds of the water storage capacity of the Ruhr basin. Reconnaissance later established that the möehne dam had also been breached over a length of 100 yards and that the power station below had been swept away by the resulting flood. The Eder dam which controls the head water of the Weser and Fulder valleys and operates several power stations was also attacked and was reported as being breached. Photographs show the river below the dam in full flood. The attacks were pressed home from a very low level with great determination and coolness in the face of fierce resistance. Eight of the Lancasters are missing.

Award presented by H.M. King George VI 22.6.1943.

BUSBY 936266 Warrant Officer Desmond Clive Camden
156 Squadron, Royal Air Force

"In recognition of gallantry and devotion to duty in the execution of air operations."

This airman was recommended for the C.G.M. on 21st May, 1943, after completing fifty three raids against all of the major targets.

LONDON GAZETTE 6.7.1943

NOTES: Killed 16.6.1943, buried in Rheinberg War Cemetary.

Award was sent to the Colonial Office 29.3.1946.

C

CAMPBELL 1555102 Flight Sergeant Stuart Somerville
39 Squadron, Royal Air Force Volunteer Reserve

This airman has proved himself to be a valiant and devoted member of aircraft crew. He has participated in many sorties, including numerous attacks on enemy shipping and throughout has displayed a high standard of navigational ability. In June 1944, when over a target in Northern Italy, his aircraft was struck by fragment of shell which started a fire. Flight Sergeant Campbell was wounded but, despite this, he succeeded in extinguishing the outburst. He afterwards navigated the aircraft home in the face of great difficulty. Towards the end of July, 1944, this airman was again a member of a crew detailed for an air operation. During the mission his aircraft was damaged by anti-aircraft fire. A fire started but he extinguished it. Although deprived of the full use of navigational aids he guided his pilot safely home. This airman has displayed a high degree of courage and resolution.

LONDON GAZETTE 24.10.1944

NOTES: Killed in action 7th September 1944, no known grave he is commemorated on the Malta Memorial, Panel 13, column 2.

Award presented to Next of Kin 29.10.1946.

CARDY Can/R.70142 Sergeant William Harry
427 (R.C.A.F.) Squadron, Royal Canadian Air Force

"In recognition of gallantry displayed in flying operations against the enemy."

Flight Lieutenant Laird and Sergeant Cardy were pilot and flight engineer respectively of an aircraft detailed to attack Kassel one night in October 1943. During the operation the bomber was hit by a hail of bullets from an enemy fighter. Nevertheless, Flight Lieutenant Laird coolly and skillfully outmaneuvered the enemy aircraft and set course for this country. Two of his crew had been killed, however, and Sergeant Cardy was wounded in the arm and in the eye. In spite of intense suffering, this gallant airman refused to leave his post and executed his normal duties until he finally fainted through loss of blood. Later, when he again recovered consciousness, he attempted to do as much as he could to assist his captain in the homeward flight. By a superb effort Flight Lieutenant Laird succeeded in reaching base where he effected a safe landing in difficult circumstances. This officer displayed outstanding skill, courage and tenacity, while Sergeant Cardy's exemplary conduct and great fortitude were beyond praise.

LONDON GAZETTE 9.11.1945

NOTES: Award effective 9 November 1943 as per AFRO 358/44 dated 18 February 1944.

Born 1920 in Cooksville, Ontario; home in PortCredit, Ontario; enlisted Galt, 28 August 1940.

Incident occurred on the night of 3 October 1943. Flt. Lt. Laird was awarded a D.F.C. for his part in this action.

Award forwarded to Canadian Commission on 20.3.1945 and presented 17th June 1945.

Enlisted in R.C.A.F. in 1940 and trained as an engine fitter. He spent 2 ½ years as ground crew in Canada before being posted to England in 1943 where he applied for aircrew duties.

CASSON 778890 Flight Sergeant John
250 (Sudan) Squadron, Royal Air Force Volunteer Reserve

One morning in May, 1944, this airman took part in an attack on mechanical transport on the Alatri-Frosinone Road. Despite intense opposing fire, Flight Sergeant Casson pressed home his attacks with great determination. Whilst making a second run over the target his aircraft was hit by a shell. Flight Sergeant Casson was badly wounded in the thigh. Although faint through the loss of blood and shock, this valiant pilot flew his damaged aircraft to base. He was unable to operate one rudder-bar owing to his exhausted condition. Nevertheless, he effected a safe landing. As he was lifted from the controls, Flight Sergeant Casson collapsed. This airman displayed courage, fortitude and devotion to duty of the highest order.

LONDON GAZETTE 23.6.1944

NOTES: Flight Sergeant Casson died of his wounds received in this action and was buried on 28th May in British Cemetery No. 12.

His award was sent by post to his Father in Southern Rhodesia on 12.4.1946.

Medals comprising C.G.M. (Flying), 1939-45 Star, Africa Star, Italy Star, Defence Medal, War Medal, offered for sale at Glendinings 7.12.1988.

CHAPMAN 1576762 Sergeant Leslie
61 Squadron, Royal Air Force Volunteer Reserve

This officer, Pilot Officer Freeman, and airman were pilot and wireless operator respectively of an aircraft detailed to attack Nuremberg one night in March, 1944. During the operation the aircraft was attacked by a fighter. It was driven off but shortly afterwards two more enemy aircraft attacked. Before they were also driven off the bomber had sustained much damage. The starboard wing, the flaps and the undercarriage nacelle were all hit by bullets. The mid-upper and front turrets were damaged. The windscreen was shattered and other parts of the airframe were shot away. Four members of the crew were wounded. Most of the navigational equipment was useless but course was set for home. Sergeant Chapman had been wounded in the back, neck and head but bravely remained at his post obtaining fixes which were of inestimable value in establishing the aircraft's position at various stages on the return flight. Finally the English coast was reached and Pilot Officer Freeman landed the aircraft safely although a tyre on one of the landing wheels had punctured. Pilot Officer Freeman displayed great skill, courage and determination throughout; Sergeant Chapman also proved himself to be a gallant member of aircraft crew. It was not until the aircraft had been safely landed that he informed his captain of his wounds. He set a splendid example.

LONDON GAZETTE 9.5.1944

NOTES: Pilot Officer Freeman was awarded the D.F.C. for this action.

Killed 1.2.1945. The aircraft he was in crash landed at Skellingthorpe after an engine failed on take-off, it exploded and caught fire killing all the crew with the exception of the rear gunner, Sergeant Hoskinson. Sergeant Chapman is buried in Whaplode cemetery, Lincolnshire.

FOR CONSPICUOUS GALLANTRY

Award present to Next of Kin 9.4.1946.

CLAYTON 998503 Warrant Officer Bernard William, D.F.C.
51 Squadron, Royal Air Force

"In recognition of gallantry displayed in flying operations against the enemy."

Recommended having completed fifty-one operations between 9th May 1941 and 16th April 1943.

LONDON GAZETTE 11.6.1943

NOTES: Recommended for a Bar to the D.F.C.

Awarded D.F.C. 15.4.1943, D.S.O. 26.9.1944.

D.S.O. awarded while serving with 617 squadron, having completed seventy-seven operations.

Award presented by H.M. King George VI 23.11.1943.

CLYNES 1377364 Warrant Officer Michael George
431 (R.C.A.F.) Squadron, Royal Air Force

"In recognition of gallantry and devotion to duty in the execution of air operations."

W.O. Clynes was recommended for his award on completion of forty-seven operations. Forty-five operations had been flown with 104 Squadron, R.C.A.F. on targets in the Middle East. On no less than four occasions, the aircraft in which he was flying had to crash land.

LONDON GAZETTE 13.8.1943

NOTES: Killed 25.11.1943, buried in the Durnbach War Cemetery, Germany. This is the nearest cemetery to Frankfurt which had been the target of the attack on which he was killed.

Award sent to Next of Kin 17.11.1944.

FOR CONSPICUOUS GALLANTRY

COLE 1600604 Flight Sergeant Anthony Clifford
622 Squadron, Royal Air Force Volunteer Reserve

In August, 1944, Warrant Officer Farquharson and Flight Sergeant Cole were navigator and wireless operator respectively of an aircraft detailed to attack Stettin. On the return flight the aircraft was intercepted and severely damaged by an enemy fighter. Although seriously wounded and in great pain, Warrant Officer Farquharson continued his navigational duties but was finally persuaded to be removed to a rest bed where he was given an injection of morphia. Meantime, Flight Sergeant Cole although injured in the thigh by a piece of shrapnel, concealed the seriousness of his wound and took over the task of navigating the aircraft back to base. The English coast was eventually crossed and a landing was made at the first available airfield. Weak from loss of blood Flight Sergeant Cole was on the verge of collapse and was removed to hospital. These airmen have completed many sorties and their gallantry and devotion to duty have been of a very high order.

LONDON GAZETTE 27.10.1944

NOTES: Warrant Officer Farquharson was awarded the D.F.C. for this action.

Action took place on the night of 29/30th August.

Award presented 4.12.1945.

COOKE Can/R.173576 Flight Sergeant Jackson Chartis
103 Squadron, Royal Canadian Air Force

"In recognition of gallantry displayed in flying operations against the enemy."

One night in October, 1944, this airman was captain and pilot of an aircraft detailed to attack Cologne. Whilst over the target considerable anti-aircraft fire was encountered. just as the bombs were released the aircraft was struck by high explosive shells. Much damage was sustained. the starboard rudder controls were severed. the petrol tanks were badly pierced and the contents streamed out. Within ten minutes the petrol supply became practically exhausted. By now, Flight Sergeant Cooke had reached friendly territory. He thereupon instructed the crew to leave the aircraft by parachute. As he prepared to leave himself, Flight

155

Sergeant Cooke saw that one of his comrades still remained in the aircraft, having accidentally released his parachute inside the fuselage. Height was being rapidly lost. Nevertheless Flight Sergeant Cooke was determined not to leave his crew member and promptly returned to the controls and attempted to effect a crash landing in a field. During his approach, with undercarriage and flaps retracted, two engines failed. Coolly and skillfully, however, this intrepid pilot achieve his purpose and effected a landing, incurring little further damage to the aircraft in his effort. This airman set a magnificent example of skill, courage and captaincy in ,most difficult and dangerous circumstances.

LONDON GAZETTE 2.1.1945

NOTES: Killed on 29th November, 1944, buried in the Reichwald cemetery, Germany.

Award forwarded to Canadian Commission 20.8.1946.

CORBIN 1295151 Warrant Officer Harold Arthur
248 Squadron, Royal Air Force Volunteer Reserve

This officer has taken part in many sorties, several of them being attacks on enemy shipping. On these operations many vessels of varying classes have been successfully attacked despite heavy enemy opposition. Throughout, Warrant Officer Corbin has displayed a high degree of skill, courage and determination.

LONDON GAZETTE 17.10.1944

NOTES: Recommended for the D.F.C.

Award presented by H.M. King George VI at Buckingham Place.

CORDER 1161447 Flight Sergeant (now Pilot Officer) Charles Clayton
No 248 Squadron

"In recognition of gallantry displayed in flying operations against the enemy."

This airman has participated in 71 operational missions, including sorties off the Norwegian coast, over the Mediterranean and over the Bay of Biscay. He has displayed great navigational skill and perfect teamwork which have made him a valuable member of aircraft crew. On one occasion, in August 1942, he skillfully located a dinghy adrift in the Mediterranean and the crew were later rescued. In March, 1943, he was the navigator of one of the section of Beaufighters patrolling over the Bay of Biscay. During the operation the aircraft sustained severe damage in an encounter with a Junkers 88, which was shot down. The situation appeared hopeless but, as the intercommunication system was unserviceable, Flight Sergeant Corder crawled through to the cockpit where he gave his pilot a course for base. Returning to his seat he attempted to signal their plight to other aircraft of the formation but his efforts were unavailing, In the meantime, the pilot was having considerable difficulty in controlling the aircraft so Flight Sergeant Corder once more crawled to the cockpit to assist. The port engine failed and the possibility of flying to this country seemed remote, nevertheless, Flight Sergeant Corder calmly continued his duties, repairing the intercommunication, obtaining bearings and doing everything within his power to assist his pilot. The aircraft, which was extremely difficult to control, was now being flown almost at sea level. When nearing the English coast the second engine caught fire while some oil in the cockpit also caught alight. Just as the pilot had decided that the damaged aircraft should be abandoned the English coast was sighted, so he struggled on. Meanwhile, Flight Sergeant Corder coolly sent out distress signals and fired Verey cartridges intermittently to attract the attention of people on shore. He guided the pilot to the lowest part of a cliff which was crossed safely and a crash-landing effected on an airfield. On impact the aircraft burst into flames but both Flight Sergeant Corder and his pilot were able to jump clear. In the face of an appalling situation, this airman displayed skill and courage in keeping with the highest traditions of the Royal Air Force.

LONDON GAZETTE 13.4.1943

NOTES: The pilot, Lieutenant Max Geudj D.F.C. was awarded the D.S.O. for this action.

Later Commissioned Pilot Officer.

Award presented by H.M. King George VI 30.11.1943.

FOR CONSPICUOUS GALLANTRY

COUGHLAN A220788 Corporal John Desmond
9 (R.A.A.F.) Squadron, Royal Australian Air Force

"In recognition of his gallantry, skill and devotion to duty, while a helicopter crewman in Vietnam."

Corporal John Desmond Coughlan enlisted in the Royal Australian Air Force on 2nd August 1960 as a trainee instrument mechanic. He became an instrument fitter in 1964 and underwent training as a crewman for Iroquois helicopters in 1965.

Corporal Coughlan recently completed an operational tour in Vietnam as a helicopter crewman with No. 9 Squadron. While being completely aware of the dangers he faced he was at all times an outstanding example of steadfastness and courage to all members of the squadron.

In particular, on 3rd October, 1967, he was crewman on a helicopter which responded to the emergency call of a United States Army helicopter gunship which had crashed in dense jungle deep in known enemy territory. On arrival at the crash site the wreckage was seen to be burning fiercely. Corporal Coughlan immediately volunteered to be winched down to search for and assist survivors with the knowledge that the crashed aircraft would almost certainly attract the attention of the enemy within a short time. Aided by a slightly inured crewman from the crashed helicopter he located and prepared the three most seriously injured survivors for winch evacuation. When their evacuation was complete he remained on the ground to search for the remaining survivors, who had wandered off in a dazed state. After locating them he prepared them for winch evacuation by other helicopters which had by then reached the scene. Throughout this entire period Corporal Coughlan was also faced with the continual hazard of exploding ammunition and rockets from the burning gunship. He was frequently forced to take cover as rounds struck trees in his vicinity.

Again, on 13th January 1968, Corporal Coughlan was the winch operator on a helicopter engaged in the night rescue of the crew and patients of a crashed United States medical evacuation helicopter. The crashed helicopter had been evacuating wounded from an army company which was in contact with enemy forces. The enemy forces continued firing during the period that the Australian helicopter was engaged in rescue operations. In order to carry out the rescue the helicopter was required to hover at tree top level, with it's landing light on, for a prolonged period.

158

While the hover was in progress it was necessary for Corporal Coughlan to lean well out of the helicopter and issue instructions to the pilot. He did this calmly and coolly, maintaining a flow of clear and concise calls without which the pilot would have been unable to maintain the precise hover required during the whole operation. Throughout this time he knew full well that he was the most exposed and obvious target for enemy fire but this did not deter him.

Corporal Coughlan, under these conditions, had a great degree of responsibility for the aircraft safety in such close proximity to obstacles. His exceptional skill and airmanship, as exemplified in this incident, was directly responsible for the successful completion of the mission under very hazardous circumstances.

Corporal Coughlan showed throughout his tour outstanding skill and devotion to duty but in the cases mentioned demonstrated resolution and courage of the highest order. It is considered that his gallantry is in the finest traditions of the Royal Australian Air Force.

LONDON GAZETTE 10.12.1968

NOTES: This was the last C.G.M. (Flying) to be awarded.

Award sent to the Foreign & Commonwealth Office 30.12.1968.

COWHAM 710111 Sergeant Arthur Humphrey
57 Squadron, Royal Air Force Volunteer Reserve

"In recognition of gallantry displayed in flying operations against the enemy."

One night in October, 1943, this Airman was the rear gunner of an aircraft detailed to attack Hanover. Shortly after the target had been bombed the aircraft was engaged by a fighter and hit by a hail of bullets which caused much damage. Sergeant Cowham was struck in the face and suffered a severe injury to one of his eyes. Although his turret was virtually wrecked he fought on with resolution and played a good part in driving off the attacker. Throughout the long journey home this brave gunner, although in intense pain and suffering from the loss of blood, refused to leave his post. Twice, subsequently, his accurate shooting prevented an enemy aircraft from closing in, while his skillful directions assisted his pilot to out-manoeuvre the enemy and fly clear. In harassing circumstances his gallant example greatly encouraged his comrades who were striving to bring the crippled bomber home. On this, his first sortie, Sergeant Cowham displayed courage, fortitude and devotion to duty in keeping with the best traditions of the Royal Air Force.

LONDON GAZETTE 19.11.1943

NOTES: Award presented 2.5.1944.

Action took place on night of 18/19th October 1943.

CRABE Can/R.205588 Flight Sergeant William Eugene
170 Squadron, Royal Canadian Air Force

"In recognition of gallantry and devotion to duty in the execution of air operations."

This airman was the mid-upper gunner detailed for a sortie one night in February, 1945. Soon after leaving the target, the aircraft sustained severe damage. The rear gun turret was wrecked. Flight Sergeant Crabe went at once to attend to the trapped rear gunner. Assisted by another member of the crew he cut away the side of the turret. He was completely exposed to the slipstream and in danger of falling and was not wearing his parachute. Heedless of this and despite intense cold, this valiant airman toiled until he succeeded in freeing the gunner and getting him back into the fuselage. Unfortunately, his comrade was dead. Although his efforts were in vain, Flight Sergeant Crabe's brave and determined bid to save his co-gunner were worthy of the greatest praise.

LONDON GAZETTE 20.3.1945

NOTES: Recommended for the D.F.M.

Award sent to the Canadian Commission 31.1.1947.

CRIDGE 1802499 Sergeant Francis William
166 Squadron, Royal Air Force Volunteer Reserve

"In recognition of gallantry displayed in flying operations against the enemy."

This officer (Sqn.Ldr. Rippingale) and airman were pilot and navigator respectively of an aircraft detailed to attack Neuss one night in

September, 1944. When nearing the target the aircraft was attacked by a fighter. The fight ended with the destruction of the enemy aircraft which exploded in the air. The bomber had sustained much damage. The mid-upper and rear turrets were wrecked, the gunner of the latter being killed. The wireless apparatus, many of the pilot's instruments and much navigational equipment was rendered useless. The hydraulic gear was put out of action, making it impossible to operate the bomb doors mechanically. Even so, Squadron Leader Rippingale calculated that if the bombs were released their weight would open the bomb doors. He gave the order and the bombs fell. A course was set for home and finally an airfield was reached and a safe landing made. In hazardous circumstances, Squadron Leader Rippingale displayed exceptional skill, inspiring leadership and great courage. Sergeant Cridge also proved himself to be a brave and devoted member of aircraft crew. In the fight he was wounded in the face, arm and the body by fragments of cannon shell. His first thought was to give his captain all the assistance of which he was capable. Although in great pain and suffering from the loss of blood he navigated the aircraft home with much skill.

LONDON GAZETTE 10.11.1944

NOTES: Sqn.Ldr. Rippingale was awarded the D.S.O. for this action.

Award presented 4.12.1945.

D

DENNIS Aus.437121 Warrant Officer Kevin John
462 (R.A.A.F.) Squadron, Royal Australian Air Force

"In recognition of gallantry and devotion to duty in the execution of air operations."

One night in March, 1945, this officer was wireless operator in an aircraft detailed to attack Frankfurt. Shortly after leaving the target the aircraft was hit and severely damaged by anti-aircraft fire. One member of the crew was killed and Warrant Officer Dennis was badly wounded. The latter was hit in both legs and most of the foot of one of them was severed. Despite his wounds and the loss of much blood, Warrant Officer Dennis continued with his duties until the aircraft had landed. Although suffering great physical distress, this officer displayed courage, determination and devotion to duty of the highest order.

LONDON GAZETTE 13.7.1945

DEW 1210365 Sergeant Fielder Bennett
78 Squadron, Royal Air Force Volunteer Reserve

These airmen, Sergeant Dew, Flight Sergeant Long and Sergeant Browne, were flight engineer, pilot and wireless operator (air) of an aircraft detailed to attached Bourg-Léopold one night in May, 1944.

When nearing the enemy coast, on the homeward flight, the aircraft was attacked by a fighter and sustained considerable damage. Two engines were put out of action and extensive fires started in the fuselage. The bomber temporarily went out of control. At this moment it was struck by bullets from another enemy aircraft. Sergeant Dew was badly wounded in the foot, thigh and arm; Sergeant Browne also sustained severe wounds in the arm and thigh. The situation was critical but although Sergeant Long ordered his crew to prepare to abandon aircraft, he attempted to regain control. He succeeded in so doing. Meanwhile, Sergeant Dew, in spite of considerable suffering and weakness through loss of blood, fought the fires and his efforts were successful; he also succeeded in re-starting one of the damaged engines. By now he was unable to move about. Nevertheless, throughout the remainder of the homeward flight he directed other of his comrades in the necessary engineering tasks. Sergeant Browne also proved himself to be a devoted member of aircraft crew for, injured as he was, and suffering acutely, he insisted on remaining by his wireless apparatus to assist his pilot on his course. Eventually, Flight Sergeant Long reached an airfield in this country and made a safe landing. In the face of a trying ordeal, these airmen displayed high courage, great skill and endurance. There example ranks high.

LONDON GAZETTE 7.7.1944

NOTES: Flight Sergeant Long and Sergeant Browne were both awarded the D.F.M.

DONALDSON 1215802 Flight Sergeant Herbert Allison
199 Squadron, Royal Air Force Volunteer Reserve

"In recognition of gallantry and devotion to duty in the execution of air operations."

This airman was the wireless operator (air) of an aircraft detailed for an attack on a target in March, 1944. Soon after crossing the enemy coast, the aircraft was hit by fire from the ground defences. Flight Sergeant Donaldson was hit in the leg by fragments of shrapnel which lodged against the bone, causing a most painful wound. Despite this, he acted with great promptitude in assisting to extinguish a fire which had commenced in the aircraft. He afterwards set to work to repair his wireless apparatus which had sustained damage. Not until this task was successfully completed did Flight Sergeant Donaldson report his injury. Later on, the aircraft again came under fire and received further damage. Although in considerable pain, Flight Sergeant Donaldson made light of his injuries and remained at his post to execute his wireless duties until the sortie was completed. He displayed fortitude, courage and devotion to duty of a high order.

LONDON GAZETTE 31.3.1944

NOTES: Medals comprising C.G.M. (Flying), 1939-45 Star, Air Crew Europe Star (clasp France & Germany), Defence Medal, War Medal, offered for sale at Buckland, Dix & Wood on 27.7.1995.

FOR CONSPICUOUS GALLANTRY

DOVE 621162 Flight Sergeant George Frederick, D.F.M.
101 Squadron, Royal Air Force

"In recognition of gallantry displayed in flying operations against the enemy."

On the night of 14th February, 1943, Pilot Officer Gates, Flight Sergeant Dove and Sergeants Williams, Bain and Airey were members of the crew of an aircraft captained by Sergeant Hazard, which was detailed to attack Milan. Whilst over the target area, the aircraft was attacked by an enemy fighter from close range. It's gunfire exploded some incendiary bombs which had failed to release and a fire quickly developed in the bomber. The fuselage became a mass of flames reaching through the mid-upper turret manned by Flight Sergeant Dove. Ammunition in the turret boxes and ducts commenced to explode in all directions. In the face of an appalling situation, Flight Sergeant Dove coolly remained at his post Although he was burned about the hands and face, he manned his guns with grim resolution skill, and accuracy. He delivered a devastating burst at the attacker which had already been engaged and hit by the rear gunner and succeeded in destroying it. Disregarding the roaring flames, he then descended from his turret and went to the assistance of Sergeant Airey the rear gunner, who had been wounded and extricated him from the rear turret. The situation had become extremely critical and Sergeant Hazard ordered the crew to prepare to abandon aircraft. When informed that one of his comrades was helpless be decided, in spite of the grave risk entailed, to attempt a forced landing. Meanwhile, Pilot Officer Gates, assisted by Sergeants Williams and Bain bravely tackled the fire with extinguishers and succeeded in getting it under control. The aircraft was now down to 8oo feet but, as the fire had subsided Sergeant Hazard quickly decided to attempt to fly the badly damaged bomber home. He regained height and displaying fine airmanship crossed the Alps in safety, although 1 engine failed whilst so doing.

On the remainder of the journey Pilot Officer Gates rendered valuable assistance to his captain and frequently ministered to his wounded comrade, although this necessitated clambering over a hole in the floor of the aircraft in darkness Aided by the skilful navigation of Sergeant Williams and good work by Sergeant Bain, the flight engineer, Sergeant Hazard succeeded in flying the seriously damaged aircraft back to this country In circumstances of the greatest danger, this aircraft crew displayed courage fortitude and devotion to duty In keeping with the highest traditions of the Royal Air Force.

LONDON GAZETTE 23.3.1943

NOTES: Pilot Officer Gates was awarded the D.S.O. and Sergeants Hazard, Williams Bain and Airey the C.G.M. for this action.

Awarded D.F.M. 18.4.1941.

DOWNTON Aus.401206 Sergeant George
1437 Strategical Reconnaissance Flight, Royal Australian Air Force

"In recognition of gallantry displayed in flying operations against the enemy."

This airman was the wireless operator/air gunner of an aircraft, which, during a flight near Cap Bon, was engaged by ten enemy fighters. In the ensuing combat, Sergeant Downton was wounded three times, while his gun became unserviceable. Despite this he coolly directed his pilot in taking the necessary evading action until the aircraft could no longer be flown and was landed on fire, in enemy territory. With complete disregard for his own safety, Sergeant Downton, who escaped serious injury in the crash, entered the blazing wreckage and assisted in extricating a member of the crew who was badly burned. He then tried valiantly to re-enter the rear of the aircraft to rescue a trapped comrade but was finally beaten by the intense heat of the conflagration. His courageous efforts in spite of his wounds were worthy of the highest praise.

LONDON GAZETTE 23.7.1943

NOTES: Enlisted 1941. Underwent training in Australia, Kenya and Rhodesia before being posted to 1437 in the Middle East in July, 1942.

Action took place on 21st April, 1943. Downton was taken prisoner along with Major Braithwaite who had been attached to the crew from 40 S.A.A.F. Spitfire Squadron. Held in Italy and Germany being released finally in May 1945.

FOR CONSPICUOUS GALLANTRY

DURRANS 1515563 Sergeant Edward Dyson

90 Squadron, Royal Air Force Volunteer Reserve

This airman was the wireless operator of an aircraft detailed for a sortie one night in April, 1944. On the return flight the aircraft was hit by anti-aircraft fire. Sergeant Durrans was severely wounded by flying fragments of shrapnel. Although suffering acutely and affected by the loss of blood, Sergeant Durrans would not leave his post and continued working his wireless apparatus until the aircraft reached the English coast. His courage, fortitude and utter disregard for his own welfare set an example in keeping with the best traditions of the Royal Air Force.

LONDON GAZETTE 9.5.1944

NOTES: Due to his injuries, Flight Sergeant Durrans was unable to attend an investiture until 5th March 1944, even then he was still on crutches.

Medals comprising C.G.M. (Flying), 1939-45 Star, Air Crew Europe Star, Defence Medal, War Medal, offered for sale at Sotheby's 29.10.1987.

E

ELCOATE 628437 Flight Sergeant Anthony Futcher, D.F.M.
156 Squadron, Royal Air Force

"In recognition of gallantry and devotion to duty in the execution of air operations."

Recommended on completion of sixty-two bombing operations.

LONDON GAZETTE 20.4.1943

NOTES: Awarded D.F.M. 18.4.1941.

ELLIS 1292427 Acting Warrant Officer Edward Sydney
625 Squadron, Royal Air Force Volunteer Reserve

"In recognition of gallantry displayed in flying operations against the enemy."

One night in December, 1943, Warrant Officer Ellis was the pilot of an aircraft detailed to attack Berlin. During the initial bombing run the aircraft was hit by anti-aircraft fire, which injured the rear gunner and rendered his turret unserviceable. Warrant Officer Ellis maintained a steady run, however, and made his first attack. Just as the first bombs had been released the aircraft was raked by bullets from a fighter and the rear gunner sustained a further injury; the mid-upper gunner was also wounded. Although the enemy delivered another long burst of fire, Warrant Officer Ellis continued his run and attacked the target exactly as planned. On leaving the target area it was discovered that much damage had been sustained. The inter-communication and hydraulic systems and the turrets were all unserviceable. The mainplane and the fuselage had been damaged, while the bomb doors could not be closed. In spite of this, Warrant Officer Ellis flew on and eventually landed his aircraft safely without the aid of flaps and in spite of punctured tyres. In harassing circumstances, this pilot displayed skill, courage and devotion to duty beyond praise.

LONDON GAZETTE 24.12.1943

NOTES: Operation took place on the night of 2/3rd December.

Later Commissioned. Awarded D.F.C. 6.6.1944.

ENGBRECHT Can/R.140754 Sergeant Peter
424 (Tiger) Squadron, Royal Canadian Air Force

As mid-upper gunner this airman has participated in several sorties and has proved himself to be an exceptionally cool and confident member of aircraft crew. On one occasion during a sortie his aircraft was subjected to fourteen separate attacks by fighters. In the ensuing fights, Sergeant Engbrecht defended his aircraft with great skill and two of the attackers fell to his guns. In June 1944 he took part in an attack on a target in Northern France. On the return flight his aircraft was attacked on two occasions by fighters. Sergeant Engbrecht engaged the enemy aircraft with deadly effect each time and his brilliant shooting caused their destruction. His feats have been worthy of the greatest praise.

LONDON GAZETTE 4.8.1944

NOTES: Award presented by the King at Skipton on 11th August, 1944.

EVANS 1604111 Flight Sergeant Dennis
250 Squadron, Royal Air Force Volunteer Reserve

"In recognition of gallantry and devotion to duty in the execution of air operations."

Flight sergeant Evans has displayed the highest standard of keenness, courage and devotion to duty. He has completed very many sorties and has at all times pressed home his attacks with great determination. In April, 1945, this airman was engaged on an armed reconnaissance in Northern Italy. A convoy of enemy vehicles were sighted. During the attack his aircraft was hit and severely damaged by anti-aircraft fire. Undeterred, Flight Sergeant Evans pressed home his attack, destroying two enemy vehicles. Later, Flight Sergeant Evans was compelled to abandon his crippled aircraft. He came down safely by parachute. Although landing in enemy territory he evaded capture and soon rejoined his squadron. He displayed great courage and tenacity throughout.

LONDON GAZETTE 20.7.1945

F

FERGUSON Aus.431444 Flight Sergeant George Bailie
466 (R.A.A.F.) Squadron, Royal Australian Air Force

This airman was the mid-upper gunner in an aircraft detailed to attack Essen one night in February, 1945. When approaching the target much anti-aircraft fire was encountered. Flight Sergeant Ferguson was struck in the face by a piece of shrapnel which crashed through the perspex screen round his gun turret. He had sustained a most serious wound. Nevertheless, he would not distract his captain. Making light of his condition, Flight Sergeant Ferguson assured him that he did not require assistance. Another member of the crew went to investigate but this brave gunner kept on his oxygen mask to prevent his comrade from seeing the extent of his injuries and reiterated that he was not in need of help. Throughout the bombing run, Flight Ferguson remained at his post. When over allied territory on the way home the captain once more called to his gunner. Owing to congealed blood in the microphone of his mask, Flight Sergeant Ferguson was unable to reply. The wireless operator was promptly sent to his assistance. When taken from his gun turret and his mask removed, Flight sergeant Ferguson's injuries were fully disclosed. A piece of shrapnel, some two inches long, was embedded in his cheek. His upper jaw had been fractured. several teeth had been knocked out. His face was very badly swollen and the right eye was completely closed. He was suffering intensely. First aid was given at once. So serious was his condition that the captain brought the aircraft down at an airfield in allied territory so that his brave comrade could receive the urgent medical attention he so urgently needed. Flight Sergeant Ferguson set a magnificent example of courage, self-sacrifice and devotion to duty.

LONDON GAZETTE 1.5.1945

NOTES: Enlisted July, 1943. Operation took place on 23rd February, 1945.

FOR CONSPICUOUS GALLANTRY

FOSS 1313625 Flight Sergeant Ronald John

224 Squadron, Royal Air Force Volunteer Reserve

"In recognition of gallantry displayed in flying operations against the enemy."

This Officer, Flying Officer Johnstone, and Airmen Sergeants Dilks and Foss, were members of the crew of an aircraft engaged on anti-submarine patrol in September, 1943. During the flight the aircraft was attacked by four Junkers 88. The captain was killed in the early stages of the combat and Flight Sergeant Foss, the second pilot, immediately took over the controls. Flying Officer Johnstone, with commendable initiative immediately went to his assistance and rendered material help in subsequent evading tactics. The enemy presses home their attack, however, and the aircraft was extensively damaged and caught fire, while several of the crew were wounded. Although the aircraft was fast becoming uncontrollable, Flight Sergeant Foss and Flying Officer Johnstone, by a combined effort, succeeded in bringing the aircraft down on the sea where it became wrecked on impact with the water. Although under water, Flying Officer Johnstone, who was himself injured, gallantly assisted two of his wounded comrades to get clear by allowing them to step on his shoulders and head and thus to scramble through a gaping hole in the submerged part of the aircraft. Meanwhile, Flight Sergeant Foss assisted other members of the crew into the dinghy. For nine days, these members of aircraft crew were adrift and during this period, Flying Officer Johnstone, Flight Sergeant Foss and sergeant Dilks displayed great courage and high morale. Throughout this trying ordeal their exemplary conduct set an example of the highest order.

LONDON GAZETTE 29.10.1943

NOTES: Flying Officer Johnstone was awarded the D.S.O. and Sergeant Dilks the D.F.M. for this action.

G

GOSLING 1159184 Warrant Officer Leonard Eric
617 Squadron, Royal Air Force Volunteer Reserve

LONDON GAZETTE 21.9.1945

NOTES: Medals comprise C.G.M. (Flying), 1939-1945 Star, Air Crew Europe Star with clasp France & Germany, Defence Medal and War Medal.

GREEN Aus.416212 Flight Sergeant Clarence Reginald
100 Squadron, Royal Australian Air Force

"In recognition of gallantry displayed in flying operations against the enemy."

On 1st December 1942, while on a reconnaissance, his Beaufort aircraft was attacked by three Japanese fighters. With expert airmanship he was able to evade the attacks and get himself into a position to repel the fighters. In the subsequent air battle his gunners were able to damage one fighter and to claim a second as 'probably destroyed'.

Later, one 8th March 1943, whilst flying escort duty in the Buna area off New Guinea, he saw a merchant ship blow up and disappear after being attacked by a formation of nine enemy bombers, escorted by fighters. These fighters then went down to strafe the survivors in the water. Although his Beaufort was out-gunned and out numbered, he took on the fighters with such daring and skill that they broke off the engagement and flew off. He continued to patrol above the survivors until they were picked up, and by doing so, saved many lives.

LONDON GAZETTE 10.3.1944

NOTES: Commissioned Flight Lieutenant January 1945. Awarded M.I.D. 4.5.1945.

H

HALL 1308178 Sergeant Edwin Thomas George
115 Squadron, Royal Air Force

"In recognition of gallantry displayed in flying operations against the enemy."

This airman was mid-upper gunner of an aircraft crew detailed to attack Cologne on the night of 28/29th June, 1943. On the return flight from the target the aircraft came under attack from two enemy fighters. The pilot, Sergeant Jolly took evasive action and both Hall and the rear Gunner, Sergeant White, opened fire. One enemy fighter broke of the attack and the second fired a burst of machine-gun and cannon which missed the bomber. This fighter was then seen to break off the attack and did not return. The first fighter then made another attack from dead astern and on opening fire killed the rear gunner, Sergeant White. And setting the fuselage on fire. Despite the fire burning in the fuselage below him, Sergeant Hall continued to fire his guns until at last the fighter was seen to enter a steep dive on fire. At this point Sergeant Hall left his turret due to the intense smoke and flames and assisted Sergeant Crowther in putting out the fire. At this point it was discovered that the rear turret had been shot away completely. After extinguishing the fire, Sergeant Hall returned to his turret.

LONODON GAZETTE 23.7.1943

NOTES: Sergeants Jolly and Crowther were awarded the D.F.M. for their part in this action.

HALL 605494 Flight Sergeant James Mansfield
180 Squadron, Royal Air Force

"In recognition of gallantry and devotion to duty in the execution of air operations."

This officer (P.O. R.M.Perkins) and airman were pilot and air gunner respectively in an aircraft detailed to attack the railway yards at Bocholt in March, 1945. During the bombing run the aircraft was hit by fire from the ground defences. Pilot Officer Perkins was severely wounded. His right thigh was smashed; he also sustained injuries to his back. His suffering became intense. Nevertheless this brave pilot, tended by Flight Sergeant Hall who stood at his side, flew the aircraft to an allied airfield. As the airfield was reached Pilot Officer Perkins was in great distress. Although the aircraft had sustained serious damage it was decided to attempt a landing. Flight Sergeant Hall assisted to remove his wounded comrade into the second pilot's seat and then himself took over the controls in an effort to bring the aircraft down. During the descent, Pilot Officer Perkins, injured as he was, advised and directed his resolute air gunner in the control of the aircraft so well that a successful crash landing was affected. Pilot Officer Perkins displayed outstanding fortitude, great courage and unbeatable determination in the face of extreme suffering. Flight Sergeant Hall also proved himself to be a valiant crew member. His coolness, courage and resource set a fine example.

LONDON GAZETTE 27.4.1945

NOTES: Pilot Officer Perkins was awarded the D.S.O. for this action.

HARTLY 1571712 Flight Sergeant Robert
9 Squadron, Royal Air Force Volunteer Reserve

As air gunner this airman has taken part in a large number of sorties against many heavily defended targets in Germany. His accuracy, vigilance and determination have been of the highest order and his devotion to duty unfailing.

LONDON GAZETTE 24.10.1944

HAYWOOD 649966 Warrant Officer Ronald
7 Squadron, Royal Air Force

"In recognition of gallantry and devotion to duty in the execution of air operations."

LONDON GAZETTE 18.1.1944

NOTES: Born in Staffordshire in 1921, enlisted in the R.A.F. in 1939.

Killed in action 14/15th January 1944, buried in the Hanover War Cemetery, Germany.

His award was presented to the Next of Kin on 12.2.1946.

HAZARD 1313768 Sergeant Ivan Henry
101 Squadron, Royal Air Force

"In recognition of gallantry displayed in flying operations against the enemy."

On the night of 14th February, 1943, Pilot Officer Gates, Flight Sergeant Dove and Sergeants Williams, Bain and Airey were members of the crew of an aircraft captained by Sergeant Hazard, which was detailed to attack Milan. Whilst over the target area, the aircraft was attacked by an enemy fighter from close range. It's gunfire exploded some incendiary bombs which had failed to release and a fire quickly developed in the bomber. The fuselage became a mass Of flames reaching through the mid-upper turret manned by Flight Sergeant Dove. Ammunition in the turret boxes and ducts commenced to explode in all directions. In the face of an appalling situation, Flight Sergeant Dove coolly remained at his post Although he was burned about the hands and face, he manned his guns with grim resolution skill, and accuracy. He delivered a devastating burst at the attacker which had already been engaged and hit by the rear gunner and succeeded in destroying it. Disregarding the roaring flames, he then descended from his turret and went to the assistance of Sergeant Airey the rear gunner, who had been wounded and extricated him from the rear turret. The situation had become extremely critical and Sergeant Hazard ordered the crew to prepare to abandon aircraft. When informed that one of his comrades was helpless be decided, in spite of the grave risk entailed, to attempt a forced landing. Meanwhile, Pilot Officer Gates, assisted by Sergeants Williams and Bain bravely tackled the fire with extinguishers and succeeded in getting it under control. The aircraft was now down to 8oo feet but, as the fire had subsided Sergeant Hazard quickly decided to attempt to fly the badly damaged bomber home. He regained height and displaying fine airmanship crossed the Alps in safety, although 1 engine failed whilst so doing.

On the remainder of the journey Pilot Officer Gates rendered valuable assistance to his captain and frequently ministered to his wounded comrade, although this necessitated clambering over a hole in the floor of the aircraft in darkness Aided by the skilful navigation of Sergeant Williams and good work by Sergeant Bain, the flight engineer, Sergeant Hazard succeeded in flying the seriously damaged aircraft back to this country In circumstances of the greatest danger, this aircraft crew displayed courage fortitude and devotion to duty In keeping with the highest traditions of the Royal Air Force.

LONDON GAZETTE 23.3.1943

NOTES: Pilot Officer Gates was awarded the D.S.O. and Flight Sergeant Dove, Sergeants Williams Bain and Airey the C.G.M. for this action.

Killed along with Sergeant Williams C.G.M. and Sergeant Bain C.G.M while taking a new bomber on a test flight, over Hornsea 20th March, 1943. Buried in Wolvercote Cemetery, Oxford.

HEWITT 622189 Sergeant Roy Kelly, D.F.M.
61 Squadron, Royal Air Force

"In recognition of gallantry and devotion to duty in the execution of air operations."

This airman was the wireless operator in an aircraft detailed to lay sea mines on the night of 10/11th March, 1943. After completing their mission and on the return flight they were attacked by four enemy fighters on three separate occasions. The aircraft suffered considerable damage and a fire broke out. Sergeant Hewitt sent distress signals after assisting to extinguish the fire.

LONDON GAZETTE 14.5.1943

NOTES: Recommended for a bar to the D.F.M.

Awarded the D.F.M. 19.3.1943.

FOR CONSPICUOUS GALLANTRY

HICKS 846405 Sergeant Edward Francis

466 (R.A.A.F.) Squadron, Auxiliary Air Force

"In recognition of gallantry displayed in flying operations against the enemy."

In April, 1943, Pilot Officer Hopkins, Flying Officer Clayton and Sergeants Hicks and Blair were air bomber, navigator, captain and wireless operator respectively of an aircraft detailed to attack a target in the Ruhr. Over Germany the aircraft was attacked by an enemy fighter. The first burst of fire from the attacker fatally injured the rear gunner and wounded the air bomber, navigator and wireless operator. The fighter made a second attack but Sergeant Hicks avoided its gunfire by turning steeply under the enemy aircraft which ass not seen again. Although the hydraulic and brake systems of the bomber were damaged causing the wheels to drop down and the bomb doors to open, the crew decided to continue their mission. Pilot Officer Hopkins, the air bomber, although suffering from a corn, pound fracture of the arm and, at times, only retaining consciousness with great difficulty, displayed unsurpassed determination by directing his pilot to the target and bombing it successfully On the return flight Pilot Officer Hopkins, Flying Officer Clayton and Sergeant Blair laboured for more than 2 hours to assist the mortally wounded rear gunner. extricating him from his turret and administering morphia; some of their efforts were made whilst flying at 15,000 feet and without oxygen. - Sergeant Hicks eventually flew the damaged aircraft to an airfield in this country where he effected a landing without the aid of flaps These members of aircraft crew displayed great courage, fortitude and determination in most hazardous circumstances.

LONDON GAZETTE 14.5.1943

NOTES: Recommended for an immediate D.F.M.

Pilot Officer Hopkins was awarded the D.S.O., Flying Officer Clayton the D.F.C. and Sergeant Blair the D.F.M. for their parts in this action.

Later commissioned. Awarded the D.F.C. 16.11.1943., M.I.D. 1.1.1945.

HILTON 1192265 Sergeant Paul Alexander
35 Squadron, Royal Air Force Volunteer Reserve

This airman was pilot of an aircraft detailed to attack Essen on the night of 2/3rd June, 1942. The target was bombed without incident and Hilton headed for home. On the return journey they came under attack from three enemy aircraft and in the ensuing combat, both inner engines were knocked out. The enemy aircraft broke off their attack. The aircraft had now dropped to 4,000 feet when the port outer engine began to fail. Sergeant Hilton gave the order to abandon aircraft. One of the crew had pulled his rip cord by mistake and so Sergeant Hilton made the decision to attempt to land on what appeared to be water below. It turned out that the water was no more than the reflection of the moon on the ground mist.

Sergeant Hilton was taken prisoner and remained in captivity until April 1945.

LONDON GAZETTE 29.3.1946

HOGG 552693 Flight Sergeant Robert Service
49 Squadron, Royal Air Force

"In recognition of gallantry and devotion to duty in the execution of air operations."
LONDON GAZETTE 14.5.1943

HOPKINS 520203 Warrant Officer Sidney Charles
214 Squadron, Royal Air Force

Warrant Officer Hopkins has a long record of operational flying. He has completed two tours of duty with Coastal Command and one in which he has been employed on bomber support duties. During this last tour all his sorties were against heavily defended targets in the heart of Germany. By his cool courage, efficiency and determination in the face of the enemy this Warrant Officer has inspired the other members of his crew with confidence.

LONDON GAZETTE 26.10.1945

NOTES: M.I.D. 11.8.1940

Medals C.G.M., 1939-45 Star, Atlantic Star (clasp France & Germany), Defence Medal, War Medal (M.I.D.) appeared for sale at Spink on 12.7.1994, and again at the same auction house on 12.3.1996.

HOWE 1333913 Sergeant John Alfred William
144 Squadron, Royal Air Force Volunteer Reserve

"In recognition of gallantry displayed in flying operations against the enemy."

As captain of an aircraft this airman took part in an attack on an enemy convoy in July, 1943. Whilst over the target the aircraft was hit by shell fire, whilst Sergeant Howe sustained a severe wound in the leg and was hit in the face. Despite this he resolutely pressed home his attack with great effect, afterwards flying the damaged aircraft to base. Sergeant Howe displayed great courage and fortitude, setting a fine example of devotion to duty.

LONDON GAZETTE 24.9.1943

HURSE Aus.410489 Warrant Officer Alexander William
75 (N.Z.) Squadron, Royal Australian Air Force

This officer, Flying Officer Zillwood, and Warrant Officer were navigator and air bomber respectively of an aircraft detailed to attack a target at Nantes. Shortly after making the attack the aircraft sustained damage. The pilot was seriously injured and was unable to execute his duties. Despite his lack of experience, Warrant Officer Hurse took over the controls and with the assistance of Flying Officer Zillwood succeeded in flying the damaged aircraft to base. These members of aircraft crew displayed exception coolness, great determination and devotion to duty in most difficult circumstances. They have completed very many sorties against heavily defended targets in Germany.

LONDON GAZETTE 21.7.1944

NOTES: Flying Officer Zillwood was awarded the D.F.C. for this action.

Enlisted January 1942, joined 75 Squadron in November 1943.

J

JEFFERIES 1313283 Flight Sergeant Arthur Harrington
Royal Air Force Volunteer Reserve

"In recognition of gallantry and devotion to duty in the execution of air operations."
LONDON GAZETTE 21.12.1945

NOTES: Killed in action on the famous Nuremberg raid in March 1944. He is buried in the Haverlee War Cemetery, Belgium.

JONES 1652870 Flight Sergeant Derrick Teify
62 Squadron, Royal Air Force Volunteer Reserve

This airman has completed a large number of day and night sorties many of which have been over mountainous terrain and in adverse weather. In May, 1945, his aircraft was hit and set on fire by anti-aircraft fire. Handing over control of the aircraft to his second pilot, Flight Sergeant Jones attempted to extinguish the flames. His efforts proved unsuccessful and he sustained burns. Upon resuming control of the aircraft, he realised that there was no alternative but to make a forced landing, the aircraft exploded. His ability and coolness undoubtedly saved the lives of his crew. This airman has set a fine example to his fellows.

LONDON GAZETTE 3.8.1945

NOTES: Later Commissioned.

FOR CONSPICUOUS GALLANTRY

JONES 1652936 Sergeant Owen Noel
90 Squadron, Royal Air Force Volunteer Reserve

"In recognition of gallantry displayed in flying operations against the enemy."

In September, 1943, Warrant Officer Denton and Sergeants Jones and Sudden were pilot, flight engineer and navigator respectively of an aircraft detailed to attack Hanover. Just after the bombs had been released the aircraft was intercepted by a Junkers 88 which made several attacks. The bomber was repeatedly hit and sustained much damage. The rear gunner was killed, while Warrant Officer Denton was hit in the leg by a bullet and sergeant Suddens was hit in the hand. Nevertheless, Warrant Officer Denton succeeded in flying clear and set course for this country. Meanwhile, Sergeant Jones, displaying praiseworthy promptitude, dealt effectively with two fires which had broken out in the rear part of the fuselage, afterwards rendering first aid to his wounded comrades. In the face of many difficulties, Warrant Officer Denton succeeded in reaching this country and successfully crash-landed the damaged bomber at an airfield. Throughout the return flight Sergeants Jones and Sudden did everything in their power to assist and proved themselves cool and resourceful members of aircraft crew. These gallant airmen set an example worthy of emulation.

LONDON GAZETTE 19.10.1943

NOTES: Warrant Officer Denton was awarded the D.F.C. and Sergeant Sudden the D.F.M. for this action.

JOUX 1151582 Flight Sergeant Edward Ernest de, D.F.M.
102 Squadron, Royal Air Force Volunteer Reserve

"In recognition of gallantry displayed in flying operations against the enemy."

Recommended for award at the end of his operational tour.

LONDON GAZETTE 12.11.1943

NOTES: Awarded D.F.M. 9.1.1942.

K

KEEN 923049 Flight Sergeant Geoffrey Frank, D.F.M.
427 (R.C.A.F.) Squadron, Royal Air Force

"In recognition of gallantry displayed in flying operations against the enemy."

One night In March. 1943, this airman Was the wireless operator of an aircraft detailed to attack Essen. Whilst over the target area the aircraft was hit by heavy anti-aircraft fire - The navigator was killed instantaneously. Flight Sergeant Keen. who was in the astro-dome. had his right foot blown off and received cuts on both legs. Disregarding his wounds. Flight Sergeant Keen regained his seat in the wireless cabin. For over two hours he laboured to repair the damaged apparatus. He could not speak to other members of the crew owing to damage to the inter-communication apparatus- Another airman spoke to him. however. on at least a dozen occasions and found him still conscious and working at his self imposed task of directing the manipulation of various installations. He also offered assistance in navigating the aircraft and actually managed to drag himself on two occasions to the navigator's compartment to obtain essential information. His courage and fortitude in such circumstances were of the highest order.

LONDON GAZETTE 23.4.1943

NOTES: Recommended for the Victoria Cross. Awarded D.F.M. 30.1.1942.

Retired from the R.A.F. as Squadron Leader.

Medals comprising C.G.M. (Flying), D.F.M., 1939-45 Star, Air Crew Europe Star, Defence Medal, War Medal appeared for sale at Christie's on 25.7.1989.

KELLY 1518651 Acting Flight Sergeant Thomas William Dennis

7 Squadron, Royal Air Force Volunteer Reserve

"In recognition of gallantry and devotion to duty in the execution of air operations."

One night in February, 1945, this airman was the navigator in one of a formation of aircraft detailed to attack an oil refinery at Bohlen.

When approaching the target the aircraft was hit by anti-aircraft fire and sustained damage. Flight Sergeant Kelly was severely wounded in the leg. In spite of this, his first thought was the fulfillment of his allotted duties . Although in acute pain he insisted on remaining at his post. Throughout the attack and on the return flight home, Flight Sergeant Kelly displayed the highest standard of skill. After the English coast had been crossed he was overcome by faintness but he had accomplished his task and navigated the aircraft safely back. This airman displayed exceptional courage, fortitude and devotion to duty.

LONDON GAZETTE 6.4.1945

NOTES: Recommended for the D.F.M. Awarded D.F.M. 17.4.1945

KNIGHT 635682 Sergeant Ernest William

432 (R.C.A.F.) Squadron, Royal Air Force

"In recognition of gallantry displayed in flying operations against the enemy."

One morning in October, 1944, this airman was the flight engineer of an aircraft detailed to attack Wanne Eickel. Whilst over the target the aircraft was badly hit by anti-aircraft fire. The bomb aimer was killed and Sergeant Knight was wounded. His injury was severe. Although suffering acutely he insisted on remaining at his post ready to give of his best to assist his captain in his attempt to fly the badly damaged aircraft home. One engine was completely out of action. whilst a second was kept functioning only by Sergeant Knight's constant attention. This airman displayed courage, fortitude and devotion to duty of a high order. His example was most inspiring.

LONDON GAZETTE 15.12.1944

L

LANGLEY N.Z.421067 Flight Sergeant Marcus Louis
489 (N.Z.) Squadron, Royal New Zealand Air Force

As pilot and navigator respectively these airmen, Flight Sergeant Langley and Parish, have participated in numerous attacks on enemy shipping and have set a fine example of skill and dash. In May, 1944, they took part in an attack on a heavily armed convoy and obtained a hit on one of the vessels. Flight Sergeant Langley also used his machine guns to good effect on two minesweepers. Some days later these airmen were again in action against enemy shipping. At the outset of the fight Flight Sergeant Langley was wounded in the throat, arms and thigh. In spite of this he pressed home his attack and afterwards flew the aircraft to base. He displayed courage and fortitude of the highest order. Flight Sergeant Parish also proved himself to be a cool and resolute member of aircraft crew. On the return flight he tended to his wounded pilot and did everything in his power to assist him in his endeavours to reach this country. He proved a tower of strength.

LONDON GAZETTE 16.6.1944

NOTES: Flight Sergeant Parish was awarded the D.F.M. for this action.

LARDEN Can/R.90883 Flight Sergeant Alan William Jessup
218 Squadron, Royal Canadian Air Force

"In recognition of gallantry displayed in flying operations against the enemy."

One night in August 1943, this airman was the bomb-aimer of an aircraft detailed for an operation against Turin. Whist over the city the bomber was subjected to accurate bursts of fire from an enemy fighter. The windscreen was shattered, the front and rear turrets were put out of action while three engines were hit, one of them being rendered useless. The navigator was killed and the pilot was wounded and lay slumped over the controls. He was removed from his position and Flight Sergeant Larden coolly took over the controls. The aircraft was down to three thousand feet and the bombs were released. Flight Sergeant Larden realized that he would be unable to gain height sufficiently to cross the Alps so decided to make for North Africa without navigator and flying a crippled bomber. The situation was serious, but displaying outstanding skill and determination, this airman succeeded in reaching an airfield in Tunisia; although he had never previously landed an aircraft, Flight Sergeant Larden came down perfectly with the undercarriage retracted. In the face of extreme peril this airman displayed courage, coolness and resource of a high order.

LONDON GAZETTE 24.9.1943

NOTES: Award effective 4 August 1943 as per AFRO 2386/43 dated 19 November 1943. Born in North Bay, Ontario, 1916. Enlisted North Bay 27 June 1941. Trained at No.3 ITS (graduated 7 November 1941), No.4 BGS (graduated 28 March1942), No.8 AOS (graduated 16 February 1942) and No.2 ANS (graduated 11 May a942). Sergeants Guy and Mithem were awarded D.F.M.'s and Sergeant Aaron a posthumous V.C. for this action.

LONGLEY 1486967 Flight Sergeant Rupert Percy
218 Squadron, Royal Air Force Volunteer Reserve

"In recognition of gallantry and devotion to duty in the execution of air operations."

This airman was the wireless operator in an aircraft detailed to attack Neuss one night in January 1945. During the operation the aircraft sustained severe damage. In spite of this the pilot succeeded in reaching Allied territory where he was forced to give the order to abandon as the aircraft had now become uncontrollable. One member of the crew, whose parachute had opened by accident inside the fuselage was therefore unwilling to jump. He asked to be allowed to strap himself to Flight Sergeant Longley's back. The latter without the slightest hesitation agreed. After the two airmen had been strapped together they made their way, in total darkness, to the jumping point. On the way the ripcord of Flight Sergeant Longley's parachute caught in a projection. Although the parachute opened he was able to catch and hold the case intact and, with his comrade on his back, jumped clear of the aircraft. Unfortunately, in the descent, his comrade fell away. Flight Sergeant Longley came down on a tall tree from which he fell to the ground and badly injured his back.

184

FOR CONSPICUOUS GALLANTRY

His action in allowing a comrade to descend with him on a single parachute, although unavailing, showed a spirit of gallantry and self-sacrifice which will long be remembered.

LONDON GAZETTE 13.4.1945

M

McGARRY 1344057 Sergeant John Patrick
70 Squadron, Royal Air Force

"In recognition of gallantry and devotion to duty in the execution of air operations."

One night in April, 1943, this airman was the navigator of an aircraft detailed to attack an enemy landing ground. During the operation the aircraft was hit by anti-aircraft fire. The pilot was severely wounded, while Sergeant McGarry was wounded in the leg. Despite his injury, this airman helped to remove the wounded pilot from the cockpit and afterwards rendered efficient first aid. Meanwhile, another member of the crew took over the control and Sergeant McGarry displaying great fortitude continued his navigational duties. In addition, throughout the return flight. he tended his injured pilot. When base was reached the pilot took over the controls to attempt a landing. Sergeant McGarry was given permission to leave by parachute but elected to stay with his pilot and a successful crash landing was made near the airfield. In perilous circumstances. Sergeant McGarry displayed courage, fortitude and coolness worthy of the highest praise.

LONDON GAZETTE 4.6.1943

NOTES: The pilot Sgt. Petrie was also awarded the C.G.M. for this action.

Killed in action 2.7.1943, no known gave. He is commemorated on the Malta Memorial, Panel 9, Column 1.

Medals comprising C.G.M. (Flying), 1939-45 Star, Italy Star, War Medal appeared for sale at Christies on 25.3.1986.

FOR CONSPICUOUS GALLANTRY

MATHERS Aus.413221 Flight Sergeant Francis Edwin
77 Squadron, Royal Australian Air Force

"In recognition of gallantry displayed in flying operations against the enemy."

One night in June, 1 943, Sergeants French and Spedie were the wireless operator / air gunner and rear gunner respectively of an aircraft piloted by Flight Sergeant Mathers, which attacked Mulheim. Whilst over the target area, the bomber was subjected to heavy fire from the ground defences and was repeatedly hit. Two engines were rendered unserviceable in quick succession, while the starboard aileron control was shot away and 3 petrol tanks were pierced all of which leaked rapidly. In spite of this, Flight Sergeant Mathers flew clear of the defences and set course for this country. On the return flight, the bomber gradually lost height and all movable equipment including the guns of the mid-upper turret and some ammunition, were jettisoned Shortly after crossing the enemy coast, the disabled aircraft was intercepted by an enemy fighter. In the ensuing engagement, Sergeant Spedie skillfully used his guns and, eventually with a devastating burst from close range, he shot the attacker down into the sea. The bomber was down to 500 feet but, displaying superb airmanship, Flight Sergeant Mathers, receiving much assistance from Sergeant French who diligently worked his wireless apparatus to obtain direction fixes, struggled on to reach an airfield near the coast. Although the undercarriage could not be lowered, this pilot successfully effected a crash-landing. In most harassing circumstances Flight Sergeant Mathers displayed exceptional skill, courage and fortitude, while Sergeants French and Spedie displayed conduct worthy of the highest praise.

LONDON GAZETTE 16.7.1943

NOTES: Sergeant French and sergeant Spedie were both awarded the D.F.M. for this action.

Killed in action 5.9.1943. He is buried in Durnbach War Cemetery, Germany.

For Conspicuous Gallantry

MAYER 1040284 Flight Sergeant Stanley
101 Squadron, Royal Air Force Volunteer Reserve

"In recognition of gallantry displayed in flying operations against the enemy."

This Warrant Officer (W.O. Walker) and airman were pilot and flight engineer respectively of an aircraft detailed to attack Hanover one night in September, 1943. In the run-up to the target, the bomber was illuminated by the searchlights and subjected to heavy anti-aircraft fire, while immediately afterwards it was attacked by an enemy fighter. The aircraft was repeatedly hit and sustained serious damage. One of it's engines was set alight but, with great coolness, Warrant Officer Walker went into a steep dive and thus evaded the fighter, whilst the force of the wind extinguished the flames. Meanwhile, a fire had started amidships. Flight Sergeant Mayer, displaying great gallantry and promptitude, made strenuous efforts to prevent the flames from spreading. He succeeded in getting the outbreak under control before he was overcome by the fumes. He was dragged clear, however, and the fire was afterwards extinguished. The situation was very serious but, undaunted, Warrant Officer Walker went on to release his bombs on the target. Displaying superb airmanship, this gallant and resolute pilot flew his crippled bomber to this country where he effected a safe landing in appalling weather. Throughout the return flight Sergeant Mayer rendered material assistance, while his exemplary conduct in the face of imminent dangers was beyond praise.

LONDON GAZETTE 2.11.1943

NOTES: Warrant Officer Walker was also awarded the C.G.M. for this action.

Killed in action 26.11.1943. Buried in Heverlee War Cemetery, Belgium.

MAXWELL Can/R.165426 Flight Sergeant Robert Burton
428 Squadron, Royal Canadian Air Force

In August, 1944, Flight Sergeant Maxwell was detailed to attack a target in Germany. When nearing the objective, his aircraft was struck by anti-aircraft fire, disabling engine and damaging the electrical system. Despite loss of height and a wound in the leg, this airman pressed on to the target where the bombs had to be released manually. Flight Sergeant Maxwell then flew his aircraft back to England and effected a safe landing. His coolness, courage and determination to achieve success have been of a high order.

LONDON GAZETTE 24.10.1944

NOTES: Awarded D.F.C. 25.9.1945.

Born 1924 in Toronto; Enlisted 12 May 1942.

Trained at No.1 ITS, No.12 EFTS and No.5 SFTS (graduated 11 June1943). Commissioned August 1944. Incident described was 25 August 1944 (target, Russelshein).

MEADOWS Can/R.191205 Sergeant George William
166 Squadron, Royal Canadian Air Force

"In recognition of gallantry displayed in flying operations against the enemy."

This airman was the rear gunner of a bomber detailed to attack Berlin one night in November, 1943. During the operation the aircraft was attacked by a fighter. Bullets from the enemy aircraft hit and damaged the mid-upper and rear turrets. One bullet struck Sergeant Meadows in the back. It was deflected by the wiring in his electrically heated clothing and came out in the groin. Another attack developed and the mid-upper gunner, the wireless operator and the navigator were wounded. Despite his injury, Sergeant Meadows remained in his turret and, by his excellent co-operation with his pilot, together with his good shooting, beat off a further 8 attacks by fighters. This airman displayed skill, courage and fortitude of a high order.

LONDON GAZETTE 24.12.1943

MEEK Can/R.138466 Warrant Officer Richard Jack
626 Squadron, Royal Canadian Air Force

"In recognition of gallantry displayed in flying operations against the enemy."

Flying Officer Breckenridge, Pilot Officer Baker and Warrant Officer Meek were pilot, mid-upper gunner and navigator respectively of an aircraft detailed to attack Berlin one night in January 1944. Whilst over the target area, the aircraft was hit by bullets from a fighter. Much damage was sustained, the wireless operator was killed and the rear gunner was wounded. Pilot Officer Baker was also wounded, being hit in the face and rendered unconscious. Nevertheless, Flying Officer Breckenridge evaded the attacker and, displaying great determination, resumed his bombing run and successfully attacked the target. Almost immediately the bomber was again hit by machine gun fire from the enemy aircraft, which had closed in. This time, Warrant Officer Meek was severely wounded, a bullet penetrated his breast bone close to the heart and another one hit him in the shoulder. Coolly and skillfully Flying Officer Breckenridge manoeuvred his badly damaged aircraft, however, and finally evaded the attacker. By now, Pilot Officer Baker had recovered consciousness and, realizing that the aircraft was unprotected, immediately made his way to the rear turret and manned it in spite of his physical suffering, the intense cold and the lack of oxygen. Pilot Officer Baker remained in the turret throughout the homeward flight, except for a short time when he left it to extinguish a fire which had commenced. Meanwhile Warrant Officer Meek, though desperately wounded and suffering intensely, refused to leave his post. Although deprived of practically all his navigational equipment, he plotted the route home with great skill. Eventually Flying Officer Breckenridge reached base where he effected a successful crash landing. His skill, courage and coolness in the face of heavy odds were worthy of the highest praise. Pilot Officer Baker and Warrant Officer Meek proved themselves to be valiant members of aircraft crew, displaying great courage, fortitude and devotion to duty. In spite of their injuries and much suffering they did all that was possible to assist in the safe return of the aircraft.

LONDON GAZETTE 22.2.1944

NOTES: Incident occurred 30/31 January 1944, Lancaster LM584 (UM-Y2).

Award effective 9 February 1944 AFRO 644/44 dated 24th March 1944. Born 1908 in Vancouver; home there (wireless engineer); enlisted there 11 November 1941. Trained at No.7 ITS (graduated 3rd July 1942) and No.5 AOS (graduated 23 October 1942).

Commissioned March 1944.

Pilot Officer Baker and Flying Officer Breckenridge were both awarded the D.F.C. for this action.

Awarded the D.F.C. as Pilot Officer 17.11.1944.

MORIARTY N.Z.421549 Flight Sergeant David John
75 (N.Z.) Squadron, Royal New Zealand Air Force

One morning in July, 1944, this airman was captain of an aircraft detailed to attack an objective in Northern France. Whilst over the target are his aircraft was hit by an anti- aircraft shell which exploded in the cockpit. Flight Sergeant Moriarty was severely inured about the face being completely blinded in one eye which was badly lacerated by flying glass or shell fragments; he also sustained a nasty scalp wound. After receiving first aid he insisted on remaining at the controls. In spite of his distress he succeeded in flying the aircraft home. This airman displayed courage, fortitude and determination of a high order.

LONDON GAZETTE 15.9.1944

NOTES: Later commissioned.

N

NORRIS 1411327 Sergeant James William
61 Squadron, Royal Air Force Volunteer Reserve

"In recognition of gallantry displayed in flying operations against the enemy."

This airman was the flight engineer of an aircraft detailed to attack Dusseldorf. Soon after crossing the enemy coast, the aircraft was attacked by a fighter and sustained damage. A few minutes later another fighter attacked. The bomber was struck by a hail of bullets. The windscreen was broken, the wireless and other important equipment were destroyed and the oxygen system was rendered useless. The pilot, the wireless operator and the flight engineer were wounded and the navigator was killed. The aircraft became difficult to control but, despite this, the pilot continued to the target, being greatly assisted by sergeant Norris, whose strenuous efforts were invaluable. Shortly after the target had been successfully attacked, the pilot collapsed owing to his wounds. Sergeant Norris took over the controls and, at times aided by another member of the crew succeeded in flying the damaged bomber to this country. When an airfield was sighted, Sergeant Norris and his comrade succeeded in rallying the semi-conscious pilot sufficiently to take over and land the aircraft safely. Not until then, did Sergeant Norris disclose that he had been wounded in the arm. In circumstances fraught with great danger, this airman displayed courage, fortitude and determination of the highest order.

LONDON GAZETTE 3.12.1943

NOTES: Flight Lieutenant Reid was awarded the V.C. and Flight Sergeant Emerson the D.F.M. for this action.

NUTTALL 1684518 Warrant Officer Squire, D.F.M.
35 Squadron, Royal Air Force Volunteer Reserve

LONDON GAZETTE 26.10.1945

NOTES: Awarded D.F.M. 12.12.1944

O

OLIVER 618877 Sergeant George William
467 (R.A.A.F.) Squadron, Royal Air Force

"In recognition of gallantry displayed in flying operations against the enemy."

One night in August, 1943, these airmen (Warrant Officer Leonard Wilson and Sergeant Oliver) were pilot and mid-upper gunner respectively of an aircraft detailed to attack Peenemunde. The objective was successfully bombed but, shortly afterwards, the aircraft was hit by cannon fire from an enemy fighter. The rear gunner was wounded, his turret was rendered useless and ammunition in the aircraft was set alight, while the elevator and rudder trimmers were shot away. In spite of these harassing circumstances, Sergeant Oliver fought the attacker with great determination and succeeded in shooting it down. He then turned his attention towards the fire which was beginning to spread and, with assistance from other members of the crew, succeeded in quelling it. Meanwhile, Warrant Officer Wilson coolly and skillfully evaded several fighters and afterwards flew the crippled bomber to base. This pilot displayed superb qualities throughout, while Sergeant Olivers courageous and skilful efforts proved of the greatest assistance.

LONDON GAZETTE 7.9.1943

NOTES: Warrant Officer Wilson was awarded the D.F.C for this action.

P

PENROSE 1113654 Warrant Officer Alan, D.F.C.

157 Squadron, Royal Air Force Volunteer Reserve

LONDON GAZETTE 21.9.1945

NOTES: Awarded D.F.C. 20.10.1944, bar to the D.F.C. 9.3.1945.

Commissioned as Pilot Officer.

PETRIE 1070296 Sergeant Thomas Parker

70 Squadron, Royal Air Force

"In recognition of gallantry and devotion to duty in the execution of air operations."

One night in April, 1943. this airman was the pilot and captain of an aircraft detailed to attack an enemy landing ground. In the run up the aircraft was hit by anti-aircraft fire but Sergeant Petrie held course and a stick of bombs was re-leased. Almost immediately the aircraft was again hit which caused it to dive steeply. Sergeant Petrie was severely wounded, his foot being practically severed, while other members of the crew were slightly wounded. Despite his injuries. Sergeant Petrie skillfully regained control of his aircraft, circled and released the remaining bombs over the target area. Course having been set for home, the injured pilot was removed from his seat and given first aid, while another member of the crew kept the aircraft on its course to base. When the airfield was reached, Sergeant Petrie who, throughout the return flight, though in considerable pain and feint through loss of blood had remained in command as captain, gave the crew permission to leave by parachute. They elected to remain. However, confident in his ability to effect a landing. By strapping him in the pilot's seat and tying his uninjured foot to the rudder bar. Sergeant Petrie was able to take over the controls. When approaching land, at a height of 3oo feet, the petrol supply ran out but a successful crash-landing was made. This gallant airman displayed great courage and fortitude in keeping with the highest traditions of the Royal Air Force.

LONDON GAZETTE 4.6.1943

NOTES: The navigator, Sgt. McGarry, who took over the controls and flew the bomber home was also awarded the C.G.M. for this action.

PIALUCHA P.781051 Sergeant Jozef
300 (Polish) Squadron, Polish Air Force

Sergeant Pialucha was flight engineer in a Lancaster bomber, piloted by Flight Sergeant Stepian, ordered to attack the German strongholds at Emiéville. On reaching the target, and on the bombing run, they were hit by flak which caused the bombing installation to become unserviceable, and they were therefore unable to release the bombs. Flight Sergeant Zentar, the rear gunner, was manouevering his turret when the flak hit and the blast blew his turret beyond its normal limits, ripping open the steel doors behind him. He was sucked out of the turret only saved from falling by his left foot which was trapped in the doorway. Sergeant Pialucha and Flight Sergeant Derewienko went to his aid but were unable to pull him back into the aircraft. As they attempted the rescue, Flight Sergeant Zentars foot began to slip from his trapped shoe as the lace began to snap. Derewienko grabbed his trousers which also began to rip. Pialucha disregarding his own safety climbed through the opening between the turret and the aircraft and holding onto the aircraft with one hand, succeeded in getting a loop of rope around Flight Sergeant Zentars body to prevent him falling, the aircraft was at this point now over the English Channel. The rope was then secured to the turret seat and Pialucha climbed back inside the aircraft and returned to his duties, assisting the pilot to get the damaged aircraft back to England. The aircraft landed at Tangmere, with a full bomb load, and Flight Sergeant Zentar, who had had to swing from side to side during the landing to avoid hitting the runway with his head, was finally rescued. There is no doubt that had Pialucha not secured the rope around Zentar he would have fallen to his death.

LONDON GAZETTE not published, award approved on 28th August 1944.

NOTES: Killed in action 1st September 1944, buried in the Belgrade cemetery.

FOR CONSPICUOUS GALLANTRY

POWELL 655888 Sergeant James Stephen
224 Squadron, Royal Air Force

"In recognition of gallantry displayed in flying operations against the enemy."

In May, 1943, this airman captained an aircraft engaged on an anti submarine patrol. During the flight a U boat was sighted on the surface of the water. In the face of fire from the vessel's guns, Sergeant Powell executed 2 vigorous attacks. Sergeant Powell was compelled to rest, as he was dazed from the concussion of a cannon shell which had burst beside his cockpit but, half an hour later, he once more assumed control and, shortly afterwards, 2 further attacks were executed On enemy submarines This airman displayed conspicuous gallantry and skill throughout

LONDON GAZETTE 11.6.1943

PREECE 934814 Flight Sergeant Ivor Ward
106 Squadron, Royal Air Force

"In recognition of gallantry displayed in flying operations against the enemy."

No further information available surrounding this award.

LONDON GAZETTE 11.6.1943

R

REARDON ASN 31143820 Sergeant James J.
558th Bomb Squadron, United States Army Air Force

ON 12th June, 1944, this airman was bombardier in a Marauder aircraft during a raid over the Normandy battle front. It was a low level sortie and it came under intense ground fire as the aircraft commenced the bombing run, and a burst of an exploding anti-aircraft shell smashed in the front of the aircraft, wounding Sergeant Reardon. He remained at his post, and successfully dropped his bombs on a concentration of enemy forces, informing no member of crew of his wounds despite a severe loss of blood. They were hit again by flak, this time a direct hit in the port engine which sent the aircraft out of control.

The pilot, Captain Thomas J.James, struggled with the controls and they were out over the channel before he managed to regain control. It was only at this point that Sergeant Reardon revealed his condition to the co-pilot who pulled him out of the shattered nose section and administered first aid. The actions of Sergeant Reardon were considered in keeping with the high standard set by his brother members of the Royal Air Force and recommended for approval of the King in January 1945.

LONDON GAZETTE Not gazetted.

NOTES: Also awarded a second purple heart for this action.

REES Aus. 415193 Flight Sergeant Daniel
460 (R.A.A.F.) Squadron, Royal Australian Air Force

"In recognition of gallantry displayed in flying operations against the enemy."

One night in August, 1943, this airman displayed superb skill when piloting an aircraft detailed for an operation against Milan. During the outward flight, two of the bomber's engines became defective but Flight Sergeant Rees continued to his far distant target and bombed it, afterwards flying the disabled aircraft to base. One night in August, 1943, Flight Sergeant Rees took part in an attack on a target at

197

Peenemunde. Whilst over the target area, the aircraft was attacked by a fighter. The attacker was driven off but the bomber had been repeatedly hit. The starboard tail plane and the trimming tabs were shot away, one engine and the hydraulic system was damaged, while one of the petrol tanks was pierced and its contents lost. Despite this, Flight Sergeant Rees coolly and skillfully flew the damaged bomber to base. This airman, who has completed many sorties, has displayed courage and tenacity of a high degree.

LONDON GAZETTE 24.9.1943

NOTES: Later commissioned.

ROBB Warrant Officer Angus
405 (R.C.A.F.) Squadron, Royal Air Force

P/O/ Van Metre and W/O Robb were wireless operator and upper gunner respectively in an aircraft detailed to attack Dessau. Whilst over the target the aircraft was attacked by three enemy fighters. The first enemy aircraft to attack was shot down by the rear gunner. W/O/ Robb engaged the second fighter. Following a short but accurate burst of fire from his guns the enemy aircraft fell to the ground. The remaining fighter attacked with great persistence. The rear gun-turret of the bomber was badly hit and set on fire. The rear gunner was trapped. P/O Van Metre and W/O/ Robb, displaying the greatest determination, immediately went to the assistance of their trapped comrade. By their joint efforts, these crew members finally extinguished the flames and extricated the rear gunner from the gun turret. P/O Van Metre had severely burned his hands. In spite of much pain he returned to his post to work at his wireless apparatus throughout the return flight. P/O/ Van Metre and W/O Robb set a fine example of courage and resolution in very trying circumstances.

LONDON GAZETTE 18.5.1945

NOTES: Pilot Officer Van Metre received the D.F.C. for his part in this action.

Medals comprising 1939-45 Star, Air Crew Europe Star (clasp France & Germany), War Medal, appeared for sale at Christie's on 3.4.1984.

ROE 1813968 Acting Warrant Officer Victor Arthur, D.F.M.

35 Squadron, Royal Air Force Volunteer Reserve

"In recognition of gallantry and devotion to duty in the execution of air operations."

LONDON GAZETTE 13.4.1945

NOTES: Awarded D.F.M. 13.6.1944. Killed action 5/6th March 1945, no known grave, he is commemorated on the Runnymede Memorial, Panel 269.

RUSSELL Can/R.120651 Flight Sergeant Joseph Vincent

15 Squadron, Royal Canadian Air Force

One night in October 1943, this airman piloted an aircraft detailed to attack Kassel. Whilst making his bombing run the aircraft was subjected to heavy fire from the ground defences, but Flight Sergeant Russell held to his course and executed his bombing attack. Almost immediately the aircraft was repeatedly hit by machine gun fire from a fighter. Extensive damage was sustained causing the bomber to become difficult to control, but displaying superb airmanship Flight Sergeant Russell flew the crippled bomber to an airfield in this country. Although almost exhausted by his efforts he succeeded in effecting a safe landing. This airman displayed outstanding courage and tenacity.

LONDON GAZETTE 29.10.1943

NOTES: Award effective 27 October 1943 AFRO 2457/43 dated 26 November 1943. Born in Lisburn, County Antrim, Ireland, 1920; home in Saskatchewan . Trained at No.7 ITS, No.16 EFTS and No.7 SFTS. Arrived at Personnel Reception Centre, in England, 1st December 1942. Further trained at No.14 (P) AFRU (23rd March to 10th May 1943) and No.30 OTU (11 May 1943). Went on to No.1651 Conversion Unit; to No.15 Squadron, 19th August 1943. Commissioned after CGM event (J18912). Killed in action with this unit, 20/21 February 1944 (Lancaster LM456); buried in Germany.

S

SCOTT 525496 Warrant Officer Hugh
223 Squadron, Royal Air Force

No information available surrounding this award.

LONDON GAZETTE 26.10.1945

SIMPSON 1594208 Sergeant George Wilfred
463 (R.A.A.F.) Squadron, Royal Air Force Volunteer Reserve

"In recognition of gallantry and devotion to duty in the execution of air operations."

One night in April, 1945, these officers (A/F.O. Cox and F.O. Wainwright) and this airman were pilot, navigator and flight engineer respectively of an aircraft detailed to attack the heavily defended oil target at Tonsberg. When nearing the target the aircraft was attacked and severely damaged by an enemy fighter. Flying Officer Cox and sergeant Simpson sustained injuries but nevertheless remained at their posts. The nose of the aircraft was shattered and gaping holes were torn in the fuselage. The windows of the pilot's compartment were blown out and much equipment was lost. The bombsight was rendered useless and it was therefore impossible to bomb the target with any accuracy. The aircraft began to lose height and it seemed as though it would have to be abandoned but Flying officer Cox succeeded in regaining control. he then skillfully manoeuvered his aircraft to enable his gunners to attack the enemy fighter which was shot down in flames. Meanwhile despite suffering intense pain from severe frost bite, caused to their hands by the bitter winds blowing through the open nose of the aircraft, Flying Officer Wainwright and Sergeant Simpson did everything possible to assist their pilot in his endeavour to fly the crippled aircraft to a friendly airfield. After much difficulty this was eventually accomplished and a skillful landing was made. The coolness and devotion to duty of these officers and this airman were an inspiration to their squadron.

LONDON GAZETTE 3.8.1945

NOTES: Acting Flying Officer Cox and Flying Officer Wainwright were both awarded the D.S.O. for this action.

Medals comprising C.G.M. (Flying), 1939-45 Star, France & Germany Star, Defence Medal, War Medal, offered for sale at Buckland, Dix & Wood on 19.4.1995.

SLOAN 1550966 Sergeant Stuart Nimmo

"In recognition of gallantry displayed in flying operations against the enemy."

One night in May, ,3, Flying Officer Bailey and Sergeants Sloan and Parslow were members of the crew of an aircraft detailed to attack Dortmund . Shortly after its bombs had been released, the aircraft was badly damaged by antiaircraft fire whilst held by the searchlights. Evasive action was taken by putting the aircraft into a steep dive but this proved ineffective and the bomber was subjected to heavy fire whilst still illuminated. The situation became critical but Sergeant Sloan, displaying superb skill and determination eventually flew clear of the defences and headed for this Country. A hatch was open and could not be closed, the rear turret door was also open and wind of great force blew through the length of the aircraft. All the lights in the navigator' s cabin were extinguished but in the face of extreme difficulty Sergeant Parslow plotted a course. On the return flight, he and Flying Officer Bailey assisted Sergeant Sloan in every way within their power and eventually this gallant airman flew the badly damaged bomber to an airfield and effected a good landing. In appalling circumstances these members of aircraft crew displayed Courage. determination and fortitude of the highest order.

LONDON GAZETTE 11.6.1943

NOTES: Flying Officer Bailey was awarded the D.F.C. and Sergeant Parslow the D.F.M. for this action.

Awarded D.F.C. 1945. After the war he flew with the Kings Flight before retiring in 1951 and was appointed M.V.O.

SMITH Aus.424847 Flight Sergeant Geoffrey Charles Chapman
156 Squadron, Royal Australian Air Force

"In recognition of gallantry displayed in flying operations against the enemy."

This airman was rear gunner of an aircraft detailed to attack Berlin one night in February 1944. When nearing the target Flight Sergeant Smith reported a fighter coming in to attack. As evading action was being taken the bomber was hit by cannon and machine gun fire from the enemy aircraft. Flight Sergeant Smith was hit by a bullet which shattered the lower part of his right leg and foot. The hydraulic gear had been damaged and his turret was rendered unserviceable. Although suffering intensely and in a dazed condition. Flight Sergeant Smith refused assistance and insisted on remaining at his post to manipulate his turret manually until he enemy coast was crossed. In most distressing circumstances, this gallant airman, whose leg has since been amputated, displayed courage and fortitude of high order. His determination to defend his aircraft until the enemy coast was crossed set a magnificent example.

LONDON GAZETTE 7.3.1944

STEERE 1460321 Sergeant Gilbert Ebenezer James
429 (R.C.A.F.) Squadron, Royal Air Force Volunteer Reserve

These airmen, Sergeants Steer, Mangione and Ritchie, were flight engineer, mid-upper and rear gunners respectively of an aircraft detailed for a sortie one night in June, 1944. Over the enemy coast the aircraft was hit by anti-aircraft fire and the pilot was mortally wounded. He gave orders to the remainder of the crew to leave by parachute but Sergeant Steere, realising that his wounded comrade would not be able to follow, disregarded the order. He went to his wounded comrade and together they succeeded in regaining control of the aircraft. Sergeant Steere then discovered that Sergeants Mangione and Ritchie had also stayed in the aircraft and were ready to assist in rendering what aid they could to their fatally injured pilot. This done, they did everything possible to assist Sergeant Steere who had taken over the controls in an effort to fly the aircraft home. Although he had no previous experience he flew to an airfield. After making contact with the ground personnel by radio telephone he circled the airfield whilst Sergeants Mangione and Ritchie gave additional first aid to the pilot and then parachuted him out of the aircraft on a static line in a last effort to save his life. Only when he was sure that his other two comrades had safely left the aircraft by parachute did Sergeant Steere then leave himself. In the face of a trying ordeal these airmen displayed great courage and devotion to duty setting an example of the highest order.

LONDON GAZETTE 21.7.1944

NOTES: Sergeants Mangione and Ritchie were awarded the D.F.M. for this action.

STUART 658038 Flight Sergeant Frederick John
426 (R.C.A.F.) Squadron, Royal Air Force

"In recognition of gallantry displayed in flying operations against the enemy."

One night in October, 1943, this airman piloted an aircraft detailed to attack Leipzig. Before the target was reached the aircraft was intercepted by a fighter which attacked with great persistence. Much damage was sustained before Flight Sergeant Stuart succeeded in flying clear. Shortly afterwards, another fighter made a series of attacks but, with superb skill, Flight Sergeant Stuart evaded them. His aircraft was badly crippled. The cockpits, turrets, hydraulic gear and other essential equipment were damaged. The petrol tanks had been pierced and one of the gunners wounded. Undaunted, this valiant pilot went on to bomb his target and afterwards flew the crippled bomber back to base where he effected a masterly landing. In the face of heavy odds, this airman set an example of courage, resolution and devotion to duty beyond praise.

LONDON GAZETTE 19.11.1943

NOTES: Killed in action 20.12.1943, buried in Rheinburg Cemetery, Germany.

T

TAYLOR 748057 Warrant Officer Harry Forbes McPherson
156 Squadron, Royal Air Force

"In recognition of gallantry and devotion to duty in the execution of air operations."

LONDON GAZETTE 20.4.1943

NOTES: Awarded D.F.C. 15.6.1943.

TICKLER 1383853 Sergeant Edward Wells
No 49 Squadron

"In recognition of gallantry displayed in flying operations against the enemy."

One night in February, 1943, Flight Sergeants Matthews and Lowans and Sergeant Silvester were members of the crew of an aircraft captained by Sergeant Tickler, which was detailed for a mine-laying mission. When well on the outward flight an armed ship opened fire on the aircraft and the rear turret was hit but the captain proceeded on his course. Visibility in the target area was poor and Sergeant Tickler had to bring the aircraft down to 700 feet to locate the objective. Whilst at this height, during the commencement of its attacking run the aircraft was engaged by the ground defences. A number of anti-aircraft guns opened fire whilst it was held in the searchlights and the bomber was hit in the navigator's compartment, the rear turret, the pilot's cockpit and in the port wing. The flight engineer was severely wounded in the head and became unconscious. Sergeant Tickler was hit in the left shoulder and side, becoming so dazed that he almost lost control of the aircraft which commenced to dive. Sergeant Matthews, with great promptitude, however, pulled back the control column and brought the aircraft back to a height of 700 feet. Displaying great fortitude, Sergeant Tickler kept to his course and the mines were dropped in the correct place. Not until this was accomplished did he inform his comrades of his injuries. On the return flight, although his left arm was entirely useless, he remained at the controls, being greatly assisted by Flight Sergeant Lowans and Sergeant Silvester who did everything possible to mitigate his task. Meanwhile, Flight Sergeant Matthews displayed great navigational ability and, although deprived of all wireless aid, he set courses which enabled his captain to reach an airfield in this country. Despite his injuries, Sergeant Tickler effected a perfect landing before collapsing over the controls. This captain displayed courage, fortitude and devotion to duty of the highest order, while the skill, gallantry and team work of his comrades, who rendered such valuable support, were worthy of high praise.

LONDON GAZETTE 2.4.1943

NOTES: Flight Sergeant John Lamont Matthews and Flight Sergeant Edward John Lowans were awarded the Distinguished Flying Medal for the same action.

Tickler was commissioned as a Flight Lieutenant following this action.

Shot down in a raid over Nuremberg and taken prisoner. Held at Stalag L1 at Barth.

TOMKINS 1579116 Flight Sergeant Frederick
180Squadron, Royal Air Force Volunteer Reserve

"In recognition of gallantry displayed in flying operations against the enemy."

In December, 1944, this airman was the wireless operator in an aircraft detailed to attack a target in the Stralen area. During the sortie the aircraft was hit by anti-aircraft fire and sustained damage. The navigator and the pilot were wounded, the latter severely. Some Verey cartridges near the pilot were set alight. The cockpit became filled with smoke which obscured most of the flying instruments. A small fire stared amidships. Flight Sergeant Tomkins saw that the navigator was dealing successfully with the fire so he promptly crawled over the bomb bay to assist the injured pilot who, by now, was in a state bordering on collapse. He rallied when succoured by Sergeant Tomkins who afterwards took over the controls and flew the aircraft to an airfield in friendly territory. Here, under the instructions of his wounded pilot, he brought the aircraft down safely. In the face of most trying circumstances, Sergeant Tomkins displayed courage, coolness and resource of a high order.

FOR CONSPICUOUS GALLANTRY

LONDON GAZETTE 23.1.1945

TOWNSEND 656738 Flight Sergeant William Clifford, D.F.M.
617 Squadron, Royal Air Force

On the night of 16th May, 1943, a force of Lancaster bombers was detailed to attack the Möehne, Eder and Sorpe dams in Germany. The operation was one of great difficulty and hazard, demanding a high degree of skill and courage and close co-operation between the crews of the aircraft engaged. Nevertheless, a telling blow was struck at the enemy by the successful breaching of the Möehne, and Eder dams. This outstanding success reflects the greatest credit on the efforts of the following personnel who participated in the operation in various capacities as members of aircraft crew.

Flight Sergeant Townsend was Captain, Pilot Officer Howard, Navigator and Sergeant Franklin, Air Bomber of an aircraft detailed to attack the Ennepe Dam. By displaying a very high degree of skill and judgement, Flight Sergeant Townsend brought his aircraft to a position from which Sergeant Franklin could hardly miss. On the way to the target, much opposition was encountered but by the display of great determination on the part of Flight Sergeant Townsend and by great navigational skill on the part of Pilot Officer Howard, their aircraft returned safely to base. I strongly recommend that the outstanding achievement of this crew be recognised by the immediate award of the Conspicuous Gallantry Medal to Flight Sergeant Townsend, the Distinguished Flying Cross to Pilot Officer Howard and the first bar to the Distinguished Flying Medal to Sergeant Franklin.

LONDON GAZETTE 28.5.1943

NOTES: This was the famous dam-buster raid led by Wing Commander Guy Gibson, a number of awards were made for this raid including the C.G.M.'s to F/Sgt. Williams and F/Sgt. Townsend, D.F.M. and the Victoria Cross to Guy Gibson.

The BBC broadcast the following announcement on the 17th May 1943, "The Air Ministry has just issued the following communique: In the early hours of this morning a force of Lancasters of Bomber Command led by Wing Commander G.P.Gibson, D.S.O., D.F.C. attacked with mines the dams of the Möehne, and Sorpe reservoir. These control two thirds of the water storage capacity of the Ruhr basin. Reconnaissance later established that the möehne dam had also been breached over a length of 100 yards and that the power station below had been swept away by the resulting flood. The Eder dam which controls the head water of the Weser and Fulder valleys and operates several power stations was also attacked and was reported as being breached. Photographs show the river below the dam in full flood. The attacks were pressed home from a very low level with great determination and coolness in the face of fierce resistance. Eight of the Lancasters are missing.

Awarded the D.F.M. 14.5.1943.

Flight Lieutenant William Clifford Townsend, C.G.M., D.F.M. (1921-1991), born at Brookend, Gloucester, enlisted in the Army in January 1941 and transferred to the Royal Air Force in the following May After completing his initial flying instruction in January 1942 and his operational training (16 OTU) in March he was posted to No. 49 Squadron (Lancasters) as a Sergeant Pilot in June. 'Bill' Townsend's first 'Freshman' mission, laying mines in the Kattegat was successfully completed on the night 18/19 September 1942 and during the following five months he flew a further 25 sorties which included bombing attacks against Wismar Osnabruck, Cologne, Genoa, Hamburg, Essen, Dusseldorf Wilhelmshaven, Bremem, Nuremburg and St.Nazaire (D.F.M). Chosen to join the newly formed 'special' 617 Squadron, Townsend was posted to Scampton 25 March 1943 and was promoted to Temporary Flight Sergeant 1 April- He led the third wave of Lancasters during Operation Chastise on the night 16/17th May when only his aircraft attacked the Ennepe Dam (C.G.M.). Was commissioned Pilot Officer in June 1943 with effect from the previous March, Flying Officer, September and Flight Lieutenant March 1945. Following the Dams raid Townsend flew a further five sorties with the Squadron before being posted to India where he finished the war as an instructor. Flight Lieutenant 'Bill' Townsend was released from the Royal Air Force in May 1946 and relinquished his Commission in 1959, retaining his rank in the Air Force Reserve.

Bill Townsend worked for a number of years with 2516 (Droitwich) Squadron Air Training Corps. He died in April 1991 his memorial service being held in Holy Trinity Church, Lickey, Birmingham included a fly-past by Tornados from the modern day 617 Squadron as a tribute to the last of the British Dambuster pilots.

Medals comprising C.G.M. (Flying), D.F.M., 1939-45 Star, Air Crew Europe Star, Defence medal and War Medal appeared for sale at Spink on 23.9.1993

TREGUNNO 1031723 Warrant Officer Sidney James
51 Squadron, Royal Air Force Volunteer Reserve

No information available surrounding this award. *Fallows Collection.*

LONDON GAZETTE 26.10.1945

TURNBULL 4343733 Warrant Officer Class 2, Lawrence William
The Glider Pilot Regiment, Army Air Corps

"For gallant and distinguished services in North West Europe."

On 24 March 1945, during the Airborne Assault across the Rhine north of Wesel, this Warrant Officer was Senior Pilot of a glider carrying a heavy load of personnel and medical equipment. Nearing the Landing Zone, whilst flying at 2,000 feet, a loose tow rope smashed across the cockpit, destroying most of the controls and breaking the fin and rudder. His glider, out of control, went down in a vertical dive but by superb work on the sole remaining control column, S.S.M. Turnbull managed to bring the aircraft back under control. At the same time, heavy small arms fire was coming up together with a substantial amount of light 20mm. Anti-Aircraft fire. The glider was hit at least five times, killing the Second Pilot and wounding two passengers. One of the wing tips was shot away and the fuselage was badly damaged. In spite of this S.S.M. Turnbull remained calm and collected and by sheer concentration on his task brought his severely damaged glider and its load down to the Landing Zone, only a hundred yards from the correct position. On the Landing Zone itself there was heavy small arms fire and the evacuation of the wounded from the glider was almost impossible. S.S.M. Turnbull organised a Stretcher Party and with complete disregard of his own personal safety successfully extricated the wounded from the aircraft. Throughout the whole flying operation and subsequently during the very difficult Landing Zone conditions, this Warrant Officer showed skill of

FOR CONSPICUOUS GALLANTRY

the highest kind and a degree of courage that was an inspiration to the personnel flying in his glider.

LONDON GAZETTE 16.8.1945

NOTES: Medals comprising C.G.M. (Flying), 1939-45 Star, Africa Star, Italy Star, France & Germany Star, Defence Medal, War Medal, General Service Medal 1918-62 (Clasps Malaya, Arabian Peninsula), appeared for sale at Spink on 17.12.1997.

V

VERTICAN 565380 Warrant Officer Harold, D.F.C.
462 Squadron, Royal Air Force

"In recognition of gallantry and devotion to duty in the execution of air operations."

This captain of aircraft has taken part in operational missions against targets in Greece, Crete, Sicily and North Africa. While engaged on a sortie in May 1943, the starboard inner engine of his aircraft failed, and Warrant Officer Vertican turned his aircraft and flew out to sea where the bombs were jettisoned. Soon the port inner engine failed and as the aircraft was gradually losing height all equipment possible was thrown overboard. Deficient of power and battling against strong winds the bomber was soon forced down to a height of 1,000 feet when a third engine failed Warrant Officer Vertican was now faced with a perilous situation but skillfully he brought the aircraft safely down on to a rough sea causing no injury to any of his crew all of whom successfully embarked in the dinghy. After 10½ days the dinghy had drifted to shore. During all this time Warrant Officer Vertican organised the consumption of the meagre rations, and did all he could to maintain the spirit of his companions at a high level which contributed much to the survival of them all. Warrant Officer Vertican displayed great courage and fortitude throughout this hazardous experience .

LONDON GAZETTE 6.7.1943

NOTES: Awarded D.F.C. 14.5.1943. Retired from the R.A.F in 1964 as Flight Lieutenant.

WALKER 1380714 Warrant Officer Joseph Samuel
101 Squadron, Royal Air Force Volunteer Reserve

"In recognition of gallantry displayed in flying operations against the enemy."

This Warrant Officer and airman (F/Sgt. Mayer) were pilot and flight engineer respectively of an aircraft detailed to attack Hanover one night in September, 1943. In the run-up to the target, the bomber was illuminated by the searchlights and subjected to heavy anti-aircraft fire, while immediately afterwards it was attacked by an enemy fighter. The aircraft was repeatedly hit and sustained serious damage. One of it's engines was set alight but, with great coolness, Warrant Officer Walker went into a steep dive and thus evaded the fighter, whilst the force of the wind extinguished the flames. Meanwhile, a fire had started amidships. Flight Sergeant Mayer, displaying great gallantry and promptitude, made strenuous efforts to prevent the flames from spreading. He succeeded in getting the outbreak under control before he was overcome by the fumes. He was dragged clear, however, and the fire was afterwards extinguished. The situation was very serious but, undaunted, Warrant Officer Walker went on to release his bombs on the target. Displaying superb airmanship, this gallant and resolute pilot flew his crippled bomber to this country where he effected a safe landing in appalling weather. Throughout the return flight Sergeant Mayer rendered material assistance, while his exemplary conduct in the face of imminent dangers was beyond praise.

LONDON GAZETTE 2.11.1943

NOTES: Flight Sergeant Mayer was also awarded the C.G.M. for this action.

Baled out after his aircraft was attacked on 26th November 1943 and was taken prisoner.

WALLACE N.Z.404104 Flight Sergeant Leslie Bruce

83 Squadron, Royal New Zealand Air Force

"In recognition of gallantry displayed in flying operations against the enemy."

One night in December, 1942, this airman was the wireless operator of an aircraft detailed to attack Munich. On the outward flight the aircraft was intercepted by an enemy fighter and subjected to a number of attacks. In the first, which was made directly from beneath the bomber, the bomb aimer was seriously wounded while Flight Sergeant Wallace received a bullet wound in the leg. Some flares inside the aircraft were set alight while the matting on the floor below the mid-upper gunner's turret and everything inflammable in close proximity became ignited and commenced to burn furiously. Despite his injury, and with complete disregard for danger, Flight Sergeant Wallace attempted to quell the flames. The heat and stifling fumes compelled him to desist several times but, undaunted he jettisoned all moveable burning material through the rear turret and finally subdued the fire. On the homeward flight, Flight Sergeant Wallace displayed great skill in obtaining fixes, sending signals and doing everything in his power to assist his pilot in flying the damaged aircraft back to this country. This airman's gallant conduct in the face of an extremely perilous situation was in keeping with the highest traditions of the Royal Air Force. He has completed numerous sorties and has always displayed exceptional devotion to duty.

LONDON GAZETTE 16.2.1943

NOTES: Later Commissioned.

WALTERS 1580298 Flight Sergeant Stanley William

44 Squadron, Royal Air Force Volunteer Reserve

"In recognition of gallantry displayed in flying operations against the enemy."

This airman has participated in a number of sorties, including attacks on Karlsruhe, Nuremburg and Munchen Gladbach. In November 1944, he was air bomber in an aircraft detailed to attack Homberg. In the vicinity of the target the aircraft came under heavy fire and was struck by high explosive shells. The cockpit was shattered. the pilot was killed and the flight engineer was badly wounded. Flight Sergeant Walters promptly assisted another member of the crew to remove his dead comrade from the pilot's seat and then took over the controls. The aircraft had sustained severe damage. One engine had been put out of action whilst a second and a third were reduced in power and vibrating badly. The hydraulic system was damaged and the flaps had edged down.

Despite this, Flight Sergeant Walters, though lesser experienced than a regular pilot, brought the aircraft to an even keel and headed for home. Although only one engine was giving full power he reached an airfield near the English coast. The aircraft was too badly damaged for Flight Sergeant Walters to attempt to bring it down safely. He gave orders for the crew to release their dead captain by parachute and then to abandon the aircraft themselves. Not until his comrades were all clear and he was satisfied that the aircraft was headed out to sea did this gallant air bomber leave himself. His cool courage, outstanding resource and determination set an example of the highest order.

LONDON GAZETTE 2.1.1945

WHEELER 1804406 Sergeant Jeffrey George
101 Squadron, Royal Air Force Volunteer Reserve

"In recognition of gallantry and devotion to duty in the execution of air operations."

Sergeant Wheeler was flight engineer in an aircraft detailed to attack the heavily defended target of Bremen in March, 1945. Whilst over the target area the aircraft was hit and damaged by enemy fire. Sergeant Wheeler was seriously wounded in the thigh. Although in great pain this resolute airman concealed the fact until well clear of the target. After receiving attention, Sergeant Wheeler insisted on being allowed to carry on with his duties. Two of the starboard engines had sustained slight damage but so well did this engineer fulfill his tasks that his captain was enabled to have full use of the four engines throughout the homeward flight. In spite of much physical distress, Sergeant Wheeler displayed outstanding devotion to duty, setting a splendid example to all. This airman has completed a large number of sorties and has invariably displayed a high degree of skill.

LONDON GAZETTE 1.6.1945

For Conspicuous Gallantry

WHITE 1383031 Warrant Officer Claude Edward
No 100 Squadron, Royal Air Force Volunteer Reserve

"In recognition of gallantry displayed in flying operations against the enemy."

One night in October, 1943, Warrant Officer White and Sergeant Dowdell were pilot and navigator respectively of an aircraft detailed to attack Leipzig. Soon after leaving the airfield, the intercommunication system became unserviceable, and later after crossing the enemy coast, one of the bomber's engines became defective. Before the propeller could be feathered, the engine burst into flames. An extinguisher failed to put out the fire completely and it burned sufficiently bright to illuminate the fuselage and tailplane. In spite of this, Warrant Officer White flew on to the target and bombed it. On the homeward flight, Sergeant Dowdell displayed exceptional skill and resource and, in spite of great difficulties, unerringly guided his pilot to base. The defective engine was still alight when the airfield was reached but Warrant Officer White effected a masterly landing. As the bomber touched down the flames from the engine shot upwards and threatened to envelop the bomber but Warrant Officer White coolly ensured that his crew safely disembarked whilst he attended to the switches and petrol cocks. In serious circumstances, this gallant pilot displayed skill, coolness and tenacity which inspired all, while Sergeant Dowdell proved a valuable member of aircraft crew and supported his captain valiantly.

LONDON GAZETTE 16.11.1943

NOTES: Sgt. Dowdell was awarded the D.F.M. for this action.

Awarded A.F.C. 1.1.1946 which was presented with his C.G.M. on 26.2.1946.

WHITE N.Z.415807 Flight Sergeant Osric Hartnell
75 (N.Z.) Squadron, Royal New Zealand Air Force

This airman was pilot of an aircraft detailed to attack Berlin one night in August, 1943. When nearing the target, the aircraft was illuminated by the searchlights and repeatedly hit by anti-aircraft fire, sustaining damage to the port main plane. Despite this, Flight Sergeant White continued his bombing run but was attacked by a fighter. The bomber was hit by the attacker's gunfire which wrecked the rear turret, killing the gunner, and causing the aircraft to dive out of control directly over the target. Nevertheless, Flight Sergeant White released his bombs and succeeded in regaining control. Considerable height had been lost but this pilot coolly and skilfully flew clear of the target area and course was set for base. Much essential equipment had been rendered useless but, with unerring skill, Flight Sergeant White flew the badly damaged bomber to base. His courage, tenacity and devotion to duty set an example of the highest order. During the return flight, Sergeants Worledge and Collins assisted their pilot in every way within their power and proved themselves most valuable members of aircraft crew, displaying great courage and resource.

LONDON GAZETTE 24.9.1943

NOTES: Sergeants Worledge and Collins were both awarded the D.F.M. for their part in this action.

WHITE 638217 Acting Flight Sergeant Thomas Emmanuel
357 Squadron, Royal Air Force Volunteer Reserve

No information available surrounding this award

LONDON GAZETTE 2.6.1944

WILKIE 1272592 Sergeant Cecil James Morley
50 Squadron, Royal Air Force

One night in June, 1943, Flying Officer Hearn and Sergeants Pointon and Wilkinson were air bomber, mid upper gunner and flight engineer respectively of an aircraft, piloted by Sergeant Wilkie, detailed to attack Cologne. Whilst over the target area, the bomber was hit by antiaircraft fire. The windscreen round the pilot's cabin was shattered and Sergeant Wilkie was blinded by flying splinters. Despite this he remained at the controls. Flying Officer Hearn and Sergeant Wilkinson were injured by fragments of shrapnel. Nevertheless, the former uncomplainingly remained at his post ready to release his bombs whilst Sergeant Wilkinson went to the assistance of his pilot and the bombing run was completed. Still unable to see, Sergeant Wilkie remained at the controls, piloting his aircraft by touch. being aided in various ways by the flight engineer and by Flying Officer Hearn who directed him in avoiding the searchlights and continuous anti aircraft fire to which the bomber was subjected. Some time later. whilst still over enemy territory. Sergeant Wilkie recovered his vision in one eve and soon succeeded in flying clear of the defences, afterwards flying the aircraft back to this country In the course of the action Sergeant Pointon had one finger severed when his turret was as damaged by a shattering blow. Although in considerable pain he remained at his post, constantly alert to the danger of fighter interference. In most harassing circumstances these members of aircraft crew displayed courage, fortitude and determination of the highest order

LONDON GAZETTE 23.7.1943

NOTES: Flying Officer Hearn was awarded the D.F.C. and Sergeants Pointon and Wilkinson the D.F.M. for this action.

WILLIAMS Aus.411624 Flight Sergeant Norman Francis, D.F.M.
35 Squadron, Royal Australian Air Force

"In recognition of gallantry and devotion to duty in the execution of air operations."

One night in June, 1943, this airman was the rear gunner of an aircraft detailed to attack Dusseldorf. During the operation, the bomber was intercepted by 2 enemy fighters. In the first encounter, Flight Sergeant Williams' turret was rendered unserviceable, while he sustained several bullet wounds in the legs and body. Nevertheless, when the second fighter attacked, Flight Sergeant Williams skillfully gave his captain directions which enabled the fighter to be evaded. Flight Sergeant Wllliams then delivered an accurate burst of fire which caused the enemy aircraft to explode in the air. The first fighter resumed the attack but, although in considerable pain, with both legs partially paralysed, Flight Sergeant Williams with a well placed burst of fire from close range shot the enemy aircraft down. Making light of his injuries be remained in his damaged turret until a landing was effected when his turret had to be cut away before be could be extricated. By his great skill, courage and determination this airman contributed in a large measure to the safe return of the bomber and its crew.

LONDON GAZETTE 6.7.1943

NOTES: Awarded D.F.M. 24.11.1942, bar to D.F.M. 18.5.1943.

FOR CONSPICUOUS GALLANTRY

WILLIAMS 1127080 Sergeant William Ernest

101 Squadron, Royal Air Force

"In recognition of gallantry displayed in flying operations against the enemy."

On the night of 14th February, 1943, Pilot Officer Gates, Flight Sergeant Dove and Sergeants Williams, Bain and Airey were members of the crew of an aircraft captained by Sergeant Hazard, which was detailed to attack Milan. Whilst over the target area, the aircraft was attacked by an enemy fighter from close range. It's gunfire exploded some incendiary bombs which had failed to release and a fire quickly developed in the bomber. The fuselage became a mass Of flames reaching through the mid-upper turret manned by Flight Sergeant Dove. Ammunition in the turret boxes and ducts commenced to explode in all directions. In the face of an appalling situation, Flight Sergeant Dove coolly remained at his post Although he was burned about the hands and face, he manned his guns with grim resolution skill, and accuracy. He delivered a devastating burst at the attacker which had already been engaged and hit by the rear gunner and succeeded in destroying it. Disregarding the roaring flames, he then descended from his turret and went to the assistance of Sergeant Airey the rear gunner, who had been wounded and extricated him from the rear turret. The situation had become extremely critical and Sergeant Hazard ordered the crew to prepare to abandon aircraft. When informed that one of his comrades was helpless be decided, in spite of the grave risk entailed, to attempt a forced landing. Meanwhile, Pilot Officer Gates, assisted by Sergeants Williams and Bain bravely tackled the fire with extinguishers and succeeded in getting it under control. The aircraft was now down to 8oo feet but, as the fire had subsided Sergeant Hazard quickly decided to attempt to fly the badly damaged bomber home. He regained height and displaying fine airmanship crossed the Alps in safety, although 1 engine failed whilst so doing.

On the remainder of the journey Pilot Officer Gates rendered valuable assistance to his captain and frequently ministered to his wounded comrade, although this necessitated clambering over a hole in the floor of the aircraft in darkness Aided by the skilful navigation of Sergeant Williams and good work by Sergeant Bain, the flight engineer, Sergeant Hazard succeeded in flying the seriously damaged aircraft back to this country In circumstances of the greatest danger, this aircraft crew displayed courage fortitude and devotion to duty In keeping with the highest traditions of the Royal Air Force.

LONDON GAZETTE 23.3.1943

NOTES: Pilot Officer Gates was awarded the D.S.O. and Flight Sergeant Dove, Sergeants Hazard Bain and Airey the C.G.M. for this action.

Killed along with Sergeant Bain C.G.M. and Sergeant Hazard C.G.M while taking a new bomber on a test flight, over Hornsea 20th March, 1943. Buried in Wolvercote Cemetery, Oxford.

WILLIAMSON Can/R.107665 Sergeant Leonard Franklin
428 (R.C.A.F.) Squadron, Royal Canadian Air Force

"In recognition of gallantry displayed in flying operations against the enemy."

In April 1943, this airman was pilot and captain of an aircraft detailed to attack Duisberg. Whilst over the target area the aircraft was hit by anti-aircraft fire. The bomber commenced to vibrate violently while the rudder bar swung loosely. Despite this, Sergeant Williamson continued his run-up and successfully bombed his target. The situation became critical and Sergeant Williamson gave orders to prepare to abandon the aircraft. As no answer was received from the rear gunner the navigator went to investigate and found that the rear turret had been blown away, the rudder was very badly damaged, and all the fuselage to the rear of the beam gun was stripped of fabric. The hydraulic system was out of action, causing the undercarriage to sag and the bomb doors to open. In spite of this, Sergeant Williamson kept the seriously damaged bomber headed for home and eventually reached an airfield where he effected a landing. In most hazardous circumstances, this airman displayed fortitude and courage of a high degree.

LONDON GAZETTE 18.5.1943

NOTES: Award effective 2 May1943 as per AFRO 1078/43 dated 11 June 1943.

Home in Regina; enlisted there 10 June 1941.

Trained at No.4 ITS (graduated 4 October 1941), No.6 EFTS (graduated 5 December 1941), and No.11 SFTS (graduated 24 March 1942).

Invested with award by King George VI, 12 October 1943.

WRIGHT 1627924 Sergeant Barry Colin
No 166 Squadron, Royal Air Force Volunteer Reserve

"In recognition of gallantry displayed in flying operations against the enemy."

This officer, Pilot Officer Catlin, and these airmen, Sergeants Wright, Birch and Hall, were pilot, flight engineer, rear gunner and wireless operator (air) respectively of an aircraft detailed to attached Leipzig one night in February, 1944. When nearing the target area the aircraft was intercepted by 2 fighters. One of them attacked from close range and the bomber was raked along the whole length of the fuselage by the enemy's bullets. Four of the crew were wounded, including Sergeants Hall and Wright, the latter being very severely injured. The aircraft sustained extensive damage, making it impossible for the pilot to take evasive action. Then, to add to the trials of the harassed crew, the bomber became fully illuminated in consequence of a short circuit occurring in the electrical system. The second fighter flew in to the attack but, although forced to operate his turret manually, Sergeant Birch met the attacker with a devastating burst fire and the enemy aircraft burst into flames and dived to the ground out of control. Only 2 of his guns were now operating but Sergeant Birch used them most effectively and drove off the other attacker. Pilot Officer Catlin then set course for home. Meanwhile Sergeant Hall set to work to repair some of the damaged equipment and later succeeded in making the intercommunication system serviceable. Badly wounded as he was, Sergeant Wright retained consciousness and could not be dissuaded from attempting to fulfill his duties. He was deprived of the use of the instrument panel which had been shot away, while 1 of the petrol tanks was empty. Nevertheless, he continued to keep the engines running at their maximum power. In his efforts, Sergeant Wright had to be supported by a comrade and 3 times fainted through loss of blood but he never wavered. In the face of heavy odds, Pilot Officer Catlin reached an airfield where he effected a masterly landing. His skill, courage and determination were beyond praise. Sergeants Wright, Hall and Birch proved themselves to be valiant

219

members of the aircraft crew and did everything within their power to assist their pilot in his endeavours to bring the crippled bomber home.

LONDON GAZETTE 17.3.1944

NOTES: Pilot Officer Catlin was awarded the D.F.C., and Sergeants Birch and Hall the D.F.M. for this action.

The aircraft was so badly damaged that the salvage crew broke it up where it stood!

Appendix A

Abbreviations

A.F.C.	Air Force Cross
D.C.M.	Distinguished Conduct Medal
D.F.C.	Distinguished Flying Cross
D.F.M.	Distinguished Flying Medal
D.S.C.	Distinguished Service Cross
D.S.M.	Distinguished Service Medal
D.S.O.	Distinguished Service Order
M.C.	Military Cross
M.M.	Military Medal
M.S.	Minesweeper
M.S.C.	Minesweeper Coastal
M.S.L.	Minesweeping Launch
M.T.B.	Motor Torpedo Boat
M.V.	Motor Vessel
M.V.O.	Member of the Victorian Order
N.C.O.	Non Commissioned Officer
P.O.	Petty Officer
P.o.W.	Prisoner of War
Po.	Portsmouth
R.A.A.F.	Royal Australian Air Force
R.A.F.	Royal Air Force
R.A.F.V.R.	Royal Air Force Volunteer Reserve
R.C.A.F.	Royal Canadian Air Force
R.F.R.	Royal Fleet Reserve
R.N.V.R.	Royal Navy Volunteer Reserve
R.N.Z.A.F.	Royal New Zealand Air Force
S.O.E.	Special Operations Executive
U.S.M.C.	United States Marine Corps
U.S.N.	United States Navy
V.C.	Victoria Cross
W.O.	Warrant Officer

Appendix B

The following is an attachment to a despatch sent by Commodore Richards to the Admiralty on March 14th 1881 and is a statement to him by Surgeon Mahon concerning the action on Majuba Hill for which William Bevis received the C.G.M.

The Camp, Mount Prospect,
March 4, 1881

Sir,

I HAVE the honour to report that on February 26th, at about 10 P.M., I left camp with the column, accompanied by Bevis, the sickberth attendant, with surgical appliances.

Surgeon Landon, A.M.D., with four of the A.H.C., also being with the troops.

The detachment from Naval Brigade, 64 in number, under Commander Romilly with Lieutenants' Trower, Scott, and myself, reached the top of Majuba Mountain at about 4 A.M., on February 27th, the last part of the route being most precipitous. Portions of the 92nd, 58th, with General Colley, first preceded us. Day broke a few minutes after we had gained the summit, and the troops were told off to their respective positions

Surgeon Landon and myself then chose a position for the hospital near the centre of the plateau, behind a ridge of rocks, and calculated to be out of the enemy's fire. A well was immediately dug near this spot, and a good supply of water was obtained at the depth of three feet.

After about an hour a few shots began to be exchanged, but none of our force were hit for about an hour. A desultory fire continued up to about 11 A.M., up to which time five of the 92nd only had been slightly wounded, and we're dressed by Landon and myself. At about 11 A.M. I went over to the west side of the plateau (see diagram) to see how Lieutenants Scott and Trower were getting on. I had hardly been there three minutes when I heard a bullet explode, close to us. I heard the General say " Captain Romilly is hit", and turning round saw General Colley kneeling by the side of the Commander, who was lying on the ground about four yards from us. I sent for a stretcher, and proceeded to dress the wound, which I found to perforate the left side of the abdomen and corning out at the loins. The bullet had only passed through soft parts, which accounts for it not exploding inside the body.

I had him carried to the hospital.

From this time up to 12 o'clock the fire continued on all sides in a desultory manner, being much brisker, however, on the east and north-east fronts. At about a quarter to 1 P.M. the Boers' fire, which up to this point had been much brisker than ours (I should say they had fired six shots to our one), almost entirely ceased. At about 1 o'clock they advanced in force on the E.N.E. front, and poured in a tremendous fire. Some blue jackets and some of the 58th were sent to reinforce the 92nd, and the Boers retired, but immediately advanced in greater numbers a little more to the left.

The fire now became so hot, and the hospital being partially exposed to it, I had the Commander removed on a stretcher by Bevis and Bone, L.S., to a sheltered spot on the south-west front.

I was returning to the hospital when I saw our force beginning a retreat, which soon became a rout. The Boers gained the rocks just above the hospital in great numbers, and poured a tremendous fire indiscriminately on everybody they saw. Dr. Landon and two of the A.H.C. were shot down whilst attending to the wounded, the former being mortally wounded.

I then went back to the Commander, and fixed my handkerchief on a stick, and held it up over him, but it was almost immediately shot away, and a hot volley fired all round us. Bevis then fixed a piece of lint on a bayonet, but was immediately shot twice through the helmet. I ordered him to lie down until the last of our men had passed us , and did the same myself. When the Boers had driven our men over the side of the hill, and had got within fifteen paces, I got up with a piece of lint in my hand, and shouted to them that I was a doctor, and had a wounded man with me. Two or three of the younger Boers wanted to shoot us, but were prevented by the elder men. The Boers then got all round us, and opened fire on our men retreating down the side of the hill.

While they were thus engaged, Bevis and myself picked up the stretcher, and carried Commander Romilly back to where the hospital was.

When about half way across we were surrounded by Boers, who were with great difficulty prevented from shooting the Commander as he lay, they being under the idea that he was either Sir Garnet Wolseley of Sir Evelyn Wood. Having assured them to the contrary I asked to see their Commander, who was pointed out to me (I think it was Ferriora). I asked him protection for the wounded, which was immediately granted. In fact after the heat of the action, the Boers, especially the elder ones, were most kind in their attention to the wounded, getting them water, and some helping to bind up their wounds. I saw no Boers killed or wounded.

It was now 2.30 P.M., and Bevis and myself with the two A.H.C. men who were unwounded, set to work to dress the wounded.

All who could walk were allowed by the Boers to make the best of their way to camp, and many did so, but I am unable to estimate the number. The prisoners who were taken by the Boers were made to assist in carrying the wounded from various parts of the hill to the hospital. But they were taken away to the Boer laager at about 6 P.M.

I had sent the Commander with four blue jackets (prisoners) on a stretcher to the spot where he had first ascended the hill. They managed to get him down safely some part of the way, but then three of them were ordered back by the Boers. However, they allowed one man to stay with him, and there they remained all night under a bush. The Commander was found by Dr. Ring A.M.D. in the morning, not much the worse, and was sent into camp where he arrived safely.

(I did not know of this until afterwards.)

At about 6 P.M. a thick mist began to come over the hill,

224

accompanied by a drizzling rain.

Bevis and myself searched as much of the hill as we could for wounded, and found two or three, but were eventually compelled to desist on account of the thickness of the mist. I had all the wounded, 36 in number, placed on one spot near the well, and luckily we found blankets and just enough waterproof sheets to cover them all. All we had to give them was water and a little opium, the Boers having taken all our brandy.

It now commenced to rain heavily, and continued to do so without intermission during the whole night, which much aggravated the suffering of the wounded. It also became bitterly cold towards morning. The darkness also was so intense that it was almost impossible to attempt to alleviate the sufferings of the wounded without stumbling over them. We had neither lantern nor matches.

Daylight returned at about 5 A.M., and with it also the Boers. I found that four men had succumbed to the inclemency of the weather during the night.

At about 6 A.M. Drs. Babbington and Ring with medical comforts, stretchers and stretcher bearers, under Lieutenant Cochran arrived. The dead were collected and placed in a row ready for internment, and the wounded, as many as possible, were placed on the stretchers, and sent down the mountain under my charge. We dressed a few wounded on the side of the hill, who had been lying there all night, but were not able to bring them on with us.

We reached O'Neill's farm, which is turned into a temporary hospital, at about 3 P.M.

I then brought on five ambulances full of wounded into camp, where I arrived at about 5 P.M., 28th February.

[For list of the killed and wounded belonging to the Naval Brigade, see Commodore Richards' return at end of papers.]

I wish to speak most highly of the conduct of William Bevis, sick-berth attendant, for his coolness and courage during the action, and the invaluable assistance he rendered me afterwards during the night, and up to the present time.

I regret to state that Commander Romilly died from mortification of the intestines at 2 P.M. on March 2nd. William Plastine, L.S., is

225

severely wounded in the abdomen, and I have little hope of his recovery. The rest of the wounded are progressing favourably. Five of the slightly wounded have been sent down to the military hospital at Newcastle, viz:- W.Kemp, G.Bridge, G.Sponder, D.Bone, F.Cross.

I am, &c.,

EDWARD E.MAHON,

Surgeon R.N.

To Commodore Richards R.N.

The above despatch was published in the London Gazette on 3rd May 1881 along with the full despatch from Commodore Richards and the full casualty list referred to in Surgeon Mahons despatch.

It was from this despatch that details were prepared for the award of the C.G.M. to William Bevis. It can be seen from this despatch when comparing it to official citations that much has to be edited and in some cases what is left can make the act of gallantry sound much less. This in some circumstances has led to recommendations being amended to lesser awards. Several of the recommendations in this work were originally recommendations for the Victoria Cross.

rinted in the United Kingdom by
htning Source UK Ltd., Milton Keynes
8UK00001B/37/A